I0126197

Inge Butter
Nomadic Connectivity

Connectivity and Society in Africa

───

Edited by
Mirjam de Bruijn and Jonna Both

Volume 3

Inge Butter

Nomadic Connectivity

An Ethnography of Walad Djifir Navigating
Insecurities in Central Africa

DE GRUYTER
OLDENBOURG

ISBN 978-3-11-221373-5
e-ISBN (PDF) 978-3-11-071468-5
e-ISBN (EPUB) 978-3-11-071480-7
ISSN 2628-6564

Library of Congress Control Number: 2023934704

Bibliographic information published by the Deutsche Nationalbibliothek
The Deutsche Nationalbibliothek lists this publication in the Deutsche Nationalbibliografie;
detailed bibliographic data are available on the internet at http://dnb.dnb.de.

© 2025 Walter de Gruyter GmbH, Berlin/Boston
This volume is text- and page-identical with the hardback published in 2023.
Cover image: A visiting family member helps feed the goats while catching up on the latest
news. Late afternoon near Fadjé. Photo: Author, 2014.
Typesetting: Integra Software Services Pvt. Ltd.
Printing and binding: CPI books GmbH, Leck

www.degruyter.com

To our children,
from Emma and Luuk to Abdusalaam, Haamid, and little Hamdaan –
So that you may know a few pieces of the puzzles which are your parents,
and create your own.

Contents

Acknowledgements

To B. and his extended family of Walad Djifir: thank you for the warm welcome and enduring patience with my many questions and mere presence. A special mention is due to B.'s wife and their children – this could not have happened without you all making space and time for me within your home and lives. The Centre du Récherche en Anthropologie et Sciences Humaines (CRASH) team in N'Djaména, specifically Djimet, Remadji, and the late prof. Khalil Alio: thank you for always having the door to the office open, creating a haven for reflection, and general socializing when needed. Andrea and Laguerre, you were the first to include me on arrival in N'Djaména in 2011 and I will always be grateful for that. May our paths continue to cross. Mirjam and her Connecting in Times of Duress research team – Adamou, Boukary, Catherina, Inge L, Jonna, Lotte, Meike, and Souleymane – what kind of a journey would this have been without you all there, going through similar obstacles, emotions, and 'eureka' moments? The African Studies Centre (ASC), its library, and ASC colleagues are always a pleasant space to return to. Mirjam, you have an admirable way of making things possible, especially when everyone else says it can't be done. Souleymane, Adama, and your wonderful children, thank you for showing me another side of Mongo and sharing your home with me. The fieldwork we carried out together in both Bangui and Mongo was enriching. In Mongo as well, I would like to thank the Summer Institute of Linguistics (SIL) and its team of super women, 'the Guéra Girls' – Andrea, Stephanie, Liz, Emma, and Caroline – for providing a calm and secure space from which to reflect and *'répose'*. Geeske (Ritske), you were the first foreigner I was put in contact with in Mongo but also the least 'foreign'. Thank you for the conversations over coffee and your household's famous salad. Your work and family are inspiring. In Bangui, Espérance and Ahmed Hamid are to thank for making it such a pleasant experience – strange words to use these days, but I do not know how else to describe the time spent there. Rogier, Ahmed Muhammed, Ghislain, and François, thank you for helping me find my bearings research-wise! To my parents, my sisters, and Bouk: I look forward to presenting this book to you as a way of finally sharing the memories which have lived in my head for years. Finally, *li-l ahl fi-l ferīkh: shukran gezīlan. Wallahi – ana ma-nansaku intu dol abadan. Wa inshallah, fi-l yawm tāni! Ogodu 'aafé.*

https://doi.org/10.1515/9783110714685-203

List of maps, tables, figures, and photographs

Maps

Tables

Figures

Photographs

https://doi.org/10.1515/9783110714685-204

All photographs were taken by the author.

On transcription choices and translation

The Chadian Arabic spoken by the Walad Djifir is a sub-group of the Baggara Arabic dialect, falling under West Sudan Arabic (Manfredi & Roset 2021). In referencing the origins of Chadian Arabic words, I have made use of both Hans Wehr's ([1979] 1994)[1] *Dictionary of Modern Written Arabic* as well as Patrice Julien de Pommerol's (1999) *Dictionnaire arabe tchadien-français*. The Chadian Arabic in this book uses Wehr's system of standard transliteration, with the following exceptions:

ذ : dh

ث : th

ج : dj

خ : kh

و : w and ū

Upon first use of a word, its origins are explained by giving the root of the word and the correct transliteration. Throughout the text, however, I have chosen to transcribe some frequently used words as the Walad Djifir pronounce them. For example, *farīq* (MSA) is pronounced *ferīkh*. Well-known words such as *sheikh*, chief, are left un-italicized and transcribed as one would pronounce the word (i.e. the ش, 'š' becoming a 'sh'). In the case of Chadian Arabic words frequently used throughout the text, the word has been italicized only upon first use. This is especially the case for the word *ferīkh*, which is used in its literal sense but also as an analytical concept. Translations from interviews in French and Chadian Arabic are mine. In most cases, I have chosen to literally transcribe the Chadian Arabic as it is pronounced by the informant, giving an English translation alongside. For names of nomadic sub-divisions I have stuck to the more formal transcription: Walad Sūrūr instead of Sourour, Matanīn instead of Mataneen.

---

1 This is the fourth edition of the dictionary, edited by J.M. Cowan.

https://doi.org/10.1515/9783110714685-205

Maps

Map 1: Chad, Cameroon, CAR.
Source: DeVink Mapdesign. Copyright: CTD/ASCL 2018.

https://doi.org/10.1515/9783110714685-206

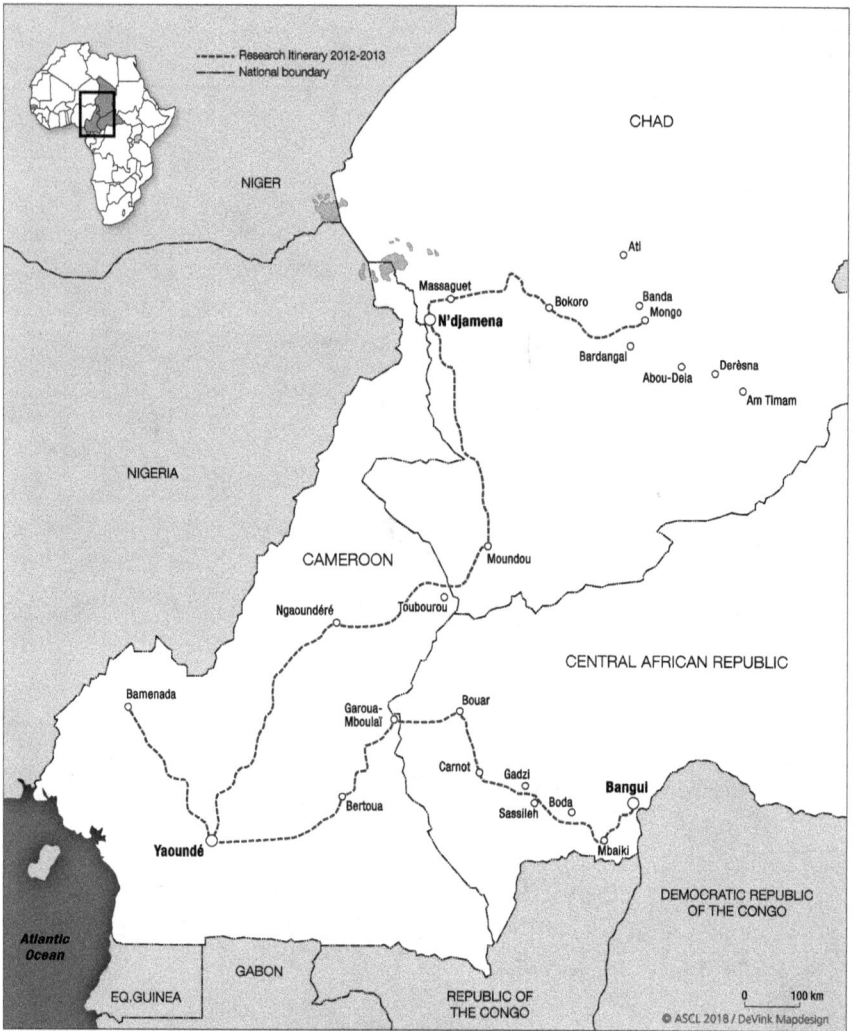

Map 2: Research itinerary, October 2012 – March 2013.
Source: DeVink Mapdesign. Copyright: CTD/ASCL 2018.

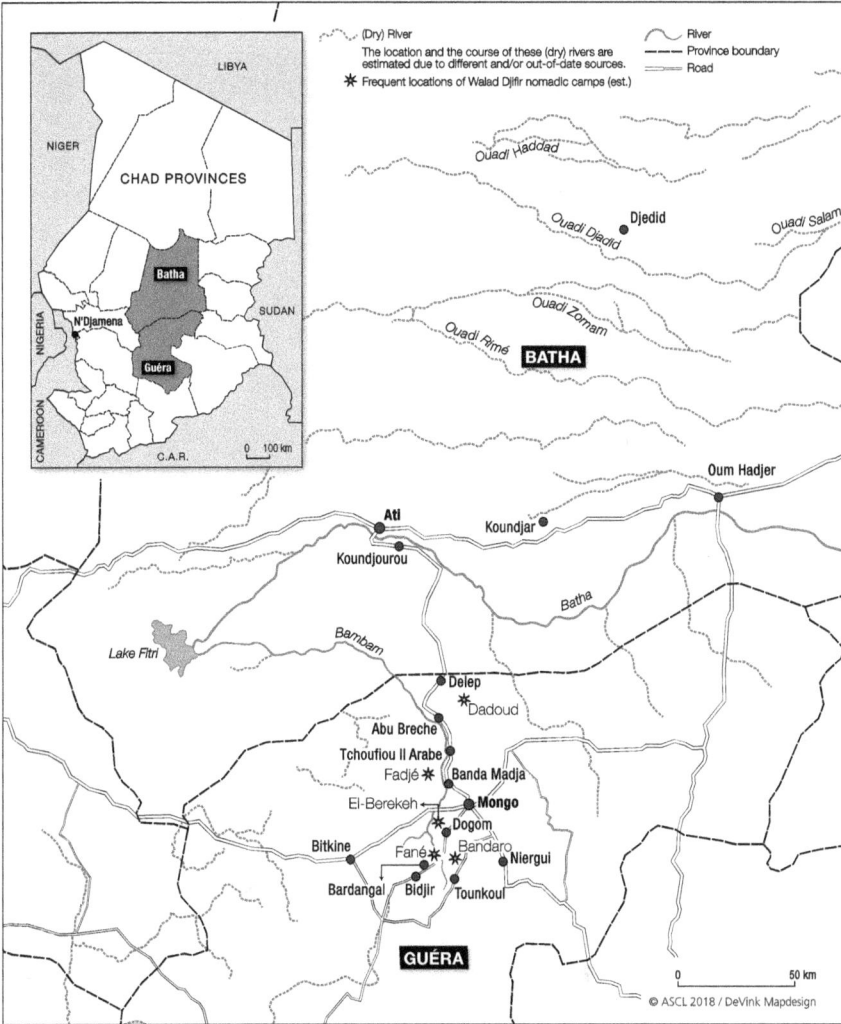

Map 3: Guéra – Batha, detail of research sites and locations of nomadic camps.
Source: DeVink Mapdesign. Copyright: CTD/ASCL 2018.

Family trees

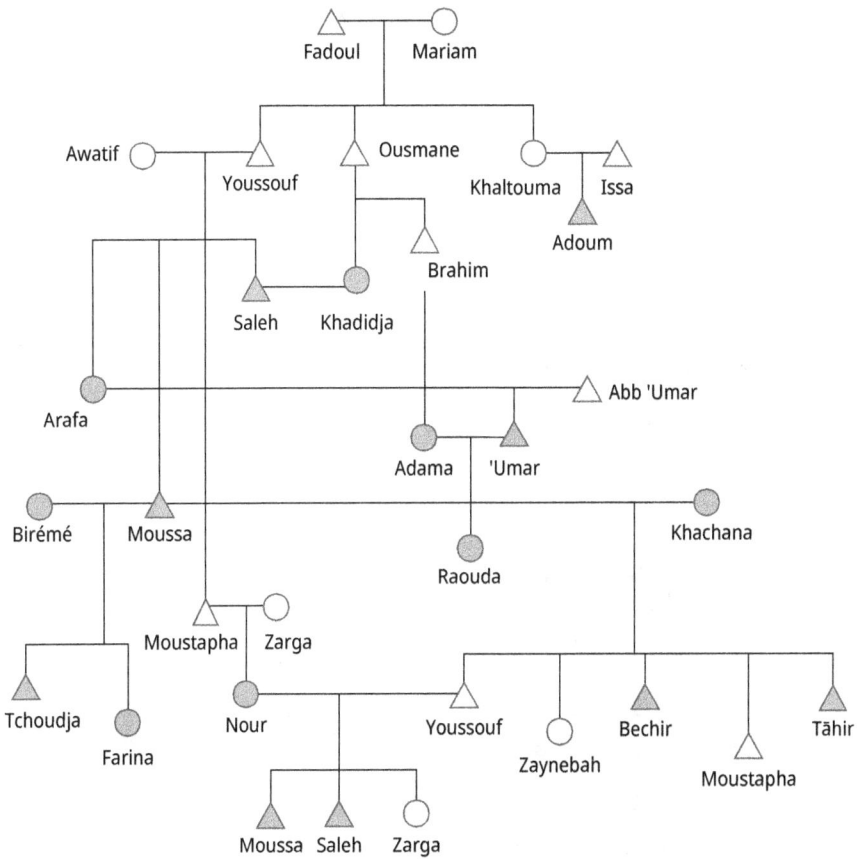

Figure 1: Family tree connecting family stayed with in 2012, including connection between Farina, her father Moussa, and Hadj Saleh.

https://doi.org/10.1515/9783110714685-207

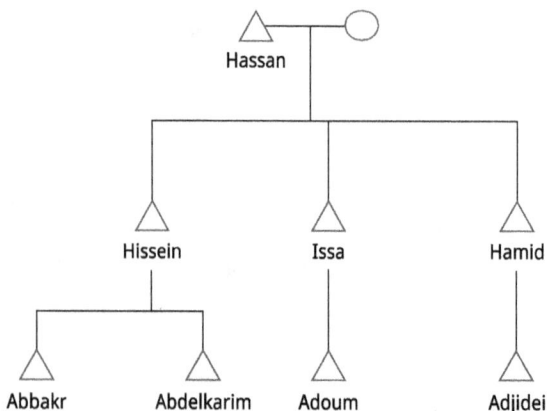

Figure 2: Family tree showing the connection between Adoum, Abbakr, and Adjidei.

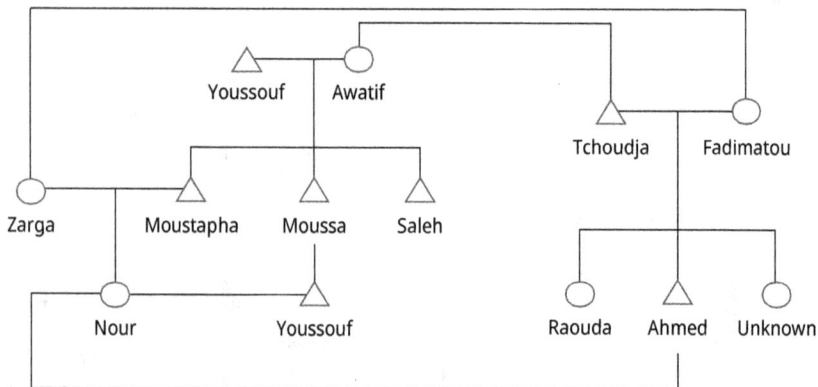

Figure 3: Family tree of Hadj Saleh and Nour's link to Hadj Tchoudja.

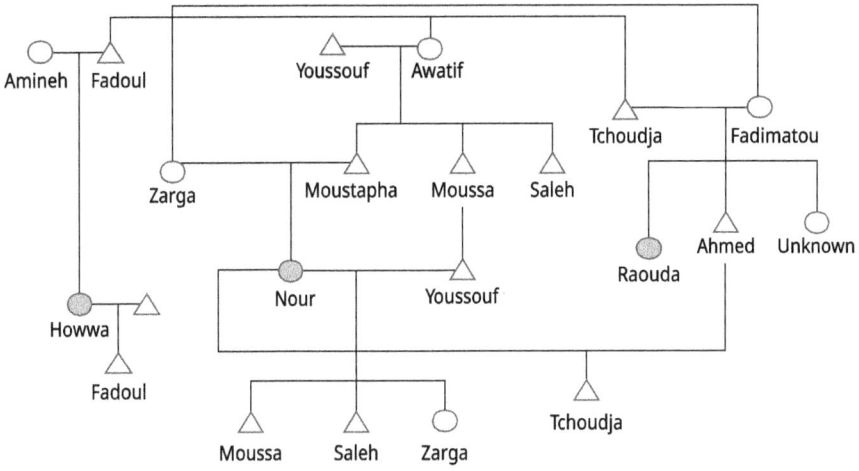

Figure 4: Family tree linking Nour, Howwa, and Raouda.

Ferīkh individuals

Abbakr	Adoum's direct cousin. Their fathers were brothers. Abbakr is based in N'Djamena and a veterinarian by training.
Adoum	Adoum left his nomadic camp as a youngster, ending up as a driver for NGOs and the state's pastoral-oriented department, living in N'Djamena with his wife and their children. Adoum's mother, Khadidja's father, and Hadj Saleh's father were siblings.
Arafa	The eldest sister of Hadj Saleh, Moussa, Moustapha, and Hassan. She used to share a tent with Nour while she was living in the ferīkh. She also spent some time visiting Moustapha and Hadj Saleh in the Central African Republic (CAR), even being sent on pilgrimage by Moustapha.
Hadj Saleh	Uncle to Nour. Brother to Moussa, Moustapha, Arafa, and Hassan (amongst others). Married to Khadidja with whom he has several children. Chef de ferīkh in Fadjé. Spent some time in CAR with his brother Moustapha.
Hassan	A younger brother of Moussa, Moustapha, and Hadj Saleh – same father, different mother. He was a traditional veterinarian, including taking care of animals who had broken or sprained something and at times applying his knowledge to his family members. Hassan passed away in 2017.
Howwa	Born and raised in Bangui where she worked a market stall in Cinq Kilo. Married and with one young son at the time of fieldwork. Her father was a brother of Tchoudja, making her and Raouda cousins.
Khachana	Mother to Nour's husband Youssouf. First wife to Moussa. Cousin to Adoum.
Khadidja	Married to Hadj Saleh with several children. Their fathers are brothers, making them first cousins. This is the preferred marriage.
Moussa	Brother of Hadj Saleh, Moustapha, and Arafa (amongst others). Married to Khachana with whom he has several children, amongst them Youssouf who is married to Nour. He also has several children (Farina, introduced in Chapter Three is one of them) with his second wife Birémé, who comes from a different tribe. Upon the death of his younger brother Hassan in 2017, he took in the latter's young wife, as is custom. She died in 2020 giving birth to twins.
Moustapha	Father of Nour. Brother of Hadj Saleh, Moussa, and Arafa. Moved to CAR and set up commercial businesses there. Passed away around 2009 after a prolonged illness.
Nour	Born and raised in Bangui. Daughter of Moustapha and Zarga. Married to her cousin Youssouf, the son of Khachana and Moussa. Mother to Tchoudja, Moussa, Saleh, and Zarga (more children were born after 2017).
Nouraddin	Chef de village of Tchoufiou II Arabe.
Raouda	Daughter of Tchoudja, born and raised in Bangui.
Tchoudja	Brother of Hadj Saleh's mother. Tchoudja migrated to Bangui sometime in the 1960s and set up commercial businesses.
Yaya	Member of the ferīkh counsel and the *khalīfa* responsible for collecting taxes on livestock sold at the weekly markets.
Youssouf	Nour's husband, son of Moussa and Khachana. Moved to a remote village in CAR upon marrying Nour.
Zarga	Nour's mother. First and only wife to Nour's father Moustapha. She remarried and had four daughters and one son. This son went on to marry Adoum's oldest daughter.

https://doi.org/10.1515/9783110714685-208

Chapter 1
Researching nomadic connectivity

On one of the many hot and dry afternoons, Adoum and I returned to Khachana's tent to find a stranger seated on a mat under one of the shady trees within the centre of their nomadic camp. He had been given a *sokhaan*[1] to wash with and a bowl containing water, milk, and grains. This mixture is a good thirst quencher, being a little bit sour, salty, and spicy. I asked Khachana who the man was and what he was doing here, and she raised her shoulders and said '*ma ne'arfa*', she did not know. The stranger was left alone for a while, until the men started returning from the *'eidd* (watering holes) and it was time for the late afternoon prayers. Brief greetings were exchanged, and those belonging to the camp sat down on a separate mat laid out by the women. Adoum later explained that when a stranger visits the *ferīkh* (nomadic camp), they are not immediately asked who they are and where they have come from.[2] In Chad, someone's physical appearance is often an indicator of his or her background, and the nomadic Walad Djifir will frequently be able to recognize which family someone belongs to within their own group. Physical traits are strong, and familial resemblances carry over to next generations. The man was wearing a white *djallabeya* and headscarf. He had come on a horse, which was tethered to a tree just outside the camp. His complexion was relatively fair, a characteristic of several nomadic Arabs. I do not remember whether he had markings on his face, a tell-tale sign for which *tribu*[3] he belonged to. Older Walad Djifir, for example, have two small parallel scars on each cheek, which has given them the nickname '*onze onze*' (eleven eleven).

The visitor turned out to be a *marabout* who was travelling from ferīkh to ferīkh to raise awareness on sending children to school. This was something we discovered only much later that evening, after another set of prayers followed by dinner. Adoum explained that guests, also when strangers, are treated with honour and respect. On many more occasions, strangers to the ferīkh were treated in this way. What interested me in these encounters was something I had also observed elsewhere in Chad. It was a certain wariness toward people one did not know, cou-

---

1 The *sokhaan* can be found in every Chadian household. They are usually made of plastic and look like a kettle, having a handle and spout. They come in various colours, sizes, and qualities. The *sokhaan* is filled with water and used to wash one's hands before a meal, for Muslims to carry out their ablutions, and also to take with you to the 'bathroom'.
2 Fieldnotes, Mongo, 28 April 2012.
3 The word *tribu* is used by Walad Djifir and other Chadians when referring to the different nomadic groups and their sub-groups.

https://doi.org/10.1515/9783110714685-001

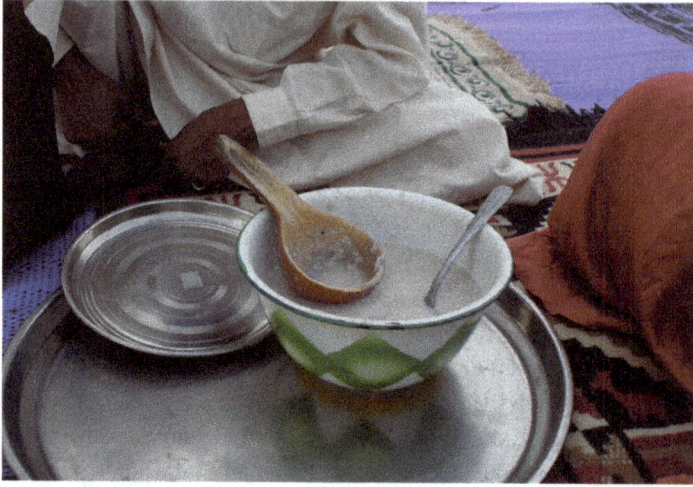

Photo 1.1: Mixture consisting of water, some grains and pepper often offered to guests, it is a bit sour, salty and sweet, Fadjé March 2013.

Photo 1.2: The *sokhaan* can be found in every Chadian household, also in the nomadic setting. They are usually made of plastic and come in various colours, sizes, and qualities. Here a man is washing before performing his afternoon prayers, Fadjé March 2013.

pled with a specific method of greeting. There is a first and extensive exchange of 'Peace be with you', 'God bless you', and other well-wishing, interrupted by brief practical questions, followed by more well-wishing for the person and their family. Only slowly does one come to know who the person is, where they are headed, and what either they want from you or you from them. When spending time next to people one does not know, as in a bus or while waiting for a tyre to be repaired along the side of the road, the conversations are minimal, with neither party liable to give away anything personal. This may not be so strange and is something I also encountered while travelling on public buses through the Sinai in Egypt, with its many checkpoints and undercover police. Yet for some reason, the evasive answering of questions and avoidance of personal matters which could identify one were very noticeable. It raises the question, what other intrinsic and expected behaviours guide Walad Djifir through their daily lives? And what happens to these behaviours under different circumstances? Circumstances coloured by sudden conflict, prolonged insecurity, or ever-changing futures. These dynamics are part and parcel of life in a nomadic camp. Just as a stranger wanders in and out of a camp, requiring its inhabitants to interact with him. So too, do many other people, goods, news, and ideas cross paths with Khachana and her family, each embodying specific dynamics of (inter)action.

✳✳✳

Khachana and Adoum are related through their parents and belong to the larger nomadic group known as the Misseria Rouges. Their extended family makes up a sub-group, the Walad Djifir, most of whom are based in central Chad. Adoum himself had left the nomadic setting as a youngster. When we met in 2011, he was based in N'Djaména with his family. We had been introduced through a mutual contact and he, in turn, introduced me to his extended family during our first trip to Ati and Mongo. It is thus somewhat serendipitously (Rivoal & Salazar 2013) that the Walad Djifir have become the subject of my explorations. On the above occasion, Khachana's nomadic camp was set up along one of the dry river beds in the Guéra region (Map 3). Adoum and I had been coming and going, visiting other camps in the vicinity and spending almost a week at a time with Khachana, before heading back to the town of Mongo to replenish our drinking water and charge batteries. Throughout these visits, interactions between family members living in nomadic camps and their family elsewhere, became more and more visible. Phones would ring and be rung when the network and credit allowed. News was sought and spread to those awaiting its arrival. Daily life was a veritable mix between the structure nomadic life entails, and moments of disruptive decisions and drama. Several such phone calls revealed a close familial connection to Bangui, with Khachana and her brother-in-law Hadj Saleh (see Family Tree in Figure 1) some of the main actors.

Between March 2012 and December 2012, Hadj Saleh's camel herd grew from a mere five or six head to at least forty. Over the next year, he would add more camels and buy plots of land in the nearby district town of Mongo. These investments were enabled by the slow but consistent selling off of cattle and land in the neighbouring Central African Republic (CAR) as a result of his brother's inheritance. Hadj Saleh was responsible for the dividing up, according to Islamic custom, of a large herd of cattle as well as of plots of land and small commercial enterprises. Ideally, the extended family wanted to move the herd of cattle north, into Chad, to be reared by their family there. Such a journey was, however, too risky and potentially very expensive – the border crossing itself would be tricky and involve bribes, let alone the travel through inland CAR, where fears of road robbers and additional 'administrative fees' are an ever-present reality (Schouten 2022). From late 2012 onwards, this fairly sudden influx of camels had consequences for the family members living and working close to Hadj Saleh, such as Khachana and her husband Moussa. The camp of those tending the camels was usually set up at a fair distance from the other camps, as camels need their space. This meant that the allocation of daily tasks performed by women, men, and children had to be reorganized – it took longer to fetch water from the well as the camels were further away. Men and boys who had previously herded the cattle now tended to the camels, staying away from their camp for more days in a row than they had previously done. The continuing familial link to CAR also had an effect on the more social and emotional aspects of people's lives. During the course of 2013, CAR underwent a coup, and what followed were months of violence whereby family members in Chad anxiously searched for news of loved ones who had fled. By March 2013, Hadj Saleh had sold off about half of the herd, receiving the profit through an Express Union transfer of three million CFA (approx. 4574 EUR). The transfer itself had been accompanied by many phone calls between a remote town in CAR, the capital of N'Djaména, and family members in the nomadic camp. The brief description of Hadj Saleh's inheritance and subsequent investments introduces the Walad Djifir as a group of people for whom mobility is a livelihood strategy inherent to their nomadic way of life, a way of life which includes transnational wage labour and commerce. This mobility involves the use of global socio-economic networks and technologies of communication.

In a globalizing Chad, an understanding of the connectivity of specific places, such as nomadic camps, provides a deeper understanding of local dynamics. Nomadic connectivity, in the case of Hadj Saleh and his extended family of Walad Djifir, encompasses a whole range of factors. Except for the works of Martin Wiese (2004, 2011) and Zakinet Dangbet (2015a, 2015b) on the Misseria, the existing contemporary studies which specifically mention the Chadian Misseria Rouges of the Batha are mainly from the Ministry of Pastoralism.[4] Dangbet's studies are an exception in that, as a historian, he made use of existing literature and archival sources

---

4 Aubague et al. (2006); Abderamane & des Fontaines (2011); Alfaroukh et al. (2011).

but also spent six months in a nomadic camp and migrating with the Salamat Arabs of the Batha in 2006. The study, published by Marty et al. (2009), focuses on understanding the Chadian transhumance system at a micro-level. In later work, Dangbet (2015a, 2015b) concentrates more on the historical and contemporary patterns of alliances and conflicts among two groups of migrating Batha Arabs between 1635 and 2012: the Misseria and the Salamat Siféra. These and other references (such as the collection of articles on Chadian nomads in general in Barraud et al. 2001 and in Alfaroukh et al. 2011) have been useful in contextualizing the accounts of the Walad Djifir. At the same time, there is still much information missing. There are older ethnographies and studies of Chadian nomadic groups,[5] though these are written in a tradition that does not reflect today's understanding of the Walad Djifir as part of a connected and globalizing world. Theirs is not a place-bound world, nor are they 'merely' nomadic pastoralists (Fischer & Kohl 2010). Instead, Walad Djifir own livestock and travel and work in different places in different capacities (wage labour, commerce). The developments in transport and communication technologies are an intrinsic part of the connected world in which these nomads carve out a living. On the other hand, they also live in a world where their transhumance and other activities are part of pre- and post-colonial histories of conflict and turmoil. This book looks at the interconnectedness of contemporary dynamics which are no longer either 'typically' sedentary or nomadic and are bound neither geographically nor economically (Azarya 1996a; Gertel 2007; Boesen et al. 2014; Köhler 2016a; Krätli et al. 2018).

The experiences encountered throughout five fieldwork periods, totalling almost twelve months between late 2011 and early 2014, were situated in people's everyday lives – that is, in everyday conversations, activities, and happenings. The result is a phenomenological ethnography of the everyday (Abu-Lughod 1991, 2008; de Certeau 2011). It tells a story of how men, women, and children go through their day living in a nomadic camp, a town, or a city: gathering wood, cooking, collecting water, coming together for meals, and so on. These lived experiences (Desjarlais & Throop 2011) include the conversations and family gatherings held when more special or less ordinary situations arise: a child gone missing, a sickness, birth or death, a marriage, conversations that brought up previous lives lived in other (foreign) places and future plans to return. And then there were the moments or days in which sudden, external, often political events impacted life – a coup with violent consequences in CAR, the loss of family and friends, uncertainty and a flight 'back' to the roots.

---

5 See Thomas (1959); Cunnison (1966, 1972); Courtecuisse et al. (1971); Zeltner (1979); Cordell (1985); Zeltner & Tourneux (1986); Brahim (1988); Hugot (1997) for fairly traditional approaches to the study of Arab nomads in Chad or as groups coming from Sudan into Chad. For other general works on the Chadian population, see Chapelle (1980); Collelo (1990).

Photography and film proved essential in capturing the details of everyday life, as well as acting as topics of conversation and discussion between family members who had been separated. Our memories and observations are a mix of sensations: sounds, smells, feelings, emotions, words, and sights (Goody 2002; Pink 2009; Stoller 2011). The visual calls up a different yet complementary emotion and narrative from the textual or verbal, through its potential linkages with other senses and discourses. In their realist function, photographs portray a visible image for something described in words, like a nomadic camp or watering hole. At the same time, they also provide a way of 'telling' a complementary story. In the case of the latter, however, it is actually the accompanying words that become complementary to the visible (in photographic form), in that they provide a way of interpreting, intersubjectively, that which may not be 'visible' but is still present and thus a part of reality (Pink 2012a, 2012b: 23–24). The visual narrative included in this book is an important part of this phenomenological ethnography of everyday connectivity. Consent was given to take and use pictures. For the purpose of this publication, a level of anonymity has been added. Individuals have been given pseudonyms. Geographical places, the names of the nomadic sub-groups, and important political leaders have not. These indicators are essential in being able to place and contextualize the ethnography. This is a way to honour the privacy of research participants while also binding the ethnography to them. The stories told here are personal, based on specific individuals and their communities. Their role in the larger scheme of things, however, is not an individual one but part and parcel of a story revealing social dynamics. Insecurity featured in many aspects of 'mundane' life, as well as throughout more extraordinary events. However, these aspects were also very much embedded in more nuanced contextual and environmental (visual) realities – lived realities in which connectivity and insecurity went hand in hand.

Looking at and beyond a context of insecurity

In Chad, conflict and politics are an almost automatic part of people's lives (Arditi 2003; Chauvin et al. 2020) – of course, for some more than for others. While staying with this group of semi-sedentary nomads, an intuitive feeling said: 'This is not what insecurity looks like, at least not in the dramatic, no-way-out, constant-state-of-fear-and-tension kind of way.' No, it was a far more subtle, though not less effective, insecurity. An insecurity which is partly inherent to a way of life and the ecology of the country the Walad Djifir find themselves in. An insecurity that includes droughts, famine, cattle disease, and general issues of health and education. The daily need to collect water, walking long distances in the heat, complaints of headaches or general *rhume* (flu), as well as pregnancy-related health issues on the part of the women – all these were issues that surfaced regularly. Yet, these are also 'normal' daily occurrences, and there are many studies which speak about pastoral-nomadic resilience and inherent mobility as coping strategies.[6] I thus consider these issues, as well as issues related to land ownership, access to watering points and grazing land, cattle theft, and strategic allegiances, as continuous insecurities.

During various fieldwork visits we heard of the occasional conflict over cattle or camels entering into someone's field and eating or destroying their crops. Walad Djifir were not involved in these instances at the time, but neighbouring groups or sedentary villagers were. These are real issues, which have caused much tension, debate, and a search for solutions at local and policy levels.[7] It is interesting that there were other conflicts or issues which took precedence among the Walad Djifir while I was there. Whether this says something about their agreements and allegiance with the sedentary villagers, or more about their control of their herds while in the vicinity of an agricultural field, is difficult to say. Certainly these conflicts occurred often in the past, and stories were told – by those remembering their childhood transhumance – of tensions running high and being chased. Problems often occur during the transhumance,[8] which is why the transhumance corridors were agreed upon. As Walad Djifir are now settled within the region, it is in their best interest to keep a healthy and friendly allegiance with their direct neighbours. Nevertheless, conflicts have arisen and do still arise between communities sharing access to agricultural and pastoral land, and to deep-water wells. Conflicts within a community itself are also common, as this book will show.

Such continuous insecurities seem almost to be *expected* insecurities – can we even speak of expected moments of crisis – although nonetheless dramatic and disruptive. What distinguishes an expected moment of crisis from Vigh's (2008) 'chronic crisis' is that the latter has a more prolonged or enduring connotation. These 'expected' insecurities, on the other hand, can come and go and are continuous in that sense, i.e. continually coming and going versus continuously present with no relief. De Bruijn & Both (2018) analyse how crises have become deeply engrained in some societies, creating a situation of insidious hardship which they

---

6 See Monod (1975); Azarya (1996b); Azarya et al. (1999); Chatty (2006); Ankogui-Mpoko et al. (2009); see van Dijk (1995) on how indigenous coping strategies can also be threatened or undermined by a combination of drought and political developments.

7 See Arditi (1999) on conflicts among the Sara and pastoralists in southern Chad; for the Misseria Rouges (Dangbet 2015a, 2015b) and Guéra and Batha specifically (Aubague et al. 2006; Dangbet 2020).

8 Transhumance is the migration of nomads and their livestock from their wet season grazing lands, to their dry season grazing lands, and vice versa. A transhumance corridor is a designated route which livestock and their herders are permitted to take while migrating, so as to avoid the devastation of agricultural fields.

convincingly refer to as 'duress'. Within this process a certain normalization is discerned, coupled with a form of deeply constrained agency. Distinguishing between different types of insecurities, within a context of duress, allows for an analysis of the nature and extent of normalization vis-à-vis 'mundane' disruptions and more 'extreme' ones.

Apart from continuous insecurities, one can also detect changing insecurities. This distinction does not necessarily imply new insecurities but rather perhaps an intensification or variation in the nature of older pre-existing insecurities. For example, family members have, for generations, travelled far and wide, whether in search of pasture or cash. The dangers of travel continue, although perhaps in different forms (e.g. due to regional dynamics and infrastructural developments). Through such technologies as the mobile phone, the experience of someone being away, and the tension and stress this may involve for those at home or away, may be altered. Family members expect periodic phone calls. They expect money to be sent home, something which is now very much possible through a mixture of formal and informal networks. Conflicts can be simultaneously more intense, quickly rallying family from all over through a phone call, and short-lived – a similar phone call to the *sous-prefet* or military can put a quick stop to anything brewing.

Events like the March 2013 coup in CAR, the death of Hadj Saleh's brother, and also other political events initiated by government leaders or rebel forces *have* shaped the environment in which people, institutions, and infrastructures exist. There is also a certain reciprocity, however, in the way political events, infrastructural developments, and civilian actions, for example, are influenced by one another.[9] What, then, is the role of the more 'mundane' daily happenings in relation to experiences of insecurity or disruption? Are choices and decisions framed differently in a context of continuous or expected insecurities, than when faced with changing insecurities? Part of the answers to these questions can be sought in a return to the 'local' – namely, to the entity known as the 'ferīkh'.

The ferīkh

In the dry season,[10] if one were to fly over the region known as Fadjé, which runs along the Bambam's dry river bed (see Map 3), one would see a chain of nomadic

---

9 See Souleymane (2017) on the relationship between communication and violence in colonial and post-colonial Chad. Djama (2010: 100) reminds us of the historical role of trade circulation and Islam in shaping political structures.

10 The dry season is approximately from February to June. When the first rains start, the camps are moved to the other side of the Bambam and road between Mongo and Ati. The terrain on that

camps dotted along it. The ferīkh is a collective word for an ensemble of nomadic tents set up together.[11] When the setting allows, tents are often set up in a circle with their openings facing outwards. This gives the women of each of the tents privacy, and allows for smaller animals to be kept safe overnight in the centre. Throughout the day men gather within the interior of the camp, given there is sufficient shade. A visitor being placed here will thus barely get a glimpse of the women going about their household chore. Tents are inhabited by family members, who share the herding of a specific group of livestock, with every married woman owning her own tent. Within the area and at walking distance from each other, one will find several other ferīkhs, inhabited by close and extended family members. This brings us to a second use of the word ferīkh. It refers to a physical nomadic camp but also indirectly to an extended family.[12]

A Walad Djifir is thus part of an extensive familial network, with complicated kinship patterns due to a preference for endogamous, parallel cousin marriages. Members of the same extended family can live spread out over various nomadic camps and still refer to themselves as belonging to the same ferīkh – that is, falling under the same *chef de ferīkh* or leader (*kabir hana ferīkh*). In Aubague et al. (2006: 69), the authors make a distinction between *iyaal raagil* [ايال راجل] (factions), the small and large *khāshim beyt* [خاشم بيت] (sub-lineage and lineage) and *qabīla* [قبيلة]

---

side is more grassy and does not turn into huge blocks of mud which are impossible to walk over. In relation to the transhumance, more seasons are distinguished (Wiese 2004): *kharīf* (rainy season), *darat* (transitional period from the rainy to the cold season), *shittéh* (cold season), *seyf* (hot and dry season), *rushāsh* (transitional period to the rainy season).

11 *farīq*, pl. *furqān* (فريق ج فرقان), band, company, troop, detachment, faction, or unit. The word فريق (*farīq*) means a team, a crew: 'a group of people that works together with one objective'. It is commonly used for sport teams. فريق كرة قدم: a soccer team (Wehr 1994). In the text, I have chosen to transcribe the word as Walad Djifir pronounce it, with a 'kh' (خ) at the end and a softer 'e': *ferīkh*. Julien de Pommerol's (1999) dictionary of Chadian Arabic–French makes the choice to transcribe the 'q' as 'g': *ferīg*.

12 Similar entities in other nomadic societies can be found. The entity which is associated with the Bedouin of Cyrenaica, *biyut*, actually comes close to that of the *ferīkh*. 'What Evans-Pritchard (1949: 56; cf. Peters 1967: 262; Peters 1960: 31) calls extended family groups (*biyut*) amongst the Bedouin of Cyrenaica [eastern coastal region of Libya] are, in fact, different levels of a nomadic community. This becomes clear in his description of them: "Their members live in the same stretch of tribal territory, move during the rains to the same grazing grounds, use the same wells during the dry season and cultivate adjacent strips of arable land. The members of a biyut have a lively sense of solidarity . . . They are jointly responsible for a wrong any one of them may commit. The smaller biyut are often identical with camps, usually from five to ten tents, in grazing grounds, and several closely related biyut camp near together in the vicinity of springs and wells in the summer, their combined camps then amounting sometimes to over a hundred tents"' (Khazanov 1994: 133). Interestingly, in Ladislav Holy's (1974: 86) study of the Berti people of Darfur, the word *farīg* is used to refer to the dry-season camp.

Photo 1.3: Men walking towards the ferīkh once the sun had cooled, October 2011. In the distance we see a chain of nomadic camps (ferīkh). Closer to the foreground, on the right, we can see how these camps are made up of several tents (*barsh*).

Photo 1.4: Close-up of a ferīkh tent and camp, with an animal enclosure (*zerrība*) in the foreground. October 2011.

Photo 1.5: The ferīkh setting in March 2014. They were located a little further away from the Bambam than previously, yet still on its western bank. The trees were a little further apart than where they had camped in early 2012 and early 2013. It is easy to distinguish the ground which has been swept clean of cow dung and vegetation.

Photo 1.6: Back of a tent with the women's cooking area shielded by the tent, Fadjé, March 2013. The area has been swept clear of dung. The blue tarps are covering sacks of grain, bought in anticipation of an upcoming wedding.

(larger overarching group or lineage). The *chef de ferīkh*, or *kabirra 'an al-ferīkh* [كبرة عن الفريخ] in Chadian Arabic, mentioned here would come closest to the leader of what they refer to as *iyaal raagil*, namely people who have the same grandfather four generations back. Several *iyaal raagil*, each with their own *chef de ferīkh*, make up the *khashim beyt* known as the Walad Djifir. Chapters One and Two will deal with the different levels of organization in more detail. In the case of the Walad Djifir, it is not so easy to distinguish where an extended family ends and a primary kin group begins.[13] There is considerable overlap; and, in general, each group of nomadic tents makes up one singular camp (ferīkh). The extended family occupying other camps in close proximity or further away also makes up a primary kin group, which varies in composition depending on the needs of the group.

Like many contemporary pastoral nomads in the Sahel region, the Walad Djifir are involved in numerous economic activities not only in various locations in Chad but also transnationally.[14] In the past, the Walad Djifir were known to migrate with their livestock, locally referred to as the *murḥal*, from areas in central Chad all the way south to the border with CAR.[15] The Arabic word *murḥal* comes from the verb *raḥala* (رحل), meaning to set out, voyage, or move away. In the context of nomadic Chad, the word *murḥal* is used to specifically signify the 'corridor' of transhumance. The verb *sāra* (سار) is used locally to indicate the act of migrating (moving with livestock). Officially, nomadic movement is said to be irregular, with the transhumance being of a more regular or fixed nature – though how regular this can really be is debatable. Partly due to severe losses of livestock in the 1970s and 1980s after periods of recurring droughts and cattle disease, many members have cut down on their transhumance activities, limiting the distance travelled with their livestock in the rainy and dry seasons.

For the past thirty years, Khachana, Hadj Saleh, and their extended family of Walad Djifir have taken to settling their nomadic camps in five specific areas in the Guéra (see Map 3), only moving camp three to four times a year. Their cattle and other livestock still travel toward far-away pastures when necessary, but the

---

13 Khazanov (1994) attempts to decipher the distinction between extended families, communities, and other classifications of social organization. Writing about primary kin groups versus the extended family, he says the following: 'Amongst nomads a primary kin group consists of closely related families which all year round, or for part of the year, pasture together and help and support each other. Such groups are, of course, considerably less stable than an individual family and all the families of a primary kin group run their own households and keep their own livestock. The primary kin group consists of several autonomous economic cells which do not automatically have the right to make claims on each other's property and labour. Thus the primary kin group must not be confused with the extended family' (p. 128).

14 See Fisher & Kohl (2010) for similar dynamics among the Saharan Tuareg; Pantuliano (2010) on the Misseriyya of Sudan; the edited volume by Catley et al. (2013) on dynamics in the Horn of Africa; and Manoli et al. (2014) in Senegal.

15 Barraud et al. (2001); Aubague et al. (2006); Dangbet (2015a); conversations with informants in 2012–2015.

majority of the family will then stay behind. Some Walad Djifir have year-round agricultural fields close to their dry- or wet-season ferīkh, in the Guéra or Batha respectively. Permanent villages, though only a handful, have also been established in the area. Nevertheless, mobility is still very much a livelihood strategy inherent to their nomadic way of life. Older Walad Djifir recount stories of earning cash in Sudan, returning to the ferīkh with a horse of their own and some change to spare.[16] Such trends have continued with several Walad Djifir working as cattle traders herding cattle to the lucrative markets of Nigeria. Others have found work guarding herds of smaller livestock and camels in the Libyan Desert. Still others make their living selling products from a stall or small shop in CAR.

The ferīkh is where all of the Walad Djifir's networks meet, and often also begin – providing the departure point of this ethnography of connectivity. The ferīkh is a physical place, embodying different social spaces through the connections it has with life 'outside' the ferīkh. This does not at all imply that a distinction can be made between life in the ferīkh and life 'outside' it. Regional and local dynamics are very much linked – especially in terms of 'everyday' life. In this sense, the 'ferīkh' is introduced as an analytical concept, in the way it functions as a network of connectivity, echoing the idea of an *éspace mobile* (Retaillé & Walther 2011). The mobile space model considers the mobility of places themselves; a 'place' can move within a given spatial structure and yet keep its intrinsic properties (ibid.: 89). Everyday life in the ferīkh is a reflection of wider dynamics, with its 'space' embracing the intricate relationships between sedentarism and mobility, the mundane and the extreme, flexibility[17] and expectations. The words of Massey come to mind: 'It is about constructing a sense of a locality's place in the world (its identity) which has the courage to admit that it's open' (1994: 117).

Cutting the network

A focus on everyday life in the nomadic camp inadvertently revealed the many ways in which that life was connected to a variety of goings-on outside of the camp

---

16 Author interviews, Fadjé, 20 March 2012.
17 Flexibility, here, is used within the context of nomadic studies and in line with de Bruijn & van Dijk (1997: 504): 'At the level of the community and the herding families it [flexibility] expresses itself not only in a geographical mobility in order to deal with ecological fluctuations, but also in the ways people relate to each other, redistribute natural resources over society, and mediate access to social resources which may provide some protection in bad times.' They go on to emphasize that with this flexibility comes an aspect of political and cultural control, to avoid chaos. See also Chapter Four for more on flexibility.

and the immediate family. It was this exact setting that would define and mark the nature and limits of the research, with common denominators such as livestock, family, land-ownership issues, and the sending of money popping up within conversations and observations. I refer to these common denominators as 'connectors' as they embody connections between life in and outside of the ferīkh setting. Each connector symbolizes and introduces a 'layer of connectivity'. Empirically following the trajectories (Schapendonk 2011) of Leaders, Cattle, Money, and Family, as they related to daily life, is the basis of this book's chapters. 'Islam' could very well have formed one of the chapters of this book. It is a veritable agent of connectivity, recognizable in every domain of life. Islam is such a given, however, that there were no direct discussions or frictions related to it within Walad Djifir daily life. Instead, Islam is a thread which runs through all of the chapters. It is present in the discussions and actions surrounding ferīkh politics, it is at the basis of the distribution of family inheritance, it informs familial expectations, and it determines the orientation towards certain countries for both religious and educative purposes. It is an intrinsic part of Walad Djifir life, forming both a context and a way of life.

The way each connector – Leaders, Cattle, Money, and Family – appears in the lived experiences of Walad Djifir reveals how they relate to and/or are influenced by different socio-political and economic aspects, and vice versa (Harvey 1993). Flows of information influence interactions surrounding connectors, as well as people's valuation for and behaviour in relation to them (Appadurai 1990, 1996; Castells 1996). They are shaped by factors such as market changes, politics, and technological changes. Connectors may then be fixed entities whose values change over time and in certain contexts, thus also changing the connectivity they embody.[18] Chapter Three, for example, looks at how Walad Djifir perceptions of cattle are related to the choices they make in terms of labour migration and wage labour – but also how experiences of the latter influence perceptions of cattle's future value. Cattle embody information on how to tend them, where and when to sell them, and so on – and this information in turn is based on past processes in which change and continuity are important elements. Walad Djifir interactions with cattle reveal tendencies embedded in power relations, access, and wealth, and vice versa. The physical place of the ferīkh thus becomes a condensation of social interrelations and networks within a specific moment. This builds on the idea of connectors as 'condensed networks', and networks as socially expanded connectors. A focus on

---

18 For studies building on the 'social life' of material and living connections, see Appadurai (1986) (social life of things); van Binsbergen & Geschiere (2005) (commodification); Elliot (2010) (nomadic commodification and social ties); de Bruijn & van Dijk (2012) (connectivity); van Dijck (2013) (social media).

connectivity – on these linkages or 'connectors' specifically – tells us something about the nature of the 'place' and ultimately of those linked to it, while not being limited to time or space (Massey 1994). The choice for 'connectors' and the conceptualization of the ferīkh as embodying various networks, and thus as a way of 'cutting the network' (Strathern 1996), defines the nature and limits of this ethnography of nomadic connectivity. By analysing the shifting systems of logic surrounding each of the connectors, I look at how they are related to decision-making processes and larger social dynamics.

Crisis and connectivity

What struck me was the constant negotiation that family members were involved in, a negotiation between security and insecurity, the self and the group, the group and the state, order and disorder, the known (predictable) and the unknown (and thus unpredictable crisis?),[19] the drive to escape while nurturing the safety of familiar ways. Another intriguing aspect was that of the simultaneous confrontation, struggle, adaptation, and empowerment of flexibility in relation to (in)security. This flexibility was mostly reflected in the (in)voluntary choices people made and their explanatory narrative of why they had done so. How, then, can we research the degree to which Walad Djifir experience disruptions (insecurity) to their everyday lives? How can we disentangle our own ideas about such abstract concepts as crisis and disruption, from the perceptions and experiences of those being researched? And what is overlooked when approaching the analysis from a crisis-perspective?[20]

A house burning down is not immediately a crisis, given a specific context (Roitman 2005). The fleeing of Khachana's daughter-in-law, Nour, and her young family from CAR after the 2013 coup (see Chapter Six) in and of itself is a crisis situation.

---

19 In his short book *Liquid Times: Living in an Age of Uncertainty*, Bauman (2007: 95) says the following: 'We are all familiar with unpleasant and uncomfortable occasions when things or people cause us worries we would not expect them, and certainly not wish them, to cause. What makes such adversities ("blows of fate", as we sometimes call them) particularly irksome is that they fall unannounced – we do not expect them to come, and quite often will not believe that they might be near. They hit us, as we say, "like bolts out of the blue" – we can't take precautions and avert the catastrophe, since no one expects a thunderbolt from a cloudless sky.'

20 I refer here mainly to the political scientists who have written on Chad, such as Buijtenhuijs (1977, 1978, 1987); Decalo (1980a, 1980b); Lemarchand (1980, 1981, 1985, 1986); Joffe (1982); Nolutshungu (1996); Azevedo (2004); Marchal (2006, 2008); Tubiana (2011); and others. For exceptions see Arditi (1999); de Bruijn et al. (2004); Behrends et al. (2007); Debos (2008, 2016); Behrends (2011); Seli (2012); de Bruijn (2014); Souleymane (2017); de Bruijn & Both (2018).

Nour was born and raised in urban Bangui but sent to live in rural Chad upon the death of her father. Both events were traumatic and stressful and involved much uncertainty for all parties involved. At the same time, the result was that Nour, her children, and husband were reunited with her father's family in Chad. They currently live in the town of Mongo, close to the nomadic camps of their families. The children go to Qur'ānic school; her husband runs a shop. Within 'the everyday', how can the interplay of crisis as context (Mbembe & Roitman 1995; Vigh 2006; Cooper & Pratten 2015) and moments of crisis then be interpreted? Or do the results of Nour's sudden move require a more nuanced concept to describe them? The cause was a crisis situation; the process was also one of relative insecurity. But the outcome? And the chronicity of the contextual crisis?

Photo 1.7: Bullet-holes of 1979 fighting in N'Djaména, taken at the home of a khalifa of the Misseria Rouge, N'Djaména, March 2014. Perceptions of Chad are often described in a context of post-conflict and insecurity. While I did not focus on such a context from the outset, these themes and historical events of violence did come up in the 'everyday' – here in the form of a way to create some privacy and protection from the wind and sun in a household setting. Those present on this afternoon could tell me exactly which weapon had made which bullet holes.

Amidst disruption there is always a choice in focus. Just as the Second World War mathematician who decided to reinforce the parts of planes that *did* make it back to Britain, the shift in focus on what *does* work and not on *what went wrong* provided a different angle of understanding. The logic was that those plane parts seemed to be most important in keeping the plane in the air. Similarly, moments of crisis can act as builders or disruptors of connectivity, depending on the 'parts' available and accessible. In Nour's case, the focus on the everyday brought to light certain elements which had the potential both to redefine pre-existing social structures, as well as to emphasize them. This ethnography shows what 'parts' or connections define how Walad Djifir like Khachana, Nour, and Hadj Saleh experience disruption. These are the same 'tentacles' that somehow anchor disruptions back into the everyday (Das 2007). We will explore how the ferīkh, and everything around it, provides a network for dealing with crisis and disruption.

The globalizing wilderness

In the case of Hadj Saleh, Khachana, and Adoum, this 'anchoring' (Das 2007) is defined by the ferīkh and that which it embodies – the extended family – but also by socio-economic ties or networks and norms and values (i.e. a frame of reference); there is a coupling of belonging and connectivity, and of space and place. For the Walad Djifir this 'home' is not necessarily a physical location but has more to do with the social relations and obligations embodied in specific connectors – whether they be people, cattle, or money. For the Walad Djifir, this belonging to the family circle (Nyamnjoh 2014) is not only an emotional factor but also a 'mentality' linked to ferīkh norms and values – providing a safety network in times of need. Observed negotiations among family members, as well as with non-Walad Djifir, reveal the dynamics associated with belonging to be non-neutral and to include moments of friction and constraint.

Take Khachana's daughter-in-law Nour, for example. How do her actions and feelings toward her family in the ferīkh relate and contribute to feelings of 'belonging' in relation to a physical territory or a more immaterial 'space'? How does the ferīkh, as an entity governed by both internal and external forces, affect the decisions made in Nour's life, decisions surrounding her assets, children, and where she settles? And how do events in her life impact on 'ferīkh life'? Analysis of such daily life encounters, through a focus on 'connectors', sheds light on the dynamics within different layers of connectivity and emotions of belonging, in a (dis)connected and networked society.

Emotions of belonging

For most nomadic populations 'place' is ever-moving but, nevertheless, does exist (Prussin 1995). This touches upon the idea of *asuf* – solitude, loneliness, home-sickness – which lives among the Tuareg (see Lecocq 2010). From early on, the Tuareg are taught how to cope and survive with the Sahara's *tenere* or wilderness. Their relation with such a tough environment is described as one of contradictory feelings.

> The Tuareg are compelled by the necessities of their life to move often, to leave continuously people whom they know and love. There is a kind of ambivalence in the Tuareg's relation with the hostile desert environment whereby awareness of being the only human (part of the essence of *asuf*, which is felt as soon as one is away from the sights, sounds, and smells of camp) is simultaneously ego diminishing and ego enhancing. Just as a seaman belongs less to the harbor where his boat is anchored than to the sea, so *tenere* [wilderness/desert] rather than his tent is the true home of the Tuareg man. (Youssouf et al. 1976: 800)

Moving away from the familiarity of the camp invokes a feeling of being alone (*asuf*), a feeling which has the effect of both enhancing and diminishing the ego. When it comes to their own environment, Walad Djifir relate to the ambivalence described above. Although currently based in a relatively populated area in Chad's Sahelian Guéra region, in contrast to the Tuareg's western Sahara setting, these contradictory feelings are defined along the lines of the physical, ecological space in which the Walad Djifir live and the feelings it creates of both endless possibilities and loneliness.

While wilderness perhaps has a somewhat negative connotation, as chaotic and perhaps even frightening, I see it more in line with nature in general as being wild or unkempt yet very much having a purpose and certain structure to it. In pastoral-nomadic studies, pastoral borderlands are often associated with being beyond the reach of the state and thus also of the development industry, (in)directly implying a level of disorder (for a refreshing alternative approach, based on the idea of the Sahel as a 'frontier' see García et al. 2023). The one does not exclude the other: wild and unstructured, order and chaos. As Marielle Debos (2016: 174) writes when describing the trajectories of Chadian civilians:

> Power relations and socio-economic hierarchies do not develop *despite* disorder – instead, they emerge and develop *from* that disorder. Social differentiation is strong. Savvy young men seldom experience social mobility with weapons in hand. However, their trajectories make sense if one considers that civilian life is often a daily combat.

In the case of the Walad Djifir, the Sahel and beyond are their *tenere* or wilderness, their space of daily 'combat' – an infinite globalizing space. The Sahel is not, if it ever was, made up of its acacia trees, wādis, and thorny shrubs alone.[21] The Sahel has held, and still holds, paths and roads; it holds nomadic camps and sedentary villages; its landscape encompasses agricultural fields and wells, with roaming livestock and wildlife. The Sahel's villages hold markets, whose products are brought in from near and far and whose prices for these products are also determined by events near and far. People are seen moving through, out of, and into the Sahel – for work, healthcare, schooling, family visits, or trade. In a sense then, the Sahel's environment could be interpreted as a multi-dimensional jigsaw puzzle – Retaillé and Walther's (2011) given spatial structure – constructed by an historical process of interactions and made up of different yet integrated pieces: ecology, infrastructure, people, but also news and ideas. Is the feeling of ambivalence shaped by a combination of these (local) pieces, creating an elaborate and complex globalizing context – one within which the individual can feel both strong and small at the same time? And is the nomadic camp merely one of the pieces of the larger environment, with the tent less of a home than the wilderness itself? Or does the wilderness become a 'home' exactly because 'the ferīkh' is moveable?

Grounded in connectivity

The idea of a certain continuity or normalization existing – throughout those extraordinary moments that *do* occur, as well as the more mundane happenings – is intriguing. While mistrust (wariness) informs behaviour when greeting strangers, the values of honour and respect hold just as much sway. There is no rudeness, even if someone is not trusted. So how do the two work together? How can both mistrust and the upkeep of certain values exist in one person? And how do the two shape and form the nature of exchange and choices made? Despite the intrinsic wariness toward the unknown stranger, methods and etiquettes for dealing with him or her exist, just as there are norms and values linked to dealing with livestock, Islamic customs, land and familial issues, or the sending of money. The logics and reasonings surrounding these moments of connectivity help structure daily life, creating connections (of belonging) within which individuals face moments of both insecurity and security.

---

21 Inspired by Lydon's (2009) descriptions of the historical connections across the Sahara, approaching it as a dynamic space with a deep history.

Photo 1.8: The Bambam *wādi* (dry river bed), Fadjé area, March 2012. The Bambam reflects how the relative wilderness (or *tenere* of the Tuareg) of the Walad Djifir's roaming grounds are not necessarily unstructured and unknown. The vast regions of the Guéra and Batha hold *wādis* which act as life sources in both dry and wet seasons. They help orientate passers-by, provide grazing areas for livestock, agricultural land for those farming, and shallow ground water in the dry season. Spatial structures exist through historical processes of interactions, between people and their environment.

The conceptualization of the term groundedness comes from wishing to find a way to describe the practical (expectations and needs) *and* more emotional aspects (such as feelings of belonging). Amidst all the possible triggers for disruption of the personal psyche, many of the Walad Djifir I encountered appeared to be 'grounded' in some way or other. Their everyday lives and subsequent decisions revolved around 'the ferīkh' and that which it stands for. It is the connections within and represented by the ferīkh which ground them – hence, grounded in connectivity. This is not to negate the very real traumas lived. It is a way of understanding what 'connections' work, so to speak, (or function) in ordinary and extraordinary situations. It allows one to touch upon the more practical aspects of daily life amidst disruption while, through the link with the 'emotion of belonging' (Yuval-Davis 2006) as a characteristic of being grounded, also creating some understanding for the agency of an individual as a person 'living life'. It is through the ferīkh and its connectivity (embodied networks and connectors), in the way that it provides a grounded space or basis for individuals and the group, that we can analyse the Walad Djifir's navigations of a globalizing Chad.

Photo 1.9: A typical guiding point in the Sahellian landscape, large trees that can be seen from miles away, Fadjé, March 2012. This tree happens to be located next to the Bambam.

The book and its chapters

The stories of several family members run throughout the various chapters, each linked to the chapter's connector. In this sense, a 'layer' of understanding is added each time, reflecting how the field presented itself to me – though I have restructured the 'order' to make it more coherent (Mintz 1989). Chapter Two introduces the 'terrain', providing historical context, and methods used. Chapter Three is the first of the 'connector' chapters, focusing on 'local leaders' as connectors while introducing and contextualizing the Walad Djifir's socio-political organization. We cannot fully understand that which the ferīkh stands for, and the ways in which its spaces are constructed, without touching upon how engrained the nomadic way of life is to those born and raised in a nomadic camp. In the case of the Walad Djifir, this nomadic way of life is linked to their livestock, making 'cattle' the second connector of focus (Chapter Four). Chapter Five focuses on the sending of money and how developing communication technologies interact with existing practices of connectivity among the Walad Djifir, within contexts of insecurity and over geographical distances. Chapters Four and Five thus show aspects of the Walad Djifir's socio-economic network, very much based within the ferīkh setting and branching 'out' from it. The final 'connector' chapter (Chapter Six) starts off in CAR, away from the physical setting of the ferīkh and Chad, only to take us back to it (as family unit) through the narratives of three women faced with disruption.

Chapter 2
Contextualizing itineraries

My first meeting with the Walad Djifir in October 2011 was something I was pretty much 'tricked' into, in the best sense of the word. As a preliminary exploration of my research-field-to-be, Adoum and I were travelling east from N'Djaména toward Mongo via Ati (see Map 1). The previous day he had already told me his *parents* (family) were from this area. This was the first time I discovered he belonged to a group of sedentary nomads, as he so accurately described them himself.[1] The following day, en route to Mongo from Ati, he asked me whether I would like to pass by and meet some of his *parents*. I said, 'Sure; why not? I would love to, if you are sure they won't mind.' No sooner said than done. Toward the end of the morning and after several phone calls, with one shouting to another – '*Weenak, where are you?! By which tree?! How much further from this village?!*' – we turned off the main road and made our way through an outstretched Savannah landscape, avoiding the thick thorny bushes. We arrived at a group of men patiently awaiting our arrival under a large tree. This was clearly not the spontaneous and unexpected visit I had thought it was going to be. After having made the proper greetings and drunk the first few glasses of sweet strong tea, Adoum asked me quietly, '*Now that we are here, how do you feel about spending the night?*' I laughed. So this is what he had probably planned since our departure from N'Djaména but what he had not dared to share with me, perhaps thinking I would be scared and say no from the beginning. I agreed and he clearly relaxed.

The rest of the afternoon was spent under the shade of two large trees. There was a lot of talk, catching up, things discussed. Adoum was asked to translate a letter written in French which concerned the registering of their number of cattle. The road maps I had with me were taken out and discussed and pored over; questions were asked, such as why certain villages were not mapped; the distances of those which were mapped were challenged or acknowledged. Toward the end of the afternoon we were led to the ferīkh. Hadj Saleh insisted I walk up to the camp with him. I remember being intrigued by this man's stance from the beginning. He had a calm presence and his hands did not show the signs of having done much of the hard physical labour involved in the tending of animals. He spoke some French

---

1 At the time of fieldwork, Adoum was in his fifties and a father of eight, based in N'Djaména. Before we met he had worked as a driver for the veterinary department in Farscha for many years, hence explaining his familiarity with this kind of terminology. He became a co-creator, providing information on the Guéra and his extended family.

https://doi.org/10.1515/9783110714685-002

as well, though he initially addressed me in Modern Standard Arabic (MSA), as opposed to the local Chadian Arabic. I have a background in Arabic, having studied both Egyptian and MSA, and the combination of this and my middle school French made fieldwork in Chad and CAR possible.

Photo 2.1: Setting of the first gathering of those with whom I would end up carrying out this research, October 2011. At the time, the camps of the Walad Djifir were located east of the road between Mongo and Ati. The car and ferīkh are pictured in the background.

Within the camp we were seated on large luxurious tapestries laid out over the regular straw mats. At a fair distance on the open square in between the tents were the other male members of the community. The late afternoon prayer was held and Hadj Saleh asked me to join them, *'Christian, Muslim, we all pray to God right?'* Never having prayed before, I graciously declined. A sheep was slaughtered just outside the compound and hung from a pole before being roasted. They were very concerned with what I should eat, Adoum insisting that perhaps *macarona* would suit me best, as the *boule* was sure to be too heavy for my stomach. I could not escape sharing some of the beloved and much revered *marara* (tripe, part of the stomach lining), but luckily the dark disguised the fact that there was nothing but sauce in the hand going from plate to mouth. After dinner, my bladder made me realize I had not yet gone the whole day. I asked Adoum where I could go and was directed to the women. This was my first real encounter with Nour, although of course I did not

Photo 2.2: Within the camp, young men are seated at a distance in the morning after our first stay, October 2011. Due to the landscape – grazing land as opposed to the more wooded area on the other side of the Bambam, which Walad Djifir prefer earlier in the year due to its proximity to ground water – there is an open feeling to this camp. Another ferīkh (camp) is visible in the distance.

realize it at the time.[2] Her first impression of me: leading me away from the camp with a torch and waiting while I went about my business. So much for first impressions . . . . It was not until the morning of the next day that I met the other women. Looking back at the photos I took at that time, I now recognize many of the women: Khadidja, Khachana, Raouda. The same goes for the men and children.

On the second visit to this same group, in February 2012, I was received with open arms, greeted by people I only vaguely recognized from the photos I had brought to distribute among them. At that time, I did not recognize any of the women. The idyllic first visit was slowly transformed into a more settled realistic stay. I now installed myself for the night on my fold-out bed just outside Nour's *barsh* (tent), no longer sleeping out in the open among the men. I had my own mat to share with others during the day and was instantly introduced to their daily life patterns, including the many young children and livestock. We took walks to the *'eidd*[3] where the livestock

---

2 This was actually a second meeting, as we had gone to see her in the late afternoon while she was sleeping, she being ill at the time. It was only much later that I pieced the encounters together and realized the woman must have been Nour during one of her ill spells.

3 *'eidd* (عد) pl. *'udūd*, a watering point, whether water is found on the surface or by digging deep (Julien de Pommerol 1999). The MSA root of the word is related to the verb *'āda - yu'ūd* (عاد - يعود)

Photo 2.3: A tent within the camp, October 2011. A shy Sassileh thought the doctor had come to give her vaccinations. Sassileh is one of Saleh and Khadidja's younger daughters and named after the town in CAR where her uncle and father spent several years. It was not until the second longer stay in early 2012 that the link with CAR was made and I learned how much time some family members had been spending there and how regular the contact was between them.

Photo 2.4: Packing up after the first morning, October 2011. Nour's little boy, Saleh, is seen playing in the foreground next to the car.

are watered. At that time, the *‘eidd* was located at a five- to ten-minute walk from the dry *wādi* and a good twenty-minute walk from the camp. The groundwater level is very high here, and the wells (*birr*)[4] the men dig are only about 4 metres deep. It takes them about two days to dig a well; and once enforced, the wells last the whole time they are in this area during the dry season, approximately from December to June. The wells provide the *hutt*[5] with water throughout the day.[6] Three *hutts* are often created around one well. They are circular in shape, slightly dug out and walled. To prevent cattle from walking right across them, a thorny bush is placed in the middle.

At first glance, this group of sedentary nomads could be considered as living an isolated existence, tending their cattle and smaller livestock, living perhaps not very differently from the way nomads lived centuries ago. But this is, of course, not the whole story. At that very first encounter in 2011, while sitting under those trees with the men, mobile phones were being charged and many would ring, often the conversations being cut off owing to the bad network. I did not yet have many questions to ask, nor did I at all know that the Nour who had led me to the 'bathroom' and who had been feeling so ill during the day had in fact recently come from CAR. Nor was I aware that many family members were or would be travelling to Libya in search of jobs. Only two years later would I even realize that several of those family members in CAR were involved in the diamond business. Sometimes, you really do need to know the answers in order to have an inkling of the right questions to ask.

---

which means 'to return' (after a long period or after a cycle). The *‘eidd* is a place where people and their livestock keep returning to over periods of time.

4 The word *bi'r* (بئر) comes from the verb *ba'ara* (بأر), to dig a well (Wehr 1994; Julien de Pommerol 1999). In the text, it is transcribed as Walad Djifir pronounce it: *birr*.

5 The origins of the word *hutt* derive from *ḥaṭṭa* (حط), to put, place down / to lower, decrease (Wehr 1994). Ex.: *maḥaṭṭ*, a place at which something goes down: The plane landed at N'Djamena airport. (حطّت الطائرة في مطار أنجمينا.) In the case of the Walad Djifir, *hutt* is used to indicate a structure where water from a shallow well is placed.

6 See Wiese (2004: 139) on the Arab Juhayna's reliance on surface water compared with the Dazagada (ibid.: 130), who exploit limited water resources during the dry season (the traditional wells they dig are about 15–20 m deep). The Arabs' use of surface water means that they are less restricted in terms of the number of livestock that can be watered, provided the water supply is large enough and the surrounding pastures provide enough space to alternate use. During the height of the dry season, the Walad Djifir often end up grazing their cattle at some distance from the camps and wells (and thus the dry river bed). This means that the cattle, and their herders, spend much time moving to and from the pasture areas. The cattle are brought to be watered during the day, setting out for the wells in the morning and sometimes arriving only late in the morning or early afternoon, only to set off again at the end of the afternoon, thus spending the night *en brousse*. Just after the rainy seasons, however, early in the year you will more often find herds kept close to the camps overnight, as there is still sufficient grazing nearby. This means that there is a lot of dung lying around.

Photo 2.5: Setting of the ferīkh in Fadjé, March 2012. Fadjé is located on the west side of the Bambam and at approximately the same height as the sedentary village Tchoufiou II Arabe. This area is wooded and becomes very muddy once the rains start, marking the time to relocate to different grounds. Notice the tents in the background, with Nour walking towards them on the left.

Photo 2.6: The back of Khachana's tent which she shared with her grandson, Nour's older son Moussa. In February-April 2012 they shared a camp and their tents were located right next to each other. The two women shared household tasks, such as the preparation of meals, with Khachana being the one to collect water once/twice a day from the ʿeidd. At the time, Arafa, Hadj Saleh's older sister, was sharing a tent with Nour.

Photo 2.7: View of Nour's tent, with boys' circumcision tent on left and Khachana's tent to the right, March 2012.

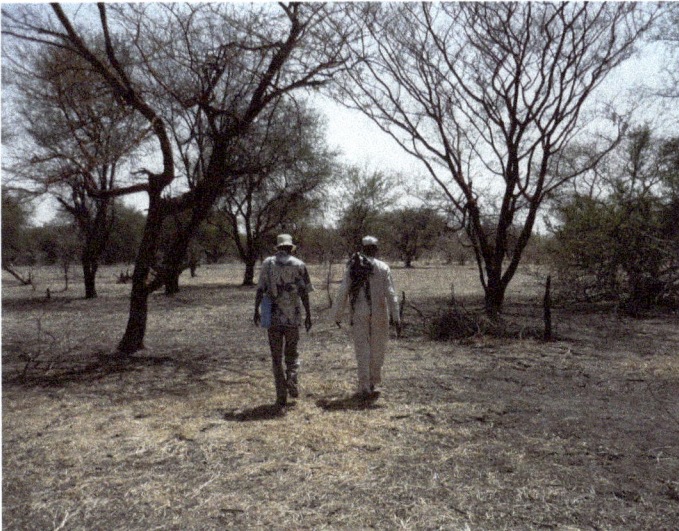

Photo 2.8: Adoum and Hadj Saleh walking back from a visit to the village, March 2012. Hadj Saleh had had a meeting to attend with other members of the ferīkh council, and we joined him. The area close to the road between Mongo and Ati and before you reach the Bambam is less densely wooded.

Photo 2.9: Cattle drinking at a *hutt* March 2013. The branches in the middle prevent the animals from walking across it and thus destroying the mud-structure.

Photo 2.10: The inside of a *birr*, March 2012. Notice how the walls at the very bottom have been fortified with branches. It takes the men two days to dig and fortify such a well. The surface water is never very clear and the branches contribute to its quality (often murky and somewhat smelly). A birr will last until the rainy season takes over, at which point a new (and shallower) well is dug.

Photo 2.11: The *'eidd* seen from a distance, March 2012. On the right is a shaded overhang under which men and children find their rest while the cattle drink and others tend to the watering. You can make out two circular shapes which are the hutts from which the animals drink.

The 'field' and its co-creation

This chapter presents 'the field', through Walad Djifir's past and contemporary itineraries. About half-way through the second fieldwork in 2012, I was asked to join a meeting of Walad Djifir elders and parents. They were gathering to discuss the new school being set up. Their chef de village Nouraddin introduced me as a researcher who was here to write down and photograph what life is like, so that their children and their children's children would have a reference to know their history by. He held up the book Pierre Hugot (1997) wrote, documenting conflicts that took place around Oum Hadjer in 1947 between the French and Misseria. In doing so, the book makes note of the various Misseria Rouges and Misseria Noires groups, indicating their leaders and their dry and wet-season grazing lands. Nouraddin wanted to use the book as proof of Walad Djifir's land ownership. In later conversations with women and men alike, a whole range of subjects were enthusiastically proposed for me to include in my studies. These ranged from how and what kind of food was prepared, to knowledge on tending livestock, photographing family members, and the documenting of whom was related to whom, and in which way. In a region where so many of its official archives have been destroyed time and again, the importance of documenting and sharing aspects of what daily life looks like is important.

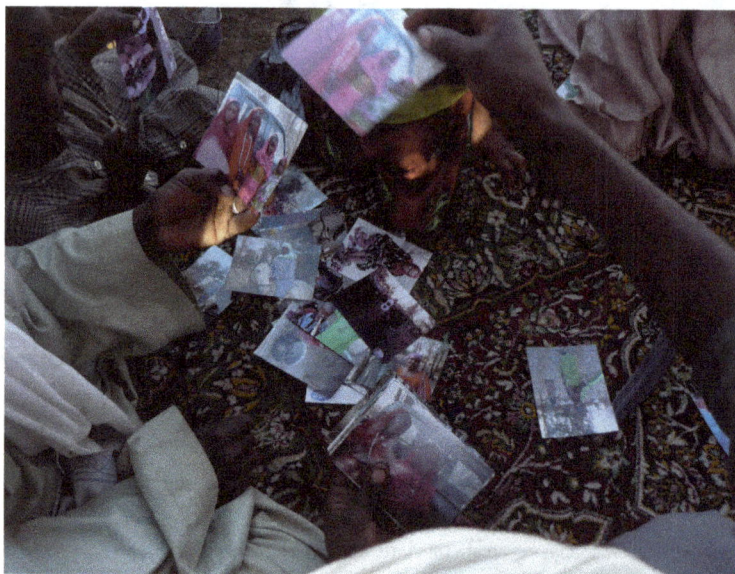

Photo 2.12: Discussing and passing around photographs, December 2012. Bringing back many of the pictures I had taken during the previous two fieldwork visits allowed me to interact in a different way with those with whom I had been living. We would talk about the people in the photographs and one subject sometimes led to another. It was also a great way to connect family members, who had not seen each other in a long time owing to physical distance.

This documenting happened in conjunction with many individuals, with some playing a larger role than others. The Matsutake Worlds Research Group's (2009) notion of collaboration as, in and of itself, being a process contributing to knowledge resonates with the idea of co-creation. Different communities provided general information and context, setting the scene and acting as passive reference points to co-interpret specific situations. With individuals, it was more of an active process of reflexivity and remembering, especially in relation to moments of crisis (Fabian 2003).[7] Taking pictures together, within the ferīkh or in a remote village in CAR, co-created moments of awareness of these physical places as spaces embodying both familiar

---

7 On how forgetting and remembering go hand-in-hand and how memory is, to an extent, constituted by forgetting, see Argenti & Schramm (2010). See also Vansina (1980); Onyx & Small (2001); Holtzman (2009); Tumblety (2013); Both (2017) for more on memory and history.

and unfamiliar dynamics (Szabó & Troyer 2017). This 'step[ping] back from the flow of everyday experience' often instigated 'spontaneous reflection and resonating sentiment', calling up questions and emotions which otherwise may not have come to light (Basso 1996: 54–55). Co-interpreting both the visible and non-visible nuanced the understanding and positioning of Walad Djifir daily life within the existing dominant visual imagery emerging from Chad and the wider region. The nomadic Walad Djifir are but a small part of the overall very diverse Chadian population. With their help, I have done my best to document and contextualize the daily lives they let me be a part of. Throughout the writing of this book Nouraddin's introduction has been a reminder of the power of the written, and a reminder of how delicate the balance is of getting the stories 'right', whatever that may entail. While research participants are not named as co-authors, with their consent, their stories and insights have contributed immensely to the existence of this book. The visual narrative shows their nomadic camps, animals, and daily lives, without giving true names. This is a way of giving them a form of ownership over the stories shared, while also protecting individual privacy. It was important to Walad Djifir that tangible words and images should exist for future generations to look back on. All contemporary Walad Djifir had some kind of anecdote related to the past. The depth and subject of such anecdotes varied greatly. Detailed anecdotes in relation to the civil war and other moments of political violence were rare. One topic which was recounted fairly frequently was that of the trauma or damage incurred after the cattle diseases of the 1970s and '80s. These anecdotal memories of Walad Djifir illustrate the local dimensions of historical 'facts' others have written about. It is the emphasis on familial or personal memories (Both 2017) which positions the way Walad Djifir narrate their own experiences of the past, in relation to existing narratives, whether these be visual or verbal.

Who are the Walad Djifir?

The Walad Djifir are a sub-group of the Misseria Rouges and claim descent from Juhaina nomadic groups who moved into Chad from the Nile Delta around the fourteenth century, after the fall of the kingdom of Nubia (Thomas 1959: 144; Zeltner & Tourneux 1986). Originating in the wider region of the Arabian Peninsula, these groups moved to Egypt and then on to Chad via the Sudan.[8] When prompted, Walad

---

8 See Dangbet (2015a: 66–67) for specifics. Le Rouvreur (1989) claims the ancestors of the Juhaina came from the Hejaz (western Saudi Arabia). Carbou (1912) specifically mentions Yemen as the ancestral homeland of the Juhaina, who then migrated onward to Egypt. Chapelle (1980) explains Arab migrations into Chad as related to the repression of Arabs, and consecutive revolts, which took place in Egypt in the fourteenth century.

Djifir themselves refer to their ancestors coming from Yemen and that the linguistic origin of the word Misseria comes from the verb *sāra*,[9] to travel. What evidence of this can we find in existing literature? This section traces their origins as described in written sources and introduces their first relations with authoritarian rule in Chad under the Ouaddaï, and later under the French.

The move into Chad

The Juhaina were the first Arabs to migrate south out of Egypt and move to Dongola 'at the great bend of the Nile' (Thomas 1959: 144), before continuing west into Kordofan and Darfur. The Misseria descend from these Juhaina, who in turn are descendants of 'Abdallah al-Juhani. It is said that his ancestry can be traced back to the uncle of Prophet Muhammed, al-'Abbas (Thomas 1959; Aubague et al. 2006).[10] It is common for nomadic groups to claim some form of descent from the Prophet or his companions, and lineages have been observed to be fluid.

The Misseria of Kordofan were initially made up of two different groups, known as the Misseria Zurg – simply known as the Misseria – and Misseria Humr, known as the Humr. The Misseria[11] and Humr[12] of Kordofan thus claim they once formed a single group with those Misseria now living in Chad and with others currently in Darfur (Cunnison 1966: 4), both descending from the common ancestor, 'Ataya.[13] This 'Ataya was from the area we now know as Yemen. Traditionally, when nomadic groups become too large or split up for any other reason, they add on contrasting names. The same might be true for the Misseria Rouges and Misseria

---

9 *sāra, yisīr* (سار يسير), to move on, set out, travel, go away (Wehr 1994).

10 'The Djoheïna [Juhaina] Arabs who migrate the Guéra are attached to the Batha region. They have Djounet as common ancestor, a descendant of Abdoullahi Ibn Ounes el Djoheïni Abd el Mottaleb, respectively the grandfather of and tutor to Muhammed. According to Le Rouvreur (1989), they came from Egypt and installed themselves in Chad's Ouaddaï region in the fifteenth century. In successive waves, other groups came to join them' (Aubague et al. 2006: 44–45).

11 To avoid additional confusion, I have chosen to use the same spelling of Misseria throughout this book. Others, like Cunnison (1966), would use a more elaborate spelling – namely, Messeriyya or Misseriyya.

12 Numerous studies have been conducted on the Humr of Sudan, who in turn belong to the Baggara Arabs – *baqqara* (بقرة) meaning 'cattle' in Arabic – and who also claim descent from pre-Islamic Arabs (Cunnison 1972).

13 Julien de Pommerol (1997) includes a list of groups with the Misseria Humr (rouge) belonging to Oum Hadjer and listed under Wulaad Atiiye, which is, in turn, listed under Juhayna.

Noirs. Some claim that the Misseria group was becoming too large and needed to split. Often what is meant here are the livestock numbers.

Looking at the linguistic origins of the word Misseria, there are two ways in which it can be transcribed: (1) as *miṢr* (مصر), the Arabic word for Egypt, *misseriyya* (مصرية) (here spelled as *misseria*) then literally meaning, 'Egyptian'; or (2) coming from the root *sāra* (سار), to travel or migrate, *misseriyya* (مسرية) then meaning those that migrate. Members of the Walad Djifir refer to the latter meaning.

It is not particularly clear from the literature whether or how the current-day Misseria Rouges and Noirs have descended from the (Misseria) Humr and Misseria (Zurg) respectively.[14] What we know is that the Humr are said to have moved west-wards into Ouaddaï around 1775.[15] Ouaddaï is currently one of Chad's districts and was also the location of the most eastern-lying sultanate to have reigned in Chad, with its capital established at what is still known as Abéché in 1850.[16] The sultanate itself was established in 1635 and continued for a good two-and-a-half centuries. Many nomadic groups remained under Ouaddaïan 'control' for years, despite their evasive tactics.

The Ouaddaïan administration installed *aqids*, who were in charge of collect-ing taxes from both sedentary and nomadic populations. The *aqid* was usually not from the same group as the one he represented but chosen from among the indig-enous groups of the region to ensure loyalty to the sultan. The *aqid* is also know as the *chef de groupe* or *chef de communauté*. Before the coming of the concept of the *chef de canton*, it was the *aqid* who acted like a *chef de guerre*. They were under the order of the Ouaddaïan *moussa*, or ruler. Under each *aqid* there were different *khashim beyt*. For example, the Misseria had an *aqid* and so did the Hamīd and the

---

14 *Ahmar* (احمر) is the Arabic word for red, *humr* (حمر) belonging to the same root of the word. *Zurg* (زورج) in turn relates to the name for those of Nubian descent in old Arabic texts. This may, however, be a coincidence. It is fairly safe to assume that the words *humr* and *zurg* have been replaced by *rouge* and *noire* respectively under French influence.

15 According to Thomas (1959), the Humr Baggara chose to move west into Darfur and Ouaddaï, from Kordofan, establishing themselves there in the middle of the sixteenth century.

16 In an interview with the then mayor of Abéché on 20 October 2011, he related how this city came to be: 'In 1850, Abéché was started as a town. Between 1820 and 1830 Sultan Mu-hammad Sherif initiated a new capital of Ouaddaï because there had been years of drought and there was no more water in the Warra. The head of the commission to find a location for the new capital was Iman al-Gazuli. He decided to follow the trajectory of the nomads, to the south of the Warra. He arrived here and found a little mountain and next to it found a herder Abu Ashee (Abéché). He found a lot of water here and decided to develop the new capital here. Al-Gazuli went back to the Sultan and together they made a plan. Turkish architects arrived and built the Palais de Sultan and made an architectural plan of the city. That is how the *ville* came to be established in 1850. The population at that time was about 12,000, made up of mixed ethnicities.'

Walad Rashīd. In turn, they were divided into six *khashim beyt*: the Walad Sūrūr, Walad Matanīn, Walad Djifir, Djarafīn, Walad Tūrki, and Walad ʿUmr.[17] Over the years, the Misseria, like other groups, split into even more factions (Table 1) owing to their having migrated far away or as a result of internal discord.[18] The factions mentioned in written sources correspond to those Walad Djifir themselves recognize and are related to questions of land rights.

Table 1: The Misseria and their khashim beyt/fellati (in 1949). Based on Hugot (1997: 121).

Misseria Noirs	Misseria Rouges	
Alaʾūn	Abideye/Habideye	Mazaknéh
Hawazmeh	Bisheshat	Nadja
Walad Abou Rahama	Djūbarat	Nawass Walad Guible
Walad Khanem	Hadjadjire	Walad Djifir
Salamanī/Hemat	Kalabīn	Walad ʿUmar
	Khozzam	Walad Sūrūr
	Matanīn	Walad Tūrki

Over time, and fleeing the Ouaddaï sultan's taxes, raids, and the demands of the *aqids*, nomadic groups moved further west, into the Guéra and Batha districts of central Chad. They could not flee too far, as other (hostile) nomadic groups were already inhabiting certain areas. The current-day Misseria, as overarching group, can be found primarily in the east along the border with Sudan, and in central Chad from the Batha down through the Guéra and into the Salamat.

In the beginning, though, the nomads would not come to the Guéra as the terrain was too much of a forest with many wild animals, making it difficult to keep their herds safe. The sedentary Hadjeray lived in or close to the mountains at this time. Under French rule, when the Hadjeray were being forced down from their mountains and establishing villages in open terrain, the land also became more

---

17 From an interview with a former *khalifa* and current *chef de raʾas* of the Misseria Rouge in N'Djaména, 1 March 2014. According to this same *khalifa*, the former name of the Misseria was Bin Ihlaal, and at that time their *moussa* was someone called Hassan Surhaan. The *khalifa* mentioned a book in Arabic which contained this information which I should photocopy from him. Unfortunately, we were unable to meet again and I have not yet been able to verify the source.

18 Special alliances exist between these factions. The Walad Djifir, for example, refer to the Walad Tūrki, who live a little further north than they do, as their 'twin'. This means that they do not intermarry. What else this 'twin-hood' means is unclear. When questioned further, Adoum was unsure what the history of this alliance was, and I did not find anyone else who knew either. From a conversation with Adoum, N'Djaména, 4 April 2012.

accessible to the nomads.[19] At present, the most prominent nomadic groups found in the Guéra are the Misseria Rouges and Noirs, the Walad Rachīd, the Djaatneh, and the Salamat Siféra. In the Batha, one will find these same groups, as well as the Sharafa, the Zioud, the Walad Himet, and the Khozzam.[20]

Administrative changes under the French

According to Thomas (1959), sections of the Misseria crossed over to the French in 1907 – escaping Ouaddaïan reign in eastern Chad – who had by this time come as far east as Lac Fitri.[21] In doing so, the Misseria installed themselves well to the west of their former homelands. Brahim (1988: 39) describes how in 1906 one of the Ouaddaï *aqids* (Ahmad Magné of the el Zabada) confiscated all of the camels of numerous Misseria sub-groups. The move away from Ouaddaïan reach followed the 1904 move of several other groups taking refuge under the French against hostile neighbours, raiders, and unreasonable tax confiscations by the *aqids*. The 1920s saw a shift in French policy when, in an attempt to improve administrative control over highly mobile Arabs, certain chiefs were awarded considerable authority (the *grand kadmul* policy).[22] In doing so, some groups became linked under one chief without there being clear family ties between them. A Humr Missairi chief, for example, was given command over all the Misseria, the independent Haimad, and even the non-Arab populations of three cantons (sedentary tribal areas) to the north of the river Batha. By 1935, due to excessive taxes imposed by these French-raised chiefs, the Misseria were dispersed over ten administrative districts, while

---

19 Fieldnotes, 11 February 2013. In his 2017 dissertation, historian Souleymane Abdoulaye Adoum describes this movement off the mountains forced by the French colonial power. For more background on the Hadjeray, especially in relation to their mobility when faced with conflict see Alio (2008).

20 Aubague et al. (2006: 45, 69), lists not exclusive.

21 The French first started taking a colonizing interest in Chad in the late 1880s / early 1890s, not establishing themselves there until 1909. As part of the AEF (Afrique Équatoriale Française / French Equatorial Africa, est. 1910), Chad was more of a strategic asset for the French, a gateway to the British Sudan. Most effort was put into developing the southern part of the country – infrastructurally and economically – though most roads (if any) were laid out for tactical (military) purposes. See Arditi (2003); Azevedo (2004); Rense (2006); Souleymane (2017).

22 The *grand kadmul* policy was an extension of indirect rule, 'a policy which respected local traditions, customary institutions and habits. In utilising the indigenous authorities it had the obvious advantage of relieving the French of many of the less important tasks of administration and reducing expenditures at a time when economies were most needed' (Thomas 1959: 149).

previously having been restricted to only one. They and other Arab nomads also altered their movements, leaving early from the north and staying longer in the south, to protect their herds from chiefs' taxes – at a cost to their own health and that of the herds. By the early 1940s, the French acknowledged the now weak position of their chiefs, both financially and socially. The chiefs were removed from their positions and replaced by new chiefs, this time those who were supported by leading sheikhs and the community (Thomas 1959; Collelo 1990: 65).[23] For administrative purposes the French had become interested in sedentarizing the nomads. In order to stimulate this, they increased the taxes on herd owners/animals and decreased taxes on straw-hut owners. The colonial administrator J. Latruffe (1949: 18) noted down several measures that needed to be taken vis-à-vis the Misseria in particular, to encourage them to be more sedentarized, e.g. by increasing the taxes of those living in tents year round without having a 'fixed' (sedentary) village. In one district, the cantonal chiefs (mostly sedentary non-Arabs) were given authority over all the residents of their canton, including Arab nomads temporarily installed there. Some chiefs deprived the Misseria of the use of pastures and wells and charged heavy fees for usage. This ended in a war between the Misseria Humr and Ratanin in 1947, in which 150 people were known to have been killed (Hugot 1997). In 1947 the French once again took away power from the chiefs, forbidding the collection of *zakaat* unless it was voluntarily paid. The French also took over many responsibilities and now had both 'civil and commercial powers'. Goudjeh Walad Hamatta, for example, was named *chef de canton* of the Misseria Rouges by the French in 1943, following the arrest of Sheikh Adoudou (aka Doudou) for not collaborating with the French (Dangbet 2015a: 214). By replacing him, they also simplified the tasks of future *chef de cantons* – sheikhs like Goudjeh Walad Hamatta would no longer have the status of *chef superieur* in the Batha region.

Independence and remembering insecurity

Following independence (1960),[24] François Tombalbaye became president of Chad, heralding the 'start' of more complex power struggles. From independence onward, Tombalbaye's regime set the tone, with political parties being banned in 1962. The years 1965–1990 were characterized by numerous rebellions, in which the Guéra

---

23 See Collelo (1990) on how the French tried to impose an administration based on territory yet ended up ruling the Arabs through their kin-based social structures; see de Bruijn (2004) for an article detailing the example of a Hadjeray family whose lives were altered due to such policies. The Walad Djifir were also affected by French changes to local leadership, as we will see later.
24 The north of Chad remained under French administration until 1965.

region played an important role (de Bruijn & van Dijk 2007; Seli 2012). It is said that Tombalbaye targeted the transhumant Batha Arabs especially, after the sedentary Moubi had rebelled against him (Lemarchand 1986: 35; Dangbet 2015a: 285–286). He wanted to prevent the Arabs migrating through the Moubi settlements joining them. This led to the arrest of three chiefs in 1965 and to the sheikh of the Misseria Rouges, Goudjeh Walad Hamatta, being placed under surveillance, even though his was known as a relatively calm community and he himself as a chief who worked with the regime and was respected by his population.

Overall, during the period 1965–1986, while under the control of Tombalbaye (1960), Malloum (1975), Goukouni (1979), and Habré (1982), the country experienced political violence by both rebels and government forces. Under Hissein Habré (1982–1990), a spider-web network of information-gathering by his secret services (the DDS, Direction de la Documentation et de la Sécurité) infiltrated the country, and numerous atrocities took place, with at least 40,000 people being known to have been killed and many more disappeared (Collelo 1990; de Bruijn & van Dijk 2007; Seli 2012; Hicks 2018). In December 1990, the MPS (Mouvement Patriotique du Salut) came to power and with it the former Chadian president, Idriss Déby Itno. The role of such foreign powers as France, the United States, Sudan, and Libya throughout the many battles for power cannot be underestimated (Azevedo 2004; de Bruijn & van Dijk 2007; Boggero 2009; Debos 2016; Hicks 2018). And, in turn, Déby himself played his fair share in regional politics (Tubiana & Debos 2017). From about 1996, when the Constitution came into force, administrative decentralization processes were implemented.

Memories of the period after colonial independence seem far away as people die young and there are only a few years between each generation. The more recent periods of civil war (1980s–1990s and early 2000) take centre stage in conversations. In his dissertation, Seli (2012) sketches the situation of repression by, and fear of, the state and its agents in relation to the Hadjeray of the Guéra, a sedentary population sharing the region with the Walad Djifir. He refers specifically to the repression of this group from 1986 onward when they lost Habré's support (p. 45). This repression has created an attitude of resistance against political authority and civil administration (van Dijk 2008: 130) and a feeling of mistrust toward anything unknown.[25] The nomadic Arabs of the Batha also suffered greatly under Habré, due to their supposed plotting against the Republic with Libyan support and the fight over pastoral resources with groups affiliated with Habré (Dangbet 2020). During

---

25 Seli goes on to question whether new technologies of communication and information, as new methods of communication, have been able to mitigate or reinforce this sentiment and social phenomenon of fear.

Photo 2.13: Saddle and knife, Fadjé, March 2013. Men will hardly travel anywhere without some kind of knife on their person. Nowadays it is forbidden to own or carry large weaponry but most nomads still carry long spears when out and about.

these waves in which Arab nomads created or broke alliances with either rebel or governmental leaders, the role of the Walad Djifir varied per individual. Some joined the military, willingly or not, and others joined rebel forces. Even Adoum joined for a short period as a youngster in 1977/8. He soon left when he realized that life as a rebel basically meant being a soldier without pay. He also claims his physique was not made for carrying large, heavy weaponry.[26]

In conversations around evening camp fires, Walad Djifir would recount the ways in which they had tried to hide from the rebels, most stories involving how they ensured noises from their livestock would not divulge their location. Rebels often came at night, and getting rid of dogs and chickens helped nomadic camps

---

26 Fieldnotes, 17 March 2012.

stay quiet overnight. Goats and sheep were often still retained, as they do not make as much noise at night. Donkeys were treated so that they would be less likely to pass gas, which normally makes them bray so loudly. Tents would be pitched in the wādis, where the sand helped camouflage them, and animals were kept under the shade of trees. On occasion, a sheep would be slaughtered and hung from a tree as a way of asking Allah for protection. Adoum says it was difficult for nomads in the time of Tombalbaye and Habré especially. They would often stay close to the government's presence (army) in an attempt to remain safe from rebel troops. During Déby's presidency, they were no longer troubled by rebels ('*ils sont parti loin*'), who had either been dispersed or had found jobs at different ministries. Adoum remembers that when he was thirteen or fourteen years old, the rebel presence was very bad; and because of their lack of firearms, the nomads could not refuse them anything.[27] These anecdotes paint a somewhat different picture from that of the stereotypical Chadian Arab: supposedly cunning, sly, and a force to be reckoned with through their possession of arms and connections to those in power. I cannot explain this discrepancy, but it does call for a little more explanation, insofar as possible. Zakinet Dangbet (2015a, 2020), for example, suggests that the involvement of Batha Arabs in armed movements may have been a defensive reaction following the creation of the FROLINAT[28] in 1966. One sees a general tendency of communities becoming more militarized around that time. While the FROLINAT was a nomadic movement, it was not of Arab nomadic origin; rather, it was initiated and dominated by Tubu–Daza–Goran nomadic groups. According to Fuchs (1996: 159), Arab nomads did not have much decisive power and were often pushed out or marginalized within the movement. They ended up establishing their own organization – the CDR[29] – with its own leaders, becoming important allies to the FROLINAT.

The Walad Djifir do not speak much about what it was like living through years of rebellions and civil war in the region, and in the country in general, post-independence. When asked, men and women alike, now in their fifties or sixties, would respond that they had been too young to really know what was going on. Given that Déby came to power in 1990, after which relative peace followed, this is difficult

---

27 Based on fieldnotes, 17 April 2012 and 20 April 2012.

28 Chadian National Liberation Front or Front de Libération Nationale du Tchad (FROLINAT), a rebel group active between 1966 and 1993. See Fuchs (1996) and Buijtenhuijs (2001) on the role of nomads in the FROLINAT and civil war, whereby it is important to mention the diverse nature of Chadian nomads in general – not all Chadian nomadic groups played a dominant role in the FROLINAT.

29 Conseil Démocratique de la Révolution/Révolutionnaire (CDR) with Acyl Ahmat Akhabach as one of its most well-known and revered leaders. Acyl belonged to one of the Misseria's sub-groups and was greatly in favour of an alliance with Libya (Lemarchand 1986: 37).

to believe. Even if they had been young during the rebellions of the 1960s, they would have been teenagers or in their early twenties during the turbulent 1970s and 1980s. With time, a few stories did surface, such as that of Yakhoub:

> Now in his sixties, Yakhoub was born in the Batha to a ferīkh in al-Masruub. He spent his childhood growing up with ferīkh life, migrating with the cattle and goats. Already at this time some Walad Djifir had started ploughing fields. When he was young, all he wanted was cattle (*tudura māl*), but Chad was poor and there was little work to be found. This was the main reason he left for Sudan when he was about sixteen years old: he wanted to make some extra money so that he could buy himself some cattle and preferably a horse as well.
>
> Yakhoub says he found Sudan more relaxed / nicer (*semeh*) than Chad at the time. Chad was a country without freedom (*istikhlaal*, lit. independence). Nowadays, there is a bit more security, but back in the earlier days there were a lot of problems. 'We had two governments,' he says, 'the rebels and the government itself.' He remembers the time of the civil conflict, although he claims that they were more involved with their own livelihood and animals than with what happened outside their world. He himself was once kidnapped by rebels and set free for a high ransom.
>
> The rebels would come to the ferīkhs in the evenings or early mornings, kidnapping people with a cord around their neck (gesticulating how he himself was tied up) and asking for ransom. They would take the kidnapped outside the ferīkh and would kill them if the ransom demand was not met. When the government would hear of the rebels having been around, they would come fully armed, punishing the people for helping them. The rebels were a mixed group of Sara, Arabs, Hadjerai – everything. When the rebels would enter the ferīkh, they would hit the men and force the women to make them '*eish* (*boule*/food). The ferīkh would be made to slaughter a sheep. Everything was done by force. They would take people here and there, two or three at a time, and take them *en brousse* for ransom. The rebels needed the money to buy food as they were not paid a salary. They would come with a lot of weapons. There were so many of them (*ḥumma kattirīn*). When asked what they did to protect themselves, he says, 'We didn't have any soldiers protecting us (*'askari maft*). There was little we could do against them, as they would do what they wanted. We didn't really change our ways. The government didn't come to protect us.' When asked whether even the women still went out in search of water, he acknowledged that, yes, they would go less often than they do now. The last time the rebels came was before Déby. 'Hissein, Idriss.'[30] 'When Déby finally came, everything became a little better. He brought us freedom', someone else adds. 'Before that, it really *ca va pas*. After Déby came, the rebels were dispersed and there are no problems like that anymore.' (Based on an interview with Yakhoub, fieldnotes, 20 March 2012)[31]

---

[30] Referring here to Hissein Habré, who was Chad's head of state from 1982 to 1990, and Idriss Déby Itno, who was Chad's president from 1990 to 2021.

[31] This anecdote comes from my fieldnotes and incorporates the words of Yakhoub, my own, and those of other people. Where I am unsure of the correct nuance in translation, I have left the original word in parentheses. At times, the original wording also reflects the level of depth in which Yakhoub talked about his experiences, as well as giving certain thoughts more emphasis – such as when the French '*ca va pas*' was used.

The older generation often claimed to have forgotten what it had been like, and only a handful were willing to talk. The general sentiment seems to be that life had continued as usual: the priorities remained with the livestock and their needs – finding grazing land and water. Sometimes, however, anecdotes of what it had been like when rebels and state roamed the region, such as the one above, surfaced during conversations about other topics. In the case of a rebel-infested zone and political strife, it is difficult to say where the general loyalties of Walad Djifir lay. On an individual level, Adoum's main motivation for joining the rebels was that he wanted to try something other than herding cattle. This was a sentiment echoed by others.

Linguistic and religious orientation

Adoum's choice of the CDR, rather than other sectors of the FROLINAT, was linked to the dominance of Chadian Arabs within it. The Walad Djifir's mother tongue is one their ancestors carried with them when migrating from Upper Egypt into Sudan in the fourteenth century, and then onwards into Chad. Their dialect is a form of Batha Baggara Arabic which in turn falls under West Sudan Arabic (Manfredi & Roset 2021).[32] The latter covers the Arabic dialects found in Nigeria, Cameroon, Chad, and the western Sudanese provinces of Darfur and Kordofan. Historically, Arabic was a vehicular language in the region, with sedentary populations incorporating it into their linguistic skillset while also keeping their ancestral language (Alio 2008). Nomadic populations tended to be less bilingual, with fewer variations to the language being made. Due to the stronger influence of local languages, the Chadian Arabic spoken by non-Arab sedentary populations in villages and urban centres is different from that spoken by semi-nomadic populations (ibid.: 4). Through Qur'anic studies, and while listening to radio broadcasts such as BBC Arabic or Al Jazeera, some of the Walad Djifir men have become verbally familiar with *fusha* and MSA. Many men, and almost all the women living in ferīkh settings, remain illiterate. This linguistic orientation towards the Arabic language is more of a determining factor than their religious affiliations when it comes to deciding where to set off to, as we will see in some of the following chapters.

Islam and being a Muslim are a large part of the daily life of the Walad Djifir. The five daily prayers are adhered to fairly strictly, and many other Islamic customs are followed – such as, the naming of a child after eight days, and the ceremonies

---

32 For a detailed, comprehensive study of the degree of diatopic variation and eco-linguistic factors within the various Baggara Arabic sub-types, see Manfredi & Roset (2021).

held after a death or during a marriage. Hadj Saleh is also a *marabout* who teaches young boys the Qur'ān when he has the time.[33] These sessions are held by the early morning camp-fire and again in the evening. On a visit to Fadjé in March 2013, one of Hadj Saleh's sons, Moustapha, was often found practising his Qur'ānic recitation and script. The hope was that he would be selected by a travelling *marabout* and invited to Egypt for further learning.

Photo 2.14: Leather bound cases for the Quran, Fadjé, March 2013. In March 2014 Hadj Saleh had moved to a ferīkh closer to Bitkine, teaching youngsters the Qurān.

Like the majority of the Muslim population in Chad, the Walad Djifir are Tijaniyya Muslims. Their orientation is primarily toward West Africa, with the most popular Sheikh Niass being based in Senegal. His image can be found on posters, calendars, and stickers throughout the country. In N'Djaména, at the time of the fieldwork, the imam was Hassan Hissein (fieldnotes, 20 April 2012). Many of the Qur'āns found in Chad come from Nigeria. Islam was present within the Guéra region at the time of the Ouaddaïan empire, which would send Islamic scholars and teachers to spread their ideas (Rense 2006: 56–57). In her chapter on itinerant Qur'ānic schools in Mongo, de Bruijn (2014: 67–68) provides a comprehensive overview of the general process of Islamization in and around Mongo, touching

---

[33] See de Bruijn (2014) on teaching the Qur'ān as an important element of Islamic education among Muslim Chadians and across the Sahel in general, and such teaching's close ties to travel by pupils and teachers.

Photo 2.15: Leather bound talisman containing Quranic verses for protection, March 2013. These are for hanging around a horse's neck. Items are often kept off the ground by placing them in trees. Islam is such a normalized part of life, it was never a point of discussion or negotiation but instead a source of guidance, support, rest, and solidarity.

upon the role of the various surrounding Islamic empires, (Muslim) Daadjo migration into the area from Sudan in the eighteenth and nineteenth centuries, and the increased presence of Muslim travelling scholars (*fākih*) and traders under French pacification of the region. From the time of the civil war (1965–1990) and mostly during the 1970s and 1980s, when rebel forces dominated the area, the conversion to Islam was stimulated not least because it opened up economic and political opportunities. The informants of de Bruijn et al. (2004: 10) noticed large changes in religious practices in the Guéra in this time, with mentions of forced Islamization varying per village. Around 1986, more Salafi and Wahhabi influences began coming into the country, coinciding with people going off to work in Saudi Arabia and with certain development aid programmes arriving in the

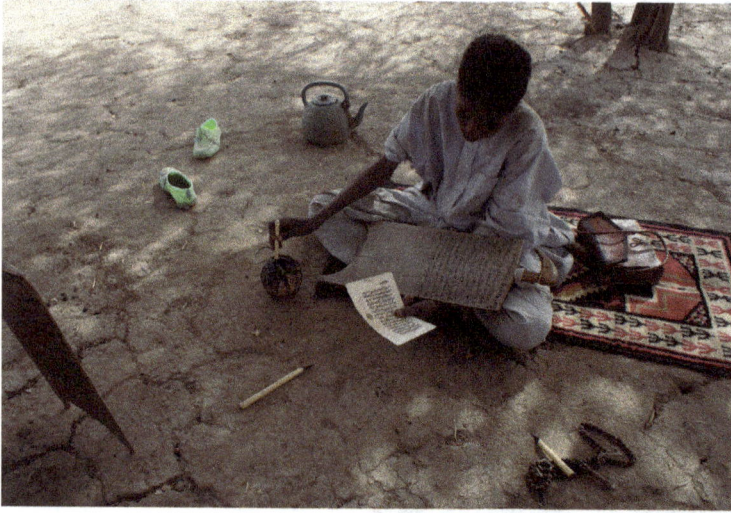

Photo 2.16: Hadj Saleh's son Moustapha practising his memorization of the Quran, March 2013. The young boys in the ferīkh would practise their recitations around a camp fire at first prayer – and at times again in the late afternoon. The rest of the day was spent tending to the animals. Hadj Saleh hoped that this particular son would be noticed by a travelling marabout and offered a scholarship to study further in Egypt.

region, building mosques and supporting educational programmes (Kaag 2007, 2012; Ladiba 2011).[34]

In the ferīkh setting, in N'Djaména, and in CAR, I did not observe a tendency toward Wahhabi forms of Islam, as have been documented amongst nomadic populations in Mali (van Dijk & de Bruijn 2023). The actions of Boko Haram and ISIS were criticized by members of the *ferīkh conseil* (advisory body) when we would hear about them on the radio. Having said that, I have not been there to observe any possible changes in Islamic practice over several generations (re-Islamization, as per Kaag 2007). At one point, I remember asking what the difference was, to them, between Wahhabi and Tijaniyya. One man said, 'They pray inside in mosques and we don't need one to pray. We could pray in a church if necessary; it doesn't matter. It is about the praying itself' (fieldnotes, 21 January 2013). Interestingly, from about

---

34 Fieldnotes, 10 April 2012; conversation with two Mazaqneh group members, Hadj Saleh and Adoum around al-Berekeh. In an *NRC* article published on 13–14 January 2018, 'Franse kapmesmoorden verdelen Tsjadische moslims', anthropologist and Arabist Dorrit van Dalen also mentions the increased trend in Wahhabism. She describes how the Chadian government acts against extremist preaching but at the same time allows the Gulf States to fund Islamic and Arabic universities in Chad, and accepts the hand-out of scholarships to Chadians wanting to study in the Gulf.

2012 onward, in addition to lobbying for the building of a deep well in their sedentary village, Tchoufiou II Arabe, there were voices who wanted a mosque to be built.
This, of course, says nothing about dogmatic orientation. The processes involved,
however, in wanting a mosque to be built or a deep well dug do bring us back to
local politics in general and to the dynamics of belonging. Most of the organizations
to which Walad Djifir would appeal were of Muslim origin, run by Turkish or Saudi
investors.

The ferīkh in place and space

Belonging has many layers and motivations – with political preferences, linguistics,
Arab 'roots', and religious affiliations being just some of them. The ferīkh has been
established as both a place and space (Gupta & Ferguson 1992, 1997; Retaillé & Walther
2011) where all these layers come together through the connectivity it embodies. The
ferīkh is in fact expanding, incorporating more physical places and long-distance
relationships. The following section describes where the contemporary itineraries
of most Walad Djifir begin, in al-Habilai, and how research was done within such an
ever-expanding transnational network which is the globalizing ferīkh.

The ferīkh in place: Al-Habilai and the creation of Tchoufiou II Arabe

Traditionally, each sub-group has its own wet-season grazing lands. Al-Habilai is the
name of the wet-season grazing land which belongs to the Walad Djifir (Hugot 1997:
162). This area of the Batha is considered their 'homeland' and refers to a specific
terrain around a deep, constructed well, situated roughly north of the road between
Oum Hadjer and Ati (Map 3). The land is used not only as pasturage but also as agricultural land, which makes it highly valuable to those looking to supplement their
livestock-based livelihood with that of grains and other food stuffs.

In the dry season, each sub-group has a different pattern of transhumance and
general region in which they settle. Zakinet Dangbet's dissertation (2015a) and the
book he co-authored with André Marty and Antoine Eberschweiler (2009), as well
as Aubague et al. (2006), provide a detailed overview with maps of the various transhumance routes in the Batha, Salamat, and Guéra. Over several generations, those
Walad Djifir who are semi-sedentary have been spending the dry-season months in
the Guéra region, some settling into permanent villages and others setting up camp
in roughly the same locations every year. In most cases, agreements have been
made between representatives of the sedentary populations who own the land and
local *chef de ferīkhs*.

So why did they choose to establish villages on land which they traditionally did not have rights to, and on which cattle can survive only during the dry season? The village (Hilleh) Tchoufiou II, for example, was established some thirty-five years ago and can be found along the road from Mongo to Ati. Walad Djifir had been coming to the region for generations prior to that. The land surrounding Tchoufiou II is more pleasant to live off during the dry season than that in the Batha (al-Habilai). Around Tchoufiou II, livestock can find grazing land, and water is close to the surface due to the nearby *wādi* (the Bambam). The Walad Djifir know the Hadjeray of the surrounding villages and they have got used to each other. It is for this reason that in the mid-1980s, following another period of drought (1984–1985), the Walad Djifir asked permission of the Hadjeray to stay and set up an official village.[35] The Dadjo I *chef de canton*, Ahmed Ibeduh, agreed; and in the following years the village was also made official at the level of the national government with, in the *gouverneur* of Mongo's absence, the *préfet* signing the document. On the land they have been granted over several years, they have divided themselves into five groups, who now live on the lands which are locally known as Tchoufiou (Fadjé), Garanek, Fané, Bandaro, and Dadoud (Eid Adoud) (see Map 3). All these places are along a tributary or main artery of the Bambam. Only the land of Garanek is located in the Batha and not in the Guéra. It was difficult to pinpoint their geographic locations owing to the uncertainty of where dry riverbeds (*wādis*) run on existing maps. The Texas Library maps which exist date from the 1970s and are too detailed to be used accurately for the making of Map 3. Pastoralist researchers in Chad have made their own maps based on GPS coordinates taken in the field, yet our cartographer did not have access to their databases. We cross-referenced these maps and notes I had made in the field, when deciding on the approximate locations of the various places in which Walad Djifir have been setting up camp.

Throughout all the fieldwork phases the set-up of camps would change, depending on the needs of the herds of cattle and camels. There were many individuals

---

35 Braukämper (2000: 45) describes a system known as *khuwa* (friendship in Sudanese Arabic), whereby alliances are created between groups, implying socio-political solidarity and rights to grazing land, etc. In the case of the Baqqara Arabs of the Sudan Belt, and especially among camel herders who travel far and wide, these alliances are not necessarily between neighbouring groups. A similar alliance was probably made many years ago between this sub-group of the Misseria Rouges and the Hadjeray and then expanded on. The word Hadjeray encapsulates a diverse group of people traditionally associated with living on or near mountains. The Dadjo are not Hadjeray, only arriving in the Guéra region in the 19th century. Socio-linguist Khalil Alio writes, "When the Dadjo arrived in the area, they occupied the northwestern plains of Abou-Telfane. Now the Dadjo live in two sous-prefectures: that of Mongo and that of Mangalmé. In the sous-préfecture of Mongo, their Canton is called Dadjo I. In the sous-prefecture of Mangalmé, their Canton bears the name of Dadjo II." (2008: 12)

whom we would see daily, passing through 'our' camp, at the *'eidd*, over a meal, just passing time in a shady spot, or on visits to a weekly market. Their mobile lifestyle, related to the care of herds or agricultural fields and also to wage labour, commerce, or study, represents the ferīkh 'in space'.

The ferīkh in space: Researching the ferīkh as a transnational network

The cases of Hadj Saleh (Introduction) and Yakhoub (this chapter) show how their lives in the ferīkh are not at all limited to it, geographically. In fact, the ferīkh itself is spread out over various geographical locations, not only in the form of its nomadic camps but also in the way its extended family members can be found far and wide – whether in the nearest town of Mongo, in the distant capital of N'Djaména, or as merchants in Bangui. It was important to follow the connections embodied in these various mobilities, leading to different people and physical locations (sites) of research and also to different perspectives and positions. My interest was not necessarily only in the trajectory itself but just as much in the different sites and the 'trajectories' these contained (Schapendonk 2011). This echoes the idea of 'ethnographies of encounter' (Faier & Rofel 2014) in how a place contains within itself clues and context, through encounters, for the various connectors followed. Fieldwork was thus not limited to the ferīkh setting but consisted of multiple sites (Marcus 1995; Olwig & Hastrup 1997). While specific field 'sites' were involved, it is ultimately the connections which could be found at these sites which were researched and which are described in this book. Methodologically, this meant 'following' (de Bruijn & Brinkman 2012; Wilson Janssens 2018) the various common variables found within these fields, which together informed networks of connections. I spent time at physical sites, allowing the various connectors to determine what other spaces needed to be visited. The chapter on livestock or cattle (Chapter Four) was started in the nomadic camps but led to local markets in Banda, Mongo, and also to the larger ones in N'Djaména. I spoke to Walad Djifir herding and owning their own cattle, as well as to large-scale cattle merchants with trans-border connections. Following the sending of money (Chapter Five) entailed visiting family members who were on the receiving end or who had previously spent time away from the ferīkh and sent money back home. Money transfer operators were visited as well as some local banks, and where possible interviews were held with their representatives. I talked to shopkeepers in the capital and Mongo, who played a role in the money chain. While following family members to CAR (Chapter Six), I spent time with those I had initially met in the ferīkh setting. They, in turn, introduced me to their family and friends in Bangui. I hung out at the Marché Soundanais, at the stall of a woman I had first met in the ferīkh in 2012 but who had since returned to Bangui. We met again the following year, in a camp for repatriates just outside N'Djaména.

Between 2011 and 2014, twelve months of fieldwork were carried out over five separate visits in and around the nomadic camps of this extended family of Walad Djifir living within the administrative boundaries of the Guéra and Batha; in Mongo, the Guéra's main town; in the capital N'Djaména; in the capital of CAR, Bangui; and a brief but important stay in a village in south-eastern CAR. While staying with the Walad Djifir, Adoum and I frequented numerous ferīkhs in the vicinity – preferably on foot when possible – and spent time in the sedentary village, Tchoufiou II Arabe. On various occasions we stayed in ferīkhs further afield (around Dadoud, Al-Berekeh, Fané, Bandaro) as well as in larger towns in the area (Mongo, Ati, Koundjar, Bardangal), this time using a car (see Maps 2 and 3). Fieldwork was of a nomadic nature – setting up camp in various locations, depending on our needs and/or where we had been invited next. The car and the relative freedom to decide our own itinerary meant we were as flexible as nomads are. We could up and leave, belongings and all, and follow them to wherever their next camp was to be set up. Although we bought our water supplies in bulk in Mongo, we too were reliant on them insofar as they determined the length of each journey into the *brousse*. Working outside urban areas meant that we came into little contact with the authorities. On arriving in Mongo, we had gone to introduce ourselves at the level of the governor, showing our letters of permission provided by both the Ministry of Higher Education (a research permit) and Ministry of the Interior (a permit to travel inland) in N'Djaména. While among the nomads, though, we felt free and more secure than when in town. They gave us protection – we were among 'family' – and they quickly knew of things happening in the vicinity.

In terms of communication, my own Dutch origins and a fair amount of Egyptian Arabic, including some MSA, meant that a 'shared interest' in cattle and a means to communicate about them were established early on with the men. As a foreign woman in a predominantly Muslim society (while amongst Walad Djifir) I could eat with both men and women alike. My 'being different' opened up possibilities, while of course also having its limits. The opening excerpt reveals how I did not get to know any of the women until my second visit in 2012. Even then, it took some of the women a while to feel comfortable enough to open up about various subjects. This also had to do with language and vocabulary, to be more precise. The men had often learned to recite and to a certain extent understand the Qur'ān and perhaps travelled further. Their daily listening to radio broadcasts in other Arabic dialects meant most were able to make sense of the Arabic I spoke, being creative in their listening skills and responses. With time it was my Arabic which adapted itself to incorporate Chadian Arabic.

The types of conversations held while in the field varied: from informal gatherings over meals, while waiting for the day to cool off, or watching out for the herds to return from the fields to be watered; to more interview-like settings, where Adoum and I would seek out a person and I had a list of questions either in my head or written down. When possible and appropriate, I would use a voice recorder to record both informal and formal conversations. I also took many photos; and from the middle of my second real fieldwork visit, I had the use of a video camera with which I recorded daily life scenes as well as interviews. The visual reveals a separate (yet complementary) emotion and narrative from the textual or verbal. Family members now living and working in urban CAR would reflect on how things had or had not changed. When showing the pictures of Nour in the ferīkh to her younger half-brother, born and raised like her in urban Bangui, he was shocked by the circumstances and the way she looked. As a way of interpreting the day's events, Adoum and I would discuss any happenings and dilemmas on our walks to another ferīkh or the *wādi*, where it was pleasant to spend the late afternoon. We did not always agree, of course, and I tried to understand people's perspectives by asking numerous questions, rather than pushing through my own opinion. On subjects such as female circumcision, we had heated discussions that made me feel sad, angry, and frustrated.[36] I also had such conversations with other members of the community, especially with the women I slept alongside and had meals with. They were moments of reflection and a chance to dig deeper or come up with new questions or lines of enquiry to follow up on. In turn, Adoum – and others – would often ask what I thought or how we would do things in the Netherlands. They were curious, for example, as to what we invested our money in and found it very strange that in the Netherlands one does not just buy land to build on. I tried to explain there is little 'free' land left and that most people need a mortgage to even consider owning their own house. Time spent in Mongo with Walad Djifir based there and with people from different walks of life, provided perspective. This

---

36 It was not something I talked about with the women, unfortunately, in the ferīkh setting; there never seemed to be a right moment and the subject of female circumcision never came up naturally. In a conversation on this subject in N'Djaména, the mother of four daughters said that it was the daughter of ten who had come to her to ask to have it performed. Her friends had been talking about it, and it was what made you a more virtuous woman (girl in her case). It was unclear what the mother was going to do, and I never managed to broach the subject with her elder daughters to ask whether they had undergone the procedure. Boys in the ferīkh are circumcised around the age of ten. On a return visit in 2012, we found two of them a bit forlorn in a specially constructed shelter, draped in decorative cloths. They were to stay in there for several days following the procedure and were not allowed out or too much interaction with the others. Peter Fuchs carried out research on various groups in Chad in the 1970s, filming aspects of their lives, including one such ceremony of female circumcision (female genital mutilation/FGM).

mutual exchange on numerous subjects provided depth to the daily observations and conversations. These encounters and interactions unearthed common denominators, discrepancies, and ultimately analytical dynamics (Faier & Rofel 2014).

Ferīkh individuals, in place and space

Numerous individuals opened my eyes to the trans-nationality of their lives. Earlier on, a distinction was made between the ways in which individuals were part of this research, as co-creators or co-interpreters. This section narrows in on a few of these individuals and the roles they played in revealing an expanding ferīkh through the relationships they kept up over geographical distances.

On that first visit in October 2011, it was of course not a random ferīkh which Adoum took me to: it was the ferīkh of Hadj Saleh ʿUmar, the *chef de ferīkh*. Hadj Saleh's father and Adoum's mother were brother and sister (see Family Tree in Figure 1). This combination facilitated my introduction to the community and the carrying out of fieldwork over the next few years. Despite being a difficult person to interview in a more formal sense, the time spent in Hadj Saleh's proximity, the conversations held during different times of the day, during a communal gathering or over a meal next to his tent, and 'following' him to CAR form a large part of my empirical data. He is an unpredictable character, with individual and communal responsibilities, a man used to making his own path. His actions were not always appreciated by the majority of his family, but it is precisely this fact that revealed the more interesting insights.

Khachana is married to Hadj Saleh's brother and it is with her and two other women that I had most of my meals within the ferīkh setting. She had the patience to listen to my questions, when there were aspects of the day's events I could not place. I could be open with her, in my quest to understand what had driven so-and-so to do this-and-that. She was always laughing, saying my name as both an exclamation and question at the same time, before answering. Khachana was more of a co-interpreter and general provider of information. She was at the centre of many individual's transnational networks, through her familial connections. One of Khachana's sons was living in CAR at the time, temporarily separated from his wife Nour. It was outside Nour's tent that my bed was set up in 2012. She shared this tent with Arafa, Hadj Saleh's eldest sister and the third with whom most meals were shared. Khachana's tent was next to theirs, in 2012, and the three women often took turns preparing the daily meals. Khachana had an informal authority, over both male and female family members, due to her age and familial relationship to those around her.

On visits in 2013 and 2014 the camp's composition had changed yet Khachana was still a part of it. Nour had returned to CAR by then, and Arafa was visiting one of her children. We were hosted by Hadj Saleh's wife Khadidja on these occasions. As *chef de ferīkh*, Hadj Saleh introduced us to 'ferīkh life' and the world connected to it. While his presence and actions determined many things, Adoum and Nour were the ones with which I had a deeper understanding and who formed the path this research took. Adoum had the role of co-creator and 'side-kick', in the sense that we formed a team and in reality took turns being each other's side-kick. He was both interpreter and the provider of access and information. His story figures throughout the book (especially in Chapter Five).

Adoum is related to this specific group of Walad Djifir through both his mother and father. He left his parental ferīkh at a young age and, after various detours, set up a home and family in N'Djaména. His transnational network included time spent in Cameroon with Mbororo (Fulani nomads), the numerous foreigners he had worked with, and the money he was being sent as go-between from Libya and CAR. The fact that we were working together and that we had the use of a car meant that he was able to spend a lot more time than he normally would have in the ferīkh and among his extended family. The setting was of course somewhat unnatural, not only through my presence but also through that of Adoum, who normally lived and worked in N'Djaména. Adoum, too, was an outsider in certain regards, having been away since his youth and no longer living the nomadic life. His advice and medi-ation were often asked, a trend which already existed before we started working together and which then continued and became more intensified. Talk of Adoum becoming the family's *chef de canton* is closely linked to this (Chapter Three). We also facilitated Nour and Hadj Saleh's travel to N'Djaména, for example, timing it to coincide with our own return (Chapter Six). Our visit to Koundjaar allowed Nourad-din and Yakhoub to tag along and speak to Abbakr Hissein, whom they hoped would help their land ownership case (Chapter Three). There is no denying that our presence, and our mobility, must have altered the course of some aspects of daily, ordinary life, as well as the more extraordinary moments. At the same time, it also very much re-enacted existing structures present in the field, including gender hierarchies and power relations. We worked well together – both enjoying being *en brousse*, preferring to sleep out under the stars rather than under a tent (even on cold nights). It was a working relationship, in the sense that I employed him for the duration of the fieldwork and provided him with food and accommodation in addition to a salary. There were many ways in which this situation could have been highly unequal (and uncomfortable) (Irwin 2006). It was my research project and I was the one that had hired him. I was in my early thirties and he somewhere in his late fifties. He was a married man of eight children, whom he provided for. At times, his frustration at being dependent on me (and others) was evident, taking the form of short, curt replies. To be fair, such moments were often mutual. Most of the time, however, we found a way to work together as equals. I too was dependent on him, on his knowledge of the terrain, on his thoughts about what was wise in a particular context, and on his access to the community. We made decisions together, and there was space to vent frustrations. The walks we would take together, sometimes without talking, helped create some distance from 'the field' – as did the occasional periods in Mongo. At the same time, he made good use of the months spent with his extended family, and they made use of his presence.

The collaboration with Nour was on a more personal level, perhaps facilitated by us both being young women who had been in contact with 'other' worlds outside of the ferīkh. With the women it generally took a longer time before we were able to have in-depth conversations, and with some women this never really worked.[37] Because Adoum was a direct family member, either as cousin, nephew, or uncle, he was able to join in on conversations with the women and often shared meals with us. Later, I did not need him to be around as much in order to have a successful conversation. It helped that a handful of the family we stayed with spoke French, in addition to Chadian Arabic. Nour, for example, was one of them. Her growing up in Bangui and being relatively 'new' to nomadic life helped us bond. She was able to explain things I wanted to understand but that the other women considered so normal that they sometimes could not grasp my questions. Next to Adoum, Nour often functioned as an unofficial translator when I was alone with women with whom I found it difficult to communicate. They in turn used her to ask me all sorts of questions, not always daring to ask me directly. The most pertinent ones being: did I have any children, why not, and what did I do about having my period? I got to know Nour and her role in the ferīkh's transnational networks while spending mornings, afternoons, and evenings together in a variety of settings. It was next to her tent in the ferīkh that I set up my own bed, and it was with her that most evening meals were eaten while there. I had the chance to travel with her to N'Djaména, spending time together there on two different occasions. In between I was able to visit her in her 'home' in a remote village in CAR, where she showed me the rooms her father had built and the photos of him and the rest of the family and friends residing in Bangui. Throughout these moments it became clear that the weight of gendered and familial expectations figure heavily in the courses her life has taken. Here Appadurai's (1997) discussion on practices of intimacy, in relation to fieldwork in a time of globalization, comes to mind. I hope to show that everyday

---

37 Many women thought I was a doctor at first, travelling with Adoum and coming to help them. This reveals something about their previous encounters with foreigners. Even afterwards, I was often asked for painkillers or medical advice by both men and women alike. I had brought along a fair amount of paracetamol and ibuprofen from home, which I was happy to hand out when Adoum and I thought it could help. When in Mongo we would sometimes ask a local nurse for advice. We would refer people on to the nearest clinic when their case seemed serious.

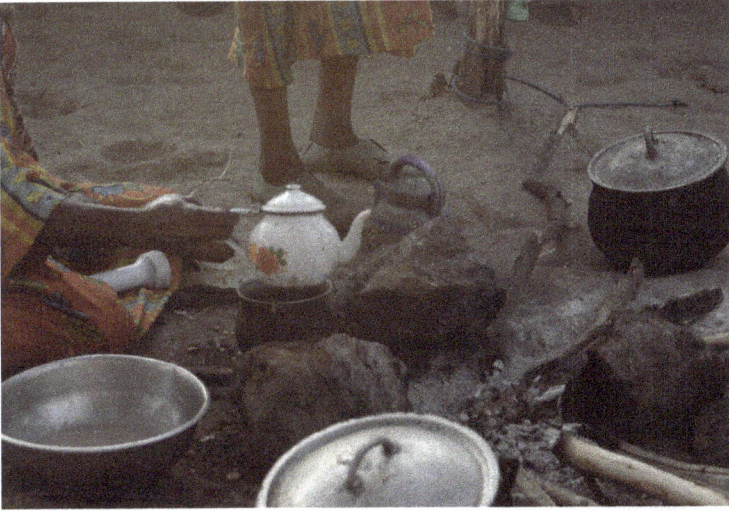

Photo 2.17: Women cooking and preparing tea, March 2013. Men and women work hard and there is not much time for lying around. The time spent cooking and eating were often ideal moments for longer conversations.

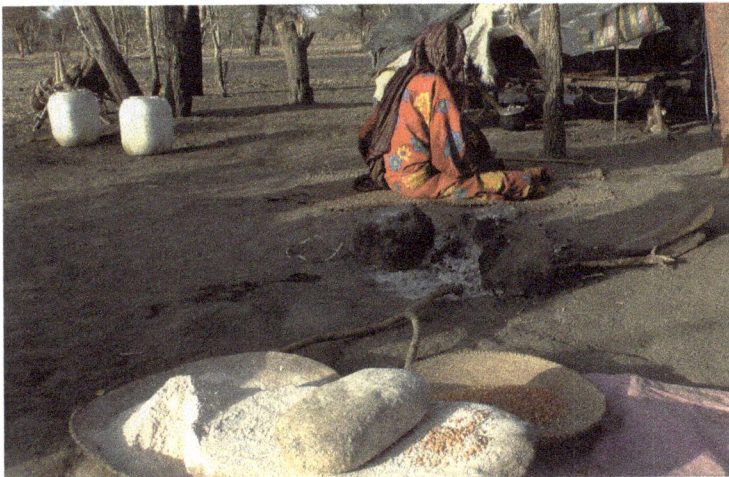

Photo 2.18: Taking a break from grinding grain into flour for the afternoon prayer, Fadjé, March 2014. Women usually pray separately, only joining the men at a distance for the main Friday afternoon prayer. You can clearly make out the three stones on which pots are placed above a fire, and the typical two *bidons* (jerrycans) of water.

social practices of intimacy span physical spaces. An intimate emotional moment, whether joyous or sad, can have its roots in practices taking place elsewhere.

***

Ethnographic research among the Walad Djifir could very well concentrate on 'just' the ferīkh and all its intricacies; but because this ferīkh life is so connected with goings-on outside of it, the field of research reflected this and thus incorporated various locations, informed by specific connectors between ferīkh life and the world 'outside'. Whatever the reasons, historically and currently – finding pasture or suitable wells, commerce, family obligations, labour migration, conflict – Walad Djifir like Khachana, Nour, Adoum, and Hadj Saleh are a mobile people living their lives over various places and spaces. There is a purpose to this mobility. Social and economic networks are engaged, to which people link up, or 'connect'. This linking up or connecting, in turn, informs feelings of and motivations for belonging. What, then, are the various 'circles of belonging' to which the Walad Djifir relate? In examining Walad Djifir's positionality toward their origins, we see a tendency to identify themselves as Arabs and Muslims. Within this identification, however, there are nuances and layers to be discerned, with motivations for belonging varying depending on the situation. A similar trend is observed in relation to socio-political structures, whether they be the state, canton, nomadic group, or familial leader. Here, factors shaping belonging are a nomadic freedom or flexibility to continue a way of life, identifying with specific pieces of land in the Guéra and Batha and adhering to familial loyalties. The next chapter will look at social organization in the context of the ferīkh and at familial expectations and obligations as sources of conflict. While there is a certain continuity to land issues between sedentary and pastoral or nomadic populations, with former agreements suddenly being overturned, nomadic pastoralists also have their own fair share of land strife among themselves.

Chapter 3
Brothers in arms

One afternoon in late April 2012, Adoum and I joined the others in visiting a ferīkh a little further up the *wādi*. We all loaded into the Toyota Hilux and set off amidst much laughter and banter. On arrival I immediately sensed a tense vibe. The mood had switched. There were several men with faces I had not seen before, even during larger gatherings for weddings or naming ceremonies. By then, most of the immediate extended family had become familiar. The younger men and I were shown to a mat out of sight of the main gathering while the others went off to greet the hosting ferīkh. On such past occasions greetings had usually been amicable, the extensive formal greeting interspersed with jokes back and forth. This was now sorely missing. The elders returned from paying their respects and we settled down for numerous cups of tea. It is usually the younger men who make the tea next to their mat. Depending on the occasion, the hosts will provide the *barada* (tea pot), tea cups, tea and of course the sugar, or the ingredients will be gifted by their guests. In the meantime a sheep was slaughtered a short distance away and portions of the *marara* (tripe, part of the stomach lining) soon passed round to each mat. A little while later large round dishes filled with *'eish*, sauce and goat meat appeared. Throughout the afternoon, the young men would come and go, visiting friends and acquaintances sitting on mats dotted around under trees some distance away. The elders, made up of members of the ferīkh's council, were involved in serious-looking discussions under the largest and shadiest tree in the vicinity. It wasn't until the next day that I could ask Adoum about it, whether something had indeed been wrong. He related the following account, of a young death and a splitting of the Walad Djifir.

In 2009, Hassan's ten-year-old son was killed in a road accident, hit while herding livestock on the road to Am Timam, in the Salamat region. Hassan is one of Hadj Saleh's younger brothers. As Islamic custom dictates, the issue was settled among those responsible and the victim's family. Hassan's family sent an envoy of five to six members of the *ferīkh conseil*[1] to collect the body and receive compensation for the loss (known as *dīya* or blood money). Traditionally, the amount of 1,500,000 CFA (2287 EUR) is distributed among the relatives. In this case, the money was not distributed evenly by Hadj Saleh, in his capacity as *chef de ferīkh*.

---

1 Unfortunately it is not clear to me what the relations are between those who were sent as envoys. Generally speaking, such things as blood money are issues dealt with by kin relations. Whether this is the case here, and how close their relationship is, is unclear.

https://doi.org/10.1515/9783110714685-003

For reasons still unclear, one particular ferīkh had refused to send a representative along with the envoy. In return, Hadj Saleh now refused to give them their full share. Instead of paying 500,000 CFA (762 EUR), he had given them 250,000 CFA (381 EUR). The situation escalated and has caused a rift in relations among members of the Walad Djifir.[2] That day of the gathering, the ferīkh who had refused to send a representative had been present.

✳✳✳

This introduction serves as a prelude to the political dynamics found within the ferīkh. It illustrates the complicated social organization within the Walad Djifir as extended family and the Misseria Rouges as a larger group. Personal conflicts (informed by a tragedy in this case) are communal property and require organized action. These communal actions, however, are not always as unanimous as they may seem; and, in this case, Hadj Saleh's individual action led to a rift within the community. While the incident took place in 2009, by 2012 the situation had still not been resolved, and Hassan had started paying off the 'debt' in person – a debt which, according to ferīkh consensus, was not his to pay but Hadj Saleh's. Through intermediation by another family member (Adoum), the situation was somewhat calmed. Adoum spent endless hours speaking to each party in turn, trying to convince them of the importance of sticking together and not creating a rift. He argued that it would not do to have other sub-groups hear of the internal discord within the Walad Djifir – they would be laughed at for letting a split happen. A separation of opposing family members within the Walad Djifir group had never happened in the history of their forefathers, and they had to be sure not to let it happen now

When Adoum went to speak to the ferīkh of the *opposantes*[3] a few days after that strange gathering in April 2012, he was gone the best part of the day.[4] Recounting the incident to me afterwards, he said he had talked partly *par force* and partly in a calm manner. He had explained that he did not think this incident was a reason to split up their *chefferie*, presided over by Adjidei. Hadj Saleh was only one man, and many of the others did not agree with his stance. After much discussion, the opposing ferīkh agreed to make up. In the presence of 'three old men with white hair' (Adoum's words), the rest of the money would at some time have to be handed over. On Adoum's

---

2 Based on fieldnotes, 26 April 2012.
3 What it means to be an *opposante* will be explained in more detail later in this chapter. For now, suffice to say that an *opposante* is one who opposes the current leader. This can occur on any level (*chef de ferīkh*, *tribu*, or *canton*). Most *opposantes* are supported (financially) by members of their community.
4 Fieldnotes, 1 May 2012.

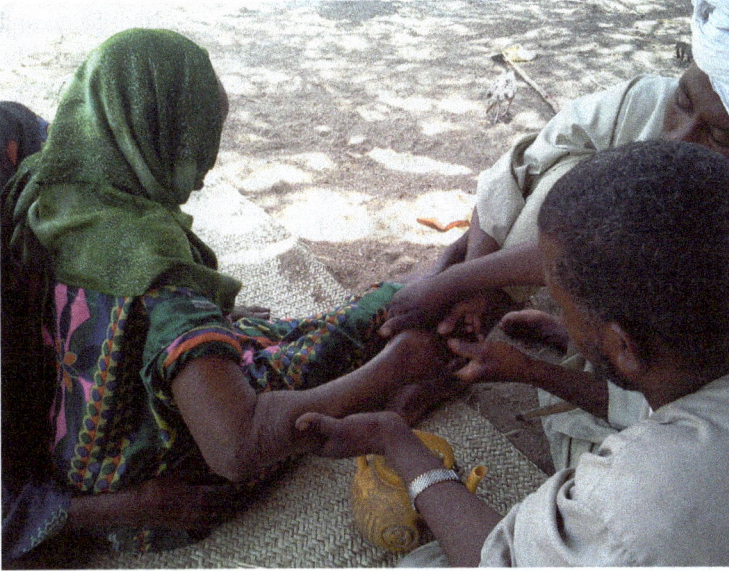

Photo 3.1: Hassan and Brahim working on Hadji Arafa's arm, April 2012. This picture was taken shortly before Hadj Saleh and Nour left for Sassileh (CAR). At the time, Hadji Arafa was very upset that Hadj Saleh refused to say goodbye to their brother Hassan and mend their differences before he left. Here, Hassan is using his knowledge of tending to the limbs of his livestock to help his elderly sister, who had fallen and broken her arm.

return from this lengthy discussion, he did not speak to the *conseil* as a whole but first took Nouraddin aside, and together they went for a long walk. He later informed Adjidei of what had been agreed with the other party, and Adjidei assured him he would ensure promises would be kept. On an earlier visit to Adjidei in mid-March 2012, Adoum had asked why he had not interfered. After all, as *chef de tribu* of the Walad Djifir, he outranked both the *chef de village* (Nouraddin) and the *chef de ferīkh* (Hadj Saleh). In the end, Adjidei agreed to pay the remaining 150,000 CFA by selling one or two of his cows. He would find his recompense by collecting among the *tribu*.[5]

In the meantime, Hadj Saleh had acquired a group of staunch supporters around him, all members of his ferīkh's *conseil* and, in general, the most outspoken ones. They stuck to their position and refused to contribute toward recompensing Adjidei. Over time, and probably due to several awkward social occasions where people were or were not greeted during larger gatherings, the ferīkh which was owed the debt became known as the ferīkh of the *opposantes*. In March 2014,

5 The use of the French word *tribu* here reflects the way the Walad Djifir refer to themselves, as opposed to my placing this categorization upon them.

the twenty-nine-year-old son of their own *sheikh* went missing. Hadj Saleh and his followers within the *conseil* refused to join the search party.[6] When, on the morning the boy had been discovered missing, Adoum and I arrived in the ferīkh and learned of what was happening, he countered the decision, claiming that it was in everyone's interest to work together, especially in a time of need. Much discussion followed, but it was enough to rally the troops to join the search. The boy – as they referred to him themselves despite his age – was found in a grave condition on the third day after his disappearance. He had undressed and would not speak. Piecing the information together, it was discovered that he had just returned from a Qur'ānic school in the eastern city of Abéché. He had come back with malaria and had already received a first *perfusion* (medical drip) at the hospital in Mongo. On the night of his return, he had got up, most probably in a fever dream, and walked away. It was a young goat herder who had found his clothes strewn about miles away; and after finding the boy, he alerted a nearby search party on horseback. During such searches, the community really comes together to help and everyone is concerned, men and women alike. These situations happen from time to time, though not always with a good outcome. Phone calls are made from ferīkh to ferīkh, and people also spread the news on horseback. Searches are organized by sending out groups of men on horseback, from early morning to nightfall. Others go on foot. It takes a lot of manpower; but in such conditions as we find in the Guéra, time is everything.

These are just a few details of a story involving many actors, factors, and much social hierarchy. It is not clear whether the animosity against that particular ferīkh was pre-dated by other events. Why, for example, did they not join the envoy when Hassan's son was killed? What is clear is that Hadj Saleh's actions soured inter-ferīkh relations even further, instead of improving them. Further time spent in the ferīkh made it clear that this souring of relations, in the aftermath of Hassan's son's death, was intertwined with a different case, namely the unjust selling of Walad Djifir land by the *chef de canton* of the Misseria Rouges.

Ferīkh politics

In both cases, the role and strategies of several leaders come to the fore. Their stories reveal normative narratives of what is good for the ferīkh or Walad Djifir in general. The connectors of this chapter are thus the various 'leaders' – an entry point to examining the nuanced complexities of social relations through their role

---

6 Fieldnotes, 8 March 2014.

in ferīkh politics. This role, which alternatively posits the community of Walad Djifir as brothers *in* or *at* arms, is part of an historical process of sedentarization and expansion. The colonial period brought changes which are reflected in the stories below. Walad Djifir claimed a place for themselves within the changing political environment of the colonial state. After independence, other processes of state-making and bureaucracy have affected how they have organized themselves within the spaces available to them. The tensions (political contestations) created by the processes involved in claiming their own space produce the connectivity (through leaders) described in this chapter

The ferīkh's socio-political organization

Traditionally, the ferīkhs were organized according to lineage and would migrate together. Nowadays ferīkhs are sometimes made up of a mixture of lineages,[7] and some groups have settled in permanent villages. The leader of a village holds approximately the same status as a *chef de ferīkh* and is known as the *chef de village*. Each *chef de ferīkh* is supported by a council (*conseil*), made up of members of his ferīkh and, if relevant, members of the sedentary village. It is the *chef de canton* that chooses which of the two or three nominees put forward by the *tribu* will become *chef de ferīkh*.[8] When issues cannot be resolved within the ferīkh's *conseil* or among the Walad Djifir in general, they are brought to the *chef de canton*.

Each *chef de canton* is responsible for his specific *canton*. Several *cantons*, in turn, make up an administrative region (governed by, in this order, a *sous-prefet*, a *prefet*, and a *gouverneur*).[9] In the case of Chad, with its intricate history of numerous ethno-linguistic groups, a *canton* is not necessarily bound by geographic markers, although most do have an historic basis in specific regions. The *chef de canton* is thus usually a member of a sub-group. A sub-group is also known as a *khashim beyt* (خشم بيت), or clan. In turn, each *khashim beyt* has a leader of its own, known as the *chef de tribu*, or *sheikh* in Arabic (شيخ). To add to the complexity of social hierarchies,

---

7 'Sometimes one family is one ferīkh. When it is a large family, they may encompass two to three ferīkhs. In this organization they used to also migrate. Now it's a mixture within each ferīkh. People from one lineage have mixed into other ferīkhs. This used to exist in the past as well but was less frequent.' From a conversation with Abbakr Hissein in N'Djaména, 25 February 2014.

8 From a conversation with Abbakr Hissein in N'Djaména, 25 February 2014.

9 Chad has eighteen regions, sixty departments, 202 *sous-prefectures* and numerous *cantons* within the latter. A region is governed by the governor and his general secretary. A department is governed by the prefect and his assistant. The *sous-préfet* governs his own *sous-prefecture*. *Cantons* follow the traditional structures of governance and are headed by chiefs belonging to the different communities.

every *khashim beyt* can be made up of several families, each with their own leader, a *chef de ferīkh*. Traditionally, the *chef de canton* of the Misseria Rouges chooses the *chef de khashim beyt* of each separate group (e.g. the Walad Djifir, Mazaknéh, Walad Tūrki). Two to three candidates are put forward or nominate themselves, and the *chef de canton* chooses from among them. It is not a process of voting. Table 2 provides an overview of the socio-political organization of the Walad Djifir.

Table 2: Socio-political organization of the Misseria Rouges (MR) in relation to the khashim beyt of the Walad Djifir (WD) (2011–2014). Sources: Brahim 1988; Aubague et al. 2006; Dangbet 2015a; own observations.

Leadership titles	Description	Position-holder b/w 2011–2014	Location
Chef de canton of the MR (aka *chef superieur*)	Leader of a canton (a territorial sub-division). Each canton is made up of several communities, and each administrative region can hold numerous cantons.	Abdoulaye Goudjeh Hamatta (since 16 April 1985/6)	Koundjaar, Batha region
Chef de canton of the WD and Dadjo I	Same as above	Youssef/Hissein Eledouh (the Dadjo chef). In 2009: Ahmad Ibeduh (fieldnotes 4 April 2012)	Mongo, Guéra region
Chef de tribu (*khashim beyt*)	Leader of a sub-group, in this case of the WD; elected but often from within the same family which already held the position. Aka *sheikh al-khashim beyt*.	Adjidei Hamid Hassan*	Fané, Guéra region
Chef de ferīkh (*iyal radjil*)	Leader of a sub-division of a sub-group, traditionally consisting of one or more lineages	Saleh 'Umar Fadoul*	Fadjé, Guéra region
Chef de village	Leader of a sedentary village	Nouraddin Ahmat*	Hilleh Tchoufioux II, Guéra region
Ferīkh conseil (*adjaouid*)	Members of a sub-division of the sub-group who act as an advisory party to the *chef de ferīkh* (and village)	Saleh 'Umar, Nouraddin Ahmat, Shamsaddin, Yaya, Alladoum (among others)*	Fadjé, Guéra region

*pseudonym

In general, *cantons* are made up of a homogenous ethno-linguistic group, with many such groups having split into several *cantons* over the years. Historically, the Walad Djifir as part of the Misseria Rouges, belonged to the *chef de canton* located in Koundjaar. Under the French, however, the situation changed a number of times. In 1911 Sheikh Adoudou succeeded his father as sheikh of the Misseria Rouges and was quick to gain French trust. Between 1932 and 1935 he was tasked with regrouping the Misseria Rouges under his authority. In 1935 he was installed as Sheikh Kabīr of both the Misseria Rouges and Noirs, as well as of the sedentary populations of Oumhadjer. Adoudou and his sons succeeded in alienating those they had been put in control over, failing to unite them in any politically stable or economically productive way. In 1943 the French administration had also had enough and re-divided the Misseria Rouges and Noirs, reinstating former *chef de tribus* and *canton*. The paternal cousins Adoum and Abbakr recall how the power over the Misseria Rouges canton came to be placed with the sheikh of the Walad Sūrūr, Goudjeh Walad Hamatta (see also Hugot 1997: 121). The town of Koundjaar, located in the Batha and falling under the canton of Assinet, became the seat of the canton of the Misseria Rouges (see Map 3). Administratively, the Walad Djifir fell under this *cantonage*. The sedentary populations took this opportunity to create their own canton, *canton des Sédentaires du Dar Misserié*. However, the rights to pasture, villages, wells, and cultivation land remained with the Arabs – a situation which still creates tensions, especially among rival *chefs de canton* (Brahim 1988: 41–44).

Upon the 1943 proclamation, the French also made it mandatory for each sub-group's sheikh to give one of their sons to be raised in Koundjaar. As son of the *chef de tribu* (Sheikh of the Walad Djifir), Abbakr was brought up in Koundjaar, alongside Goudjeh's own son and current *chef de canton*, Abdoulaye Goudjeh. Abbakr's father was succeeded by the latter's younger brother: Adoum's father. The current sheikh of the Walad Djifir is Adjidei, the son of the brother who followed Issa 'Umar.

Land strife and strengthening allegiances

By March 2012 it had been three years since the Walad Djifir had left the canton of Abdoulaye Goudjeh.[10] As *chef de canton*, Abdoulaye Goudjeh had begun giving away – or rather selling – land to other sub-groups. In the case of the Walad Djifir, he had forcefully taken a piece of Habilai and sold one part to the Walad 'Umar and another part to the Mazaknéh, in exchange for money and livestock (*'boeufs vivres'*,

---

10 Fieldnotes, 4 April 2012.

in the words of the Walad Djifir). The incident occurred in the month of October, when most of the Walad Djifir can be found on their dry-season lands in the Guéra. It had started out with a visit to the terrain from the *chef de tribu* of the Walad 'Umar. As most people do not live on al-Habilai year-round, a guard is appointed to protect their terrain, the focal point of which is now a deep, constructed well. This guard, a brother of Abbakr Hissein named Abdelkarim Hissein Hassan,[11] received the aforementioned visitor. The chef of the Walad 'Umar claimed that a specific part of the terrain belonged to the Walad 'Umar. The guard denied this: 'Since my father, I have never heard of such a thing – that there were Walad 'Umar in this area.' A meeting was organized with the Walad 'Umar, Walad Sūrūr, and Walad Djifir. The Toumaï, who are not Misseria Rouges, were called in by the Walad Djifir to act as witnesses and to confirm the identity of the rightful owner. The chef of the Walad 'Umar refused to accept this, even after they had sworn on a copy of the Qur'ān. Here the information on what happened next is somewhat unclear. However the meeting went exactly, the outcome was one with which the Walad Djifir did not agree. When they voiced this, soldiers and gendarmes arrested them and placed them in the full sun[12] for twenty-five minutes, after which they were released. The indignity of having been held unjustly is what everyone remembers most when recounting the story.[13] One may assume that the Walad 'Umar (the Mazaknéh were not mentioned in this situation) were directly supported by Abdoulaye Goudjeh when placing their claim on the terrain.

In the beginning, attempts were made to resolve the issue directly with the two sub-groups who had occupied the land, and with Abdoulaye Goudjeh himself. None of the parties would budge; and as a protest and out of desperation, the Walad Djifir left the *canton* of the Misseria Rouges and joined that of the Dadjo.[14] When Abdoulaye Goudjeh heard of the definite transfer, he undertook several steps to try to win them back. He first visited the Dadjo *chef de canton* to persuade him to give him back his people. The Dadjo chef advised him to go and speak to his own people instead of coming to him. He then offered the *ferīkh conseil* ten million CFA, or whatever they wanted. The Walad Djifir refused every amount proposed – 'even 14 and 20 million', as one person recounted. Abdoulaye Goudjeh then decided to visit

---

11 Same father, different mother. See Figure 2.

12 Perhaps an unnecessary reminder: temperatures in Chad during the day, in the sun, reach the mid-40s Celsius, if not more – also in October. Also a note on soldiers, gendarmes, and police: the police play a role in towns and villages, while the gendarmeries are responsible for the security *en brousse*.

13 Based on a conversation with Adoum, Yakhoub, and Nouraddin in Tchoufiou II Arabe, 13 April 2012.

14 The Dadjo make up a large part of the sedentary population of the Guéra.

the *préfet* in Mongo to lodge a complaint. When this complaint arrived at the level of the Walad Djifir, Hadj Saleh called Adoum for advice. Adoum told him that they should go to see the local (and only) political party, the MPS (Mouvement Patriotique du Salut).[15] The case was put forward and an appointment was made to which Abdoulaye Goudjeh was also invited. At this appointment, Abdoulaye Goudjeh was told that the MPS had brought democracy, which meant that every Chadian has the right to live where he wants, whether this is on a mountain or in a tree.[16] So if a *chef de canton*'s people wanted to leave his *canton*, they were free to do so. Following this meeting Abdoulaye Goudjeh retracted his complaint and returned to the Batha, where he continues to negotiate with those who left – although this now happens in a more passive manner. In the meantime, those groups that had sworn on the Qur'ān that a part of al-Habilai had always belonged to them and not to the Walad Djifir left the territory. Adoum joined several others to confirm this. No one is allowed to touch the land until the Walad Djifir have decided whether they will continue to fight for it or not. The land is guarded by the same man as mentioned earlier, Abdelkarim Hissein Hassan, and his family.

On a visit to Koundjaar on 11–12 April 2012, Adoum and I stayed in the *chef de canton*'s compound following an invitation from Abbakr Hissein and Abdoulaye Goudjeh himself. In accordance with French regulations, Abbakr Hissein, as son of a *chef de tribu*, had been raised in the household of the *chef de canton* in Koundjaar, together with the sons of other sub-groups (*khashim beyt*). In practice, this meant that he had been sent to school, which greatly influenced the possibility of his education in Romania as a veterinarian, his subsequent work as such in the Ministry of Pastoralism, and later ministerial posts under both Habré and Déby.[17] In 2012 he still occupied a seat in the Conseille de Presidence. His being raised alongside Abdoulaye Goudjeh (*'ils sont ensemble depuis'*), together with his political function, partly explain his loyalty to the man. His family *en brousse*, however, do not understand why he fails to take their side and to oppose Abdoulaye Goudjeh. Adoum explained that it was politics. If Abbakr does not report certain developments to the *gouverneur* of the Batha, there will be consequences to be faced.

---

15 The MPS was created in Darfur in 1990 and was initially supported by France, Sudan, and Libya (Debos 2016: 63).

16 This is literally what was said; conversation with Adoum, 4 April 2012.

17 'There was a policy by many communist countries to offer scholarships to potential allies, thus maybe not on a country-specific level in the case of Chad, but certainly as part of a wider strategy.' From a conversation with Prof. Dr. Andrea Behrends, fieldnotes, 28 March 2012. Abbakr, now retired, lives in N'Djaména but tries to visit the Batha regularly, on private and state business. On the occasion of our joint visit, he had taken his wife and children along with him.

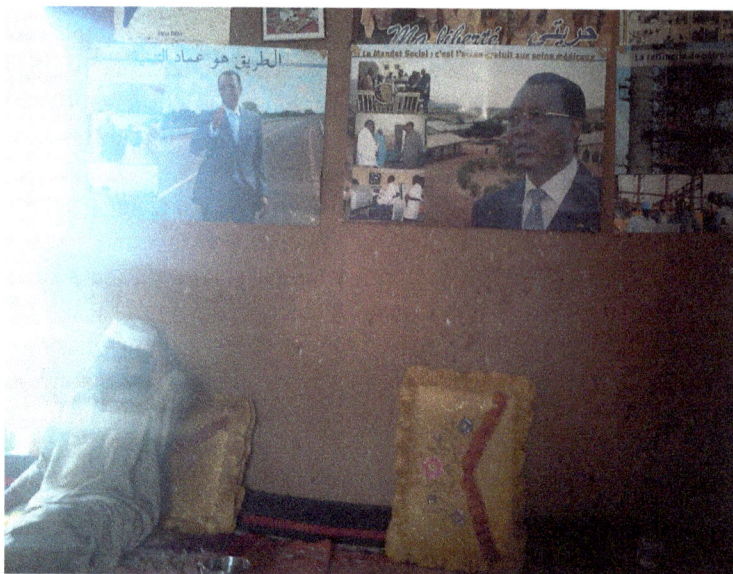

Photo 3.2: Visit to the home of chef de canton of the Misseria Rouges in Koundjaar, April 2012. We were invited by Adoums's cousin, who had been raised alongside the current chef de canton, and joined by Yakhoub and Nouraddin. The building was built over fifty years earlier by Abdoulaye Goudjeh's father. It is a square building with entrances to the front and rear. The traditional building style, using mud, wood, and branches, means that it stays relatively cool during the day – its high ceilings allowing the hot air to rise up and escape through the small window slits under the roof. Neither Yakhoub or Nouraddin ever spoke with the chef de canton directly. Instead, we spent most of the afternoon hanging around, with Adoum and his cousin discussing the land situation and trying to mediate the more fierce reactions of the other two men.

On the way to Koundjaar, we had run into Nouraddin and Yakhoub, who, after hearing where we were heading, decided to take advantage of the occasion (car transport and the added benefit of Abbakr's presence). They hoped they could talk to Abbakr about the land issue, refusing to speak directly to their former *chef de canton*. In practice, this led to a somewhat awkward (and to me almost funny) rotation of who would be inside the *chef de canton*'s main building at the same time. The building in which the *chef de canton* held office was built over fifty years ago by Abdoulaye Goudjeh's father. It is a square building with entrances to the front and rear. The traditional building style, using mud, wood, and branches, means that it stays relatively cool during the day – its high ceilings allowing the hot air to rise up and escape through the small window slits under the roof. The floors are covered by rugs – some of which seem to be specifically *à la mode*, as they are the same ones Abbakr, Adoum, and Hadj Saleh own and use for special occasions.[18] The rest of Abdoulaye Goudjeh's household is spread out over a large compound, housing his three wives and their children. He used to have four wives, but one left. Each wife has her own enclosed compound. On this occasion, we spent the night in the second wife's compound. In honour of Abbakr's visit, a calf was slaughtered.[19] Several armed men in army uniform were in the compound at the time of our visit. They were not there to guard the *chef de canton* – he hardly has any weapons of his own – but on a separate governmental mission.

Returning to the reason for Nouraddin and Yakhoub's presence in Koundjaar: the Walad Djifir's *conseil* had agreed that if Abdoulaye Goudjeh did not come up with a solution within three months from then, they would group themselves and attack. Luckily, an attack never occurred. However, on our way back from Koundjaar, we learned that the Mazaknéh had grouped themselves in Oum Hadjer in preparation for an attack on the very same Abdoulaye Goudjeh. They too had a land issue with their *chef de canton*. In the case of the Mazaknéh, he had allowed the mobile telephone company Tigo to build an antenna on their land. The *chef de canton* had received money from Tigo in return. His argument was that the land belonged to the canton as a whole, giving him this right. The Mazaknéh did not agree and thus had prepared an attack. News travels fast, and before the attackers could properly leave Oum Hadjer, they were detained by government forces. Having learned of the situation, Abbakr informed the Gouverneur of Ati, who in turn called the *sous-préfet* of Oum Hadjer. Adoum explained that these situations happened often and that it was a tactic sometimes to get the issue brought to court. By being arrested for an attack, the Mazaknéh would now be brought before the Court of Judgement in N'Djaména. To my question about why they did not just approach the court directly, he answered: 'That's now how we are. We will first try to solve it with the person or group. If that doesn't work, we fight for our right.' On our return to Fadjé we heard that the Mazaknéh were also grouping together in Mongo.

When presented with the proposed plan of action, Abbakr did not agree with them. Nouraddin, speaking for the *ferīkh conseil*, had hoped Abbakr would raise their issue at a national level. The ever-diplomatic Abbakr, however, remained very calm and passive during this heated yet low-voiced discussion and advised them to, instead of taking up arms, build a case proving the land had always been theirs.

---

18 This specific rug is imported from Libya. Adoum advised Hadj Saleh against buying such an expensive rug for use in the ferīkh, as he claimed they would not know how to care for it properly.
19 By the time we left the next morning, the left-over calf's meat that had been hung out to dry was already being taken off the lines – this is how dry the air is in Koundjaar!

He suggested a book written about the Misseria Rouges in colonial times, which mentioned which lands belonged to which sub-group. It was the book written by Pierre Hugot in 1997, dealing with the situation as it was in 1947 in relation to the Misseria Rouges, based on colonial archives and most probably on the work of Courtecuisse et al. (1971). When I later found the book at Librairie La Source in N'Djaména and brought it back to Tchoufiou for Nouraddin, we found that, indeed, the Walad 'Umar are never mentioned in it in relation to al-Habilai. In fact, according to Hugot's sources, in 1947 their terrain was far from that of the Walad Djifir. It is important to note that it is sometimes difficult to prove which land belongs to which group of people.[20] This is especially the case because much of such ownership has been passed down orally, and archives – if there were any – have been destroyed during the various rebellions.

By switching to the Dadjo canton, certain benefits have arisen. The Walad Djifir have had a sedentary village along the road to Ati for thirty years. The village is known as Tchoufiou II Arabe and is just a few kilometres north of the Dadjo village, Tchoufiou. Tchoufiou 'Deux' Arabe, simply 'Tchoufiou' from now on, has fairly recently been given official status by the local Mongo government officials, and with this official status the inhabitants have been able to apply for a public school.[21] The process was a long and tiresome one, with a lot of reluctance on the part of the neighbouring Hadjerai population; but on Monday 19 March 2012, the first school day became a fact. Walad Djifir parents had joined forces to raise the money for a classroom to be built. They also constructed a *kouzi* (round hut made of stone bricks and a straw roof) for the teacher and jointly paid his salary.

The Walad Djifir are not the only ones who see the benefit of splitting from their former *chef de canton* and joining that of the Dadjo. Another sub-group experienced a similar problem not long after and requested to join the Dadjo canton and be given land. They were refused by the Dadjo, however, and told to go back and talk to their former chef. Although relations between the Walad Djifir and the Dadjo chief are relatively stable and peaceful, the Dadjo chief is still dealing with issues which arose when he gave the Walad Djifir land. He does not want to add to this by taking on another group.

---

20 De Bruijn & van Dijk (2007: 62); Van Dijk (2003); de Bruijn (2004). Souleymane (2017) highlights how this remains a problem in the Guéra and Sido areas, where refugees are encroaching on land. The few archives that used to exist have been destroyed.

21 For a discussion of problematics and trade-offs with this format of schooling, see Swift (2011); Siele et al. (2013); Köhler (2016a: 150–155).

Photo 3.3: The new school at Tchoufiou II Arabe, March 2012. The school was an initiative of the parents. The teacher is paid by the parents and offered a home (kouzi) and food.

Photo 3.4: A second classroom was soon added to the school in Tchoufiou, which we visited in January 2013.

Photo 3.5: Parents (men) clearing the grounds before the first day of school, March 2012. Many members of the ferīkh council as well as some other parents helped sweep up and clear any prickly branches so that the children could play outside during recess.

Photo 3.6: The village of Tchoufiou II Arabe, May 2012. It houses a mixture of nomadic tents and permanent huts made with bricks and straw roofing.

Photo 3.7: Grain storage in *dabanga*'s at Tchoufiou, December 2012. Another benefit of having permanent villages is being able to store own's own grain.

Old leaders and new *'opposantes'*

In March 2014 Abdoulaye Goudjeh's *cantonage* was increasingly finding itself in troubled water. This tendency to malpractice by Abdoulaye Goudjeh had affected his relationship with other sub-groups under his *cantonage* and, consequently, opposing *chef de cantons* had arisen. There were already four or five[22] – three of which had official backing by the state, although it is not clear what this means exactly. Abdoulaye Goudjeh's actions are not the only reason for this rise in *opposantes*. In the whole of Chad this tendency can be found, a tendency linked not only to issues of income but also to injustices carried out by these leaders and/or their designation as such in the first place.

In colonial times, a *chef de canton* was given a salary. After independence, this practice was suspended for a while, or the salary was negligible. With the influx of petrol revenues, salaries once again became worthwhile.[23] Under the French, then

---

22 Fieldnotes, N'Djaména, 13 May 2012.
23 With a decline in the oil sector and the empty treasury, we can only guess what consequences this may have for future motivations. From 2016 onward, the frequency of protests and strikes

Habré, and up until fairly recently – before the coming of petrol as state revenue – taxes were paid for both people and cattle. These taxes were collected by the *chef de khashim beyt*, who would pass them on to the *chef de canton*, who in turn would hand them over to the *sous-préfet*. Nowadays, the *khashim beyt* pays them out directly to the *sous-préfet*, as large portions were 'getting lost' in transit – namely, at the level of the *chef de canton*. It is said that the *chef de khashim beyt* is known to sometimes keep some of the tax revenue aside, leaving the *sous-préfet* to make up the difference out of his own salary.[24] Nevertheless, the post of *chef de canton* is first and foremost a political one – it is the state which appoints a *chef de canton*, thus also holding the power to dismiss and replace them from their post. A certain affinity with the current political powers (MPS) is necessary.

In terms of the appointment of a new *chef de canton*, it is said to cost two million CFA to put someone's name forward at the level of the state. In order to do so, one thus needs to be either well endowed or have the financial support of others. In general, a new *chef de canton* should be brought forward by his *tribu*. While in practice this does still happen in some cases, in other cases it is the aspiring *chef de canton* who rallies support among his *tribu* and is, more often than not, well connected to certain members of N'Djaména society.

'Chaque chefferie cherche un canton'

The first successful *opposante*[25] to Abdoulaye Goudjeh was Muhammed al-Tubukh,[26] currently an officially recognized *chef de canton* of the Mazaknéh. Another such *opposante* is Muhammed Souleymane, a member of the Matanine *khashim beyt*. Muhammed Souleymane lives in a three-storey house in N'Djaména and makes his living as a successful merchant.[27] Like so many Chadian children, he was placed

---

increased. These protests were often a reaction to months of salaries not being paid to government workers and teachers.

24 From a conversation with Abbakr Hissein, N'Djaména, 25 February 2014. In 2012, the tax per person was 500 CFA – just under one euro. Fieldnotes, 7 March 2012.

25 The sub-title above refers to the numerous *opposantes* with Adoum commenting: 'Every *chef-ferie* is looking for a [to make their own] *canton*.'

26 There is some discrepancy as to the name of the *chef* of the Mazaknéh. In fieldnotes, Oyo village, 18 March 2014, the name of the Mazaknéh *chef de canton* is said to be Mahamat al-Kabbak. While in a conversation with a Mazaknéh, Zamzam of Mongo, on 15 February 2013, he is named as Muhammad al-Tubukh. Adoum referred to him as Muhammad al-Takas.

27 This is exactly how his existence was introduced: *trois étages!* Although N'Djaména is a fast-developing city, especially since Chad's oil exploitation took off in 2003, multi-storey buildings have only started springing up more frequently as of 2010, usually for commercial or governmental

under the care of a *marabout*. As *muhadjireen*, children take part in Qur'ān lessons in the early morning, afternoon, and evenings, while begging for food the rest of the day. The exact sequence of events is unclear, but at one point he had started selling three or four litres of *essence* (petrol) to get by. Slowly but surely he was able to ascend and to develop a steady business. He now owns a petrol station (not an official one but functioning nonetheless) and has built a nice house, both in Ati. Muhammed was able to come to N'Djaména with the help of Abbakr Hissein, who helped him obtain the right papers to be able to work as a merchant. His petrol station in N'Djaména is well frequented by government *fonctionaires*. More recently, he has moved on to the building of schools in the interior of the country, obtaining a state contract to build a total of 200 schools. When we discuss the man's ambitions, Adoum says, *'Il a jeté la tasse'* (lit. 'He has thrown away his bowl'), referring to the silver bowl the *muhadjireen* carry around when begging for food – he has left his *maraboutage* far behind. Although he is well known, the state acknowledges his position as such; he has submitted the necessary paperwork, though his position has not yet been officially declared. Nevertheless, he is still invited to all state occasions where *chefs de cantons* are requested to be present, such as for a *defilé* for the president or on one of Chad's national days. One such important day, especially for nomadic communities, is the yearly festival in Wadi Djadid. On this occasion, the state donates cattle, camels, sheep, rice, flour, and sugar to the various *chefs de canton* and their people.

Table 3: Chefs de canton Misseria Rouges (including opposantes), 2014.

Chefs de canton Misseria Rouges	Location *sous-prefecture*	*Khashim beyt*
Abdoulaye Goudjeh (official, colonially appointed)	Koundjaar	Walad Sūrūr; colonially appointed
Mahamat al-Tubukh *(opposante)*	Wadi Djadīd	Mazaknéh; since 2003
Capitaine Baïne *(opposante)*	Assinet	Adjadjiré; since 2001
Muhammed Souleymane *(opposante)*	N'Djaména	Matanīn

purposes. Private properties consisting of multiple storeys are still fairly rare, though were definitely becoming much more prominently visible by October 2017. Fieldnotes, 21 January 2013. See Table 3 for an overview of *chefs de canton* including the *opposantes*.

It was this Muhammed Souleymane who approached Adoum on several occasions, finally convincing him to meet him at his house. Here he tried to convince Adoum that he and his *parents*, the group led by Adjidei, needed to leave the Dadjo canton and join his instead. He argued that the Misseria Rouge as a group needed to stick together – they belonged together and not with the Dadjo. 'You live in N'Djaména, Adoum; you are an intellectual, not like your family *en brousse*.' Adoum replied that this was something the *parents* would decide together. When he related his conversation with Muhammed Souleymane to them over the phone and again on one of our visits to Fadjé in 2013, they answered that this was a decision that they had to reflect on calmly and slowly. Now was not the moment to act – '*avec "x" temps*', translated Adoum.

Adoum himself believes that for now they are fine where they are with the Dadjo. In his opinion, over time they should decide whether to stay with the Dadjo, whether to create their own canton, or whether to join the new *opposante*, a Walad Djifir. Ideally, they would want to have a *chef de race*,[28] who would function like a *chef de canton*, to whom they could approach to settle internal disputes. Only if a solution could not be found within the group would they put the case forward to the Dadjo *chef de canton*. In reality, the position of *chef de race* is equal to that of *chef de tribu*, which is now held by Adjidei. Adjidei, however, is not seen to be an assertive leader. To deal with things on the level of a *chef de race* (i.e. canton), they would require someone else.[29] According to the *conseil*, this someone else should be Adoum Issa 'Umar himself.

By early 2014, Adoum had been told by his family in Fadjé that he himself should step forward as their *chef de canton*. Their plan was to then leave the Dadjo canton and join him. Adoum has refused to accept the proposition, but they are convinced that, with time, he will accept. When asked if there was no one better suited, Adoum replied that the problem is that there are very few family members who can read and write French.[30]

Taking the legal route

The Adjadjiree are another of the Misseria Rouges' sub-groups who left their former canton, namely that of Abdoulaye Goudjeh, around 2001 to recreate their own.

---

28 The position of *chef de race*, like that of *chef de canton* and so on, was created under the French. A *chef de race* is like a *chef de canton* but without the *canton*. In most cities, one will find a *chef de race* for each, what Chadians refers to as 'ethnic' group. In practice, however, here too we see the tendency to split up resulting in several *chefs de race* per *tribu*.

29 Conversation with Adoum, 21 January 2013.

30 Conversation with Adoum, 21 February 2014.

In an interview[31] with Capitaine Baïne, the current Adjadjiree *opposante chef de canton*, he explained that his family had been leaders (*'agiib*) long before the colonial powers came and placed another family in power. Their *sous-préfecture* is at Assinet (Batha Est); and according to him, the colonial archives in Paris show that the *cantonage* of the Misseria Rouges used to belong to them. Since 2013 they have filed official paperwork at the Ministry of Interior, claiming their canton back. Submitting such a claim is free of charge. It seems that only in the last few years, people have started reclaiming their former, mostly pre-colonial, rights. At independence, the Chadian government took over the existing colonial structures of governance. For a long time afterward, the government was more like a dictatorship – there was no possibility for people to exercise their own rights, according to Capitaine Baïne. In the last few years, this has become possible. The multiplication of administrative chiefs may not be a recent phenomenon, but the judicial act of challenging the existing chiefs is.

Capitaine Baïne grew up as a nomadic child – behind his family's livestock, as they often say. Life was good, he recollects. On 2 April 1979 he left the ferīkh to join the rebels. He left because life for nomadic people had become difficult (*şa'b*). He noticed that nomads were not being given the same rights as others in Chad: there was no schooling provided for them, and they were being marginalized. He joined the rebels to gain literacy skills and to help reverse the nomads' inferior status. When the rebels were overrun by Déby in 1990, many were incorporated into the state army. This was also the case for Capitaine Baïne. He retired from his army post in 2011. The knowledge he gained during this time has made him aware of his and his people's rights. By approaching and becoming a part of the state's power, people have thus received rights and are now aware of these rights. The claim was submitted in 2013. Speaking in early 2014, Capitaine Baïne says patience is of key importance. It has always been that way. 'We will talk and discuss and wait until we find a solution. We prefer the fair [legal] course of action; it is very important to us. And it is our right. Carrying out this process the legal way will help us in the long run.' His advice echoes that which Abbakr Hissein had given Nouraddin.

Leaders as strategy and resource

What is interesting here is who these opposing *chef de cantons* are and how leadership figures are seen, in a way, as a strategy and resource by the community. As

---

31 Interview held in March 2014 in Mongo, together with colleague Souleymane Adoum Abdoulaye.

might already have been deduced from the stories of Muhammed Souleymane and Adoum himself, being connected to the right people plays a role. But who are these 'right' people, and is this all? There is a real inclination to put those forward who speak French, have some form of non-Arabic education, and generally have ties with those in N'Djaména. Having a leader literate in French facilitates communication with authorities. On the very first visit in October 2011, for example, Adoum was asked to read a letter which Yaya had received. Yaya is the *khalīfa* and responsible for collecting taxes on livestock sold at the weekly markets. The letter informed the community of taxes to be paid per head of cattle. There are other ways to find out what the letter said, and I suspect that whoever handed it to Yaya probably explained its contents to him. Nevertheless, having someone who could read and speak French within the community would be an obvious benefit. The cases of the Adjadjiree and of Abdoulaye Goudjeh, show the importance of having a leader who knows how to navigate the legal system and who has contacts in N'Djaména who may aid their cause.

Leaders thus form a 'resource', if you will, with specific qualities and are utilized to perform a specific role. The leader-as-resource is managed by the community, while there exists at the same time a certain dependency on one another. A leader is nothing without his following, and loyalties can change – as the numerous cases of opposing *chefs de canton* show. There is often a financial aspect to these positions, not only the raising of money to put forward a new *chef de canton*, but also traditionally the collection of taxes and access to these kinds of 'income' later on. Perhaps the tasks of these newly chosen leaders are slightly different from what they used to entail – of this I am unsure.[32]

The changes in choice of leaders – based not only on lineage, but also on their capabilities, skills, and connections, next to their general character – can be seen as a strategy which embodies both flexibility and control. Through choosing certain individuals, the Walad Djifir (and other sub-groups) show the ability to be flexible while hoping to increase the control they have over their own lives. There are, however, numerous strategies from which individuals and communities can choose, and there is no set format.

In 2017, Adoum did not taken up the position his family would have liked him to. Even in 2022, his role as mediator still exists; yet owing to his current job – the transportation of people and goods from N'Djaména to Ati, and between the various weekly markets around Ati – he often does not have the time or mobile network

---

32 It is not clear to me how this would be arranged. When discussing the various new and opposing *chefs de canton*, this aspect did not arise and I neglected to focus on it myself. It would be strange for Adoum to be the one to collect taxes while living in N'Djaména, so it is likely that a different structure would have been created.

to be in such close contact as he was when permanently based in N'Djaména, or indeed during the various periods of fieldwork with me. Adoum's current employment is partly a result of Chad's economic decline – he would have preferred a job as a driver for one of the NGOs or other aid organizations based in N'Djaména, but he says there are not that many positions available – and those that exist are usually given to family or friends. It is difficult to get your foot in the door without the right connections. This seems ironic when one remembers that Adoum's extended family had asked him to become their new *chef de canton*, and it shows how relative this connectivity is.

Nevertheless, the cases of Abdoulaye Goudjeh, Hadj Saleh, and Adoum himself are examples of how those in various positions of leadership can have both a connecting and disconnecting role, roles which they themselves take up or which are placed upon them as a result of decisions they have made.

In a way, a focus on leaders as both connectors and disconnectors reflects the histories of mobility and fluidity we often find in nomadic societies. Cordell explains how this need for flexibility with security provides a way of understanding the 'local histories characterised by confusing and seemingly contradictory narratives of raids and counter-raids, of pacts made and pacts broken' (1985: 322–323). In certain contexts, ferīkh members pull their strengths together and are as close as can be (fusion). In other cases, for whatever reasons, they 'fight' each other. In a way, they are brothers in arms (fighting a common battle), but also brothers *at* arms (fighting each other). Throughout the other chapters, this dualism – or paradox even? – returns in some form or other, informing choices which are either for or against the consensus of the group, the ferīkh, or that of an individual family member. Fission and fusion.

Brothers in *and* at arms: On fission and fusion in a modernizing Chad

The Walad Djifir have faced several challenges in terms of leadership strife, land use, and the subsequent forming or strengthening of allegiances. The cases described in this chapter show the structure and functioning of the ferīkh as a non-isolated unit. The consequences of a very personal tragedy – namely, the accidental death of Hassan's son – is simultaneously a communal tragedy with monetary implications for the ferīkh, and also very much a test of solidarity and social cohesion. This is a test which Hadj Saleh and company, in this specific case, failed to pass – according to Adoum and others – and which has resulted in a rift between members of the same *khashim beyt*, ultimately leading to the creation of an opposing *chef de ferīkh*, who is contemplating splitting from Hadj Saleh's group and joining another (*opposante*) *chef de canton*.

The drivers of ferīkh politics are closely linked to the navigation of social cohesion and power relations. These are in turn related to kinship relations, enforced by cattle distribution and land-use rights, and by shared Islamic norms and values. While the events which have led up to this potential divide are probably more numerous than I was able to discover, by focusing on people, namely 'leaders', there is room for individual choices which are not only linked to familial obligations.[33]

Returning first to the case of the death of Hassan's son as one illustration of socio-political relations within the ferīkh, we will add to the complexity of family and allegiances. Hassan 'Umar and Hadj Saleh 'Umar are in fact brothers, Hassan being the youngest son of their father and a different mother. On his own departure to CAR in May 2012, Hadj Saleh had refused to acknowledge his younger brother's departure greeting. He had even been rude and told him to go away when he had come to visit him. This action caused their eldest sister much distress. Hassan had been able to come up with most of the money owed to the other ferīkh. Hadj Saleh had been furious when he discovered Hassan had done this without his explicit blessing. In a way, Hassan had shown himself as the better man – in the end it is his *own* son whom he will never see again.[34] Members of the *conseil* (Alladoum, Shamsaddin, and Yakhoub specifically) still agreed with Hadj Saleh. When I asked Adoum how a *marabout*, which both Hadj Saleh and Abou Ramla are, could agree to this and what the '*grand' ferīkh marabout* had to say about it all, he replied that even the *grand marabout* had talked until he was tired ('*il a parler fatigué*'). They would not listen to him. Adoum was greatly affected by the situation and feared it would break up the family.

In the case of Abdoulaye Goudjeh, another kind of injustice lies at the foreground – namely, that of land dis-ownership. The themes of a perceived injustice and calling on certain family members – brothers, if you will – to aid the community's cause seem to run through both case studies. By highlighting the actions of certain individual leadership figures, the non-coherence and unambiguity (see Cordell 1985; Debos 2016) of these actions come to the fore: people are contradictory in nature, interpreting the importance of certain values in different ways.

In the case of Hassan's son, the issue has caused a certain divide (fission) among the community. Nomads' moments of fission are often related to the size or composition of a herd, with camps splitting up to accommodate the larger numbers of cattle or to allow camels the space they need. I explore other forms fission may take – not just the physical splitting up of a group but the splitting of opinion and the

---

[33] Debos (2016: 120) draws a distinction between the effects of actions and the intentions behind them.

[34] In October 2017 on a visit to N'Djaména, I learned that Hassan had passed away.

(re)actions involved. This places the emphasis – of the result of fission and fusion processes – on social relations and the creation of opportunities through the desta-bilization of existing hierarchies (Brenner 2001).

The land issue with Abdoulaye Goudjeh, in turn, has resulted in a feeling of needing to unite (fusion). At the level of these leaders, their actions and choices seem to be between protecting the cohesion of the group, and making choices, indi-vidual or otherwise, which break the group apart. Interestingly, these almost con-tradictory reactions can and do exist at the same time.[35]

Traditionally, the idea of fission and fusion in relation to pastoral-nomadic groups has usually been in reference to exactly that: the group. With these case studies, I question whether such processes can also take other forms or be dis-cerned at other levels of social organization. At its most basic, human geographers see scale as a form of hierarchy whereby there is a fluidity of movement across the scales, and the scales themselves should not be seen as fixed entities (see Smith 1996; Marston 2000; Brenner 2001). I am borrowing this notion of 'scale' yet using the actions of individuals and communities to define and construct what the scales themselves are made up of.

The actions of ferīkh members at these various 'scales' – individual, family, and larger group – are framed and also situated within specific geographical and non-geographical spaces. Spatially, there are different levels of interaction and deci-sion making: the level of the family, or brothers even (i.e. Hadj Saleh and Hassan); the level of the ferīkh (i.e. Hadj Saleh, the *conseil*, and the *opposante*); the level of local politics (i.e. the *chefs de canton* of the Misseria Rouges, the Dadjo, and the *opposante*); and the level of national politics (involving decisions made in colonial times, the working of the justice system, and proving the right to land). Various actors, ranging from individuals to families and groups, make different decisions at these different hierarchical levels. A hierarchy which is in the eye of the beholder, as well as dependent on the situation. The interplay between notions of loyalty and security, informing feelings of belonging, impacts how people deal with these differ-ent levels, whereby one should always leave some wiggle room for the role of pride.

Throughout the negotiation and decision-making processes of the Walad Djifir, multiple spatial units are established. Arguments are made as to where loyalties should lie: with certain individuals due to their lineage or reputation, or with the

---

35 See Rosen (2017: 37) referring to Evans-Pritchard (1940: 142–144) on 'the odd contradictions that may arise when two low-level segments are in conflict with one another at one level, but in alliance at some higher level'. See Djama (2010: 108) on the 'balance of power', a structural model of political equilibrium between social groups: 'the members of a kinship group may fight against one another in the course of a conflict but will join forces against another more distant group in genealogical terms'. Here Djama revisits the writings of I.M. Lewis.

larger group. There is a certain ambiguity to this process whereby the spatial scales of existing hierarchies become destabilized, providing individuals with opportunities to create new combinations of social relations (Gille & Ó Riain 2002: 278). Hadj Saleh's individual actions have caused some to question his position as leader, while others have even gone against his decisions. At the same time, he is still sheikh, and so not much has changed. His actions, however, have created opportunities for the agendas of those he slighted and who have now decided to join the *opposante* – new combinations of leadership are forming while old patterns of entitlement are sometimes fallen back upon. The allegiance with the Dadjo is another example of shifts in the legitimacy of leadership and the opening up of opportunities. It is socio-historical processes such as these, even if they are unambiguous and perhaps exactly because of this, through which the ferīkh as spatial form 'is established and differentiated as a unit of socio-spatial organisation, activity, conflict, struggle, discourse and/or imagination' (Brenner 2001: 599).

How then can all of this help us understand what the ferīkh as a place and space entails? Smith (1996: 71) argues for the continued importance of fixed spaces and places, explaining how the relationship between the fluidity and fixity of space is itself restructured, though not in a uni-directional manner. Returning to the case studies, the notion of the ferīkh is conceptualized in different ways in different situations (scales), reinforcing what it stands for as opposed to rendering it obsolete. Is the ferīkh, then, as a socially constructed space, one which binds the Walad Djifir together – whether through cohesion (fusion) or friction (fission)? I would say that it is.

That which causes this cohesion or friction to come about is in part determined by the actions of individuals, such as leaders, and the communal reactions to them. These reactions take place in reference to what is deemed to create security mixed with a certain pride and sense of being wronged. The functioning of the ferīkh thus exists through the choices people make and their perspectives on how things should be in reference to individual and collective grievances, of wrong and right, and of wants for the future, such as schooling and security for their children. Even though the ferīkh functions as a network within which people justify their actions, this does not mean disparities and ambiguity do not exist. There is, one may say, a certain fission and fusion in the way Walad Djifir as a sub-group, members of an extended family, and even individuals (leaders and non-leaders) relate to this network when justifying their decisions.

***

The naming of Goudjeh Walad Hamatta as *chef de canton* by the French placed in his hands a certain power to make decisions regarding land use and ownership – a power which currently resides with his son. His son's actions have led to a change in leadership alliance on the part of 'his' subjects. While Koundjaar remains an important historical seat of power for the Misseria Rouges, having jurisdiction over the terrain to which the Walad Djifir feel they belong (al-Habilai), this has not prevented Walad Djifir from seeking security with a different canton. As such, leaders are connectors to the modern state, embodying a connectivity that both connects and causes disruption. Sjeikh Goudjeh Hamatta as *chef de canton* of the Misseria Rouges is a good example of this, as are all the *opposantes*. Through their leaders, Walad Djifir access services such as schools, healthcare, and the construction of a deep well. Even if not directly provided by the state, the leader's status and place in its structures do determine their success. One cannot have a school without the right to be on the land it is to be built. Similarly with wells. Walad Djifir recognized the benefits early on, of curating a relationship with the state and its representatives.

These dynamics of socio-political strife, and the creating of connections with those in power, do not constitute a new phenomenon. Instead, they are characterized by a certain historical continuity (of fission and fusion) in which Walad Djifir position themselves towards the modern state and changing bureaucracies. Chapter Three describes how Walad Djifir's predecessors moved their livestock and families further from the increased structural presence of the Ouaddaï empire. The historical process of expansion and sedentarization, especially in colonial times, brought changes culminating for Walad Djifir in their current (2011–2017) predicament of numerous *opposantes*, an allegiance with the Dadjo *canton*, and disagreement with their former *chef de canton*. Along the way, choices made were also very much strategies to secure their futures – a way of connecting to the changes around them. In reaction to a modernizing and globalizing world, their nomadic sedentarization process involved making adjustments to the length and duration of their transhumance, tending agricultural fields, and creating a handful of permanent villages. Were these necessary changes relatively successful when compared to other nomadic groups' contestations with the state apparatus? Despite an increase in structural presence, by the Chadian state, Walad Djifir mobility has not been sacrificed. Their sedentarization has not influenced their continuous ability to remain mobile and expand their networks. Throughout the chapters this historical process of connecting to changing bureaucracies and state structures is a common thread and overarching context. The next chapter further explores dynamics of modernization and globalization by focusing on the shifting trends towards livestock and making a living. It introduces another of Hadj Saleh's brothers, Moussa, and their familial connection to the CAR.

Chapter 4
The walk of life

Farina:[1]	*Wadeet as-sirī ma'a ad-djamal. Ad-djamal bas akheer.*
	I want to migrate [travel] with the camels. The camels are the best.
Inge:	*Leeh?*
	Why?
Farina:	Because we can place our things on their backs.
Adoum:	And which milk do you think is the tastiest?
Farina:	*'an al ghanam bas helu, al-labn.*
	That of the goats is good, the milk.
Inge:	What would you like to do when you are older?
Farina:	*Biyimshu al-'eidd, ma' Bechir.*
	Go to the watering hole with Bechir.
Inge:	And where is Bechir now?
Farina:	*Al-waqt da, Bechir saarih. Bechir maashi babi' al-natron min al-hilleh. Al-beyt da 'an Birémé. Timillah bi-l'eish. Kaan imbakr tisurtuh, timshu bi-ha. Tisrah aleena. Tisrah leku bi-lghanam walla djamal. Hija matifatish al-khanazai. Timillah foq al-'eish.*
	At this time, Bechir is travelling. Bechir has gone to the village to buy natron. That house is Birémé's. She is preparing food. When tomorrow Bechir leaves again, he will take it with him. He will travel with the goats or camels. She is getting the sheep [now]. She will give them food.
Adoum:	*Almi bishribu ween?*
	Where do they drink water?
Farina:	*Foq al-'eidd.*
	At the 'eidd.
Adoum:	*Kaan inti kabiri, tisrah bi shunuh?*
	When you are big/older, what will you travel [migrate] with?
Farina:	*Tisrah bi-djamal walla baqqar. Ammi biyamilluh 'eish.*
	I will travel with camel or cattle. Mama will make the *boule* [also when she is older].

– Conversation with Farina, five/six years old, 9 March 2014

✳✳✳

The conversation above, with a niece of Hadj Saleh (see Figure 1), is illustrative of how engrained the nomadic way of life already is at a young age. A life which is

---

1 At the time of this conversation in 2014, Farina was a five- or six-year-old girl. She had been living in the same encampment (ferīkh) as I was on my stay with them in 2012, so we saw a lot of each other. She shared a tent with her mother (Birémé), older brother (Tchoudja), and father (Moussa). In 2014, she had lost neither her curiosity nor her mischievous look, compared to the three-year-old I first met in October 2011 and came to know better in 2012.

https://doi.org/10.1515/9783110714685-004

part of an historical process that includes adapting to changing political structures (Chapter Two) and ecological, environmental, and economic changes. Children's games often consist of mimicking the daily activities of their elders – using a long stick to simulate the shaking down of edible leaves for the goats and sheep to eat. From a young age, children are familiar with the ferīkh's daily activities and are encouraged to help out. They sit alongside their elders when discussions are held on decisions that need to be made. Livestock, livelihood, and social organization go hand in hand, but both are of course not limited to the domain of the ferīkh alone. As discussed in the previous chapter, those living in the ferīkh do not do so as isolated units, and livestock provide one of the reasons for socio-economic interactions with the world outside the physical ferīkh. Where in the past live-stock were the primary source of sustenance, nowadays livestock have become commodified, and other sources of sustenance are sought. With this transforma-tion, the value of cattle in a cultural sense and the relations that are informed by this value are shifting. This chapter explores a number of cases which reflect these shifting values, as part of a modernizing and globalizing process of eco-nomic change.

Economic relations are embedded within society and are part of a system with specific conditions. Connectors, in turn, are defined by their own intrinsic proper-ties as well as by the meaning they are given by others. This echoes the idea of the hybrid as an object having both properties which define it and vice versa – that

Photo 4.1: Farina and one of the ferikh elders playing with a cricket, October 2011. At our first meeting Farina was two or three years old and already so curious about the things around her, not at all shy like most of the other young children.

Photo 4.2: Farina bringing the goat's milk she has milked to Nour, May 2012. From a very early age children help with daily chores, games often mimicking aspects of tending to the animals.

is, they can both carry a 'flow' and stop it (Strathern 1996). Perceptions and attitudes toward cattle can thus help explain the actions of individuals and groups;
they reveal such things as kin relations and are simultaneously explained by these
same kin relations. Livestock are inherent to pastoral life and provide a focus in the
interactions with external forces. The idea of a 'cattle complex' is not necessarily
relevant to the Walad Djifir. Instead, cattle are predominantly seen in terms of economic rationality, as well as being a source of prestige. I am unsure if I would go as
far as calling it a 'mercenary attitude' concerning cattle (Braukämper 1996: 64), but
they do regularly sell a percentage of their herds.

Cattle, therefore, are the common denominator of this chapter. The attitudes
of people, in this case the Walad Djifir, toward cattle bring out different themes,
which are interwoven within various domains – the familial, economic, social,
and even political. These themes emerge in the way people explain the decisions
they or others have made vis-à-vis making a living. By opening with the short conversation between Adoum, myself, and Farina, I wished to start at the base, there
where cattle – indeed livestock in general – form a primary subject of attention and
knowledge for those Walad Djifir brought up and still living in the ferīkh setting.
Our conversation hints at the role of women and children, as well as the framing
of future expectations. When visiting the ferīkh it is clear that livestock largely
determine how and where camp is set up, and how long young men and boys will

be away to find suitable grazing. Intertwined with livestock are such subjects as transhumance, the need to be flexible, the role of kin relations in how herds are grouped and split up, and the devastating effects of droughts and diseases.

The young life of Farina is already linked to the more 'extraordinary' globalizing wilderness we spoke about in Chapter One. At the time of our conversation, her father was in charge of a large portion of the camels her uncle had bought as part of an inheritance – an inheritance which would be shared among the family members according to Islamic law; an inheritance which was based on the assets of another of Farina's uncles, who had been living and working as a merchant in CAR.

Kin and cattle: Adaptation and flexibility

Farina's father, Moussa, is a man whose body shows the signs of hard labour. His back plagues him and his hands are arthritic.[2] From 2011 to 2012, Moussa shared a ferīkh with his younger brother Hadj Saleh, taking care of their joint herds. He is married to two women, the first his direct cousin Khachana, and the second is Birémé, a woman from a different sub-group. Moussa no longer herds the cattle to and from their grazing lands, yet he does actively help out at the 'eidd (عيد). The daily watering of the cattle at the 'eidd is hard work, pulling up the 40-litre sacks of water from their shallow wells. In a way, cattle require the most work, along with goats and sheep. Cattle need to graze and drink water every day; and as the dry season continues, they need to be led further and further away for suitable pastures. This latter task is most often carried out by the younger boys, allowing the elderly men to rest during the evenings. In turn, the herder boys rest at the 'eidd during the day. Camels on the other hand can go for a week without water, and they tend to be herded by one person. Depending on how densely populated the area is, camel herders will either roam around the relative vicinity of the ferīkh or stay away for up to five or seven days at a time before returning to the watering holes in the vicinity of the ferīkh.

Early in 2014, Moussa and his young family (with his second wife, Birémé) had been put in charge of a large herd of camels. Together with newlywed son Bechir (from his first marriage), he now lived at some distance from the other camps. His son herded goats and sheep, staying away two to three nights at a time but

---

2 A study conducted amongst Fulani (593) and Arab cattle breeders (377) and Arab camel breeders (122) of Chari-Baguirmi and Kanem prefectures showed that joint pain and back pain represented 11.6% and 10.8% respectively of the health issues found amongst those over forty-six years of age (Schelling et al. 2005: 21). Sixteen out of eighteen people with arthritis in the knee were cattle breeders.

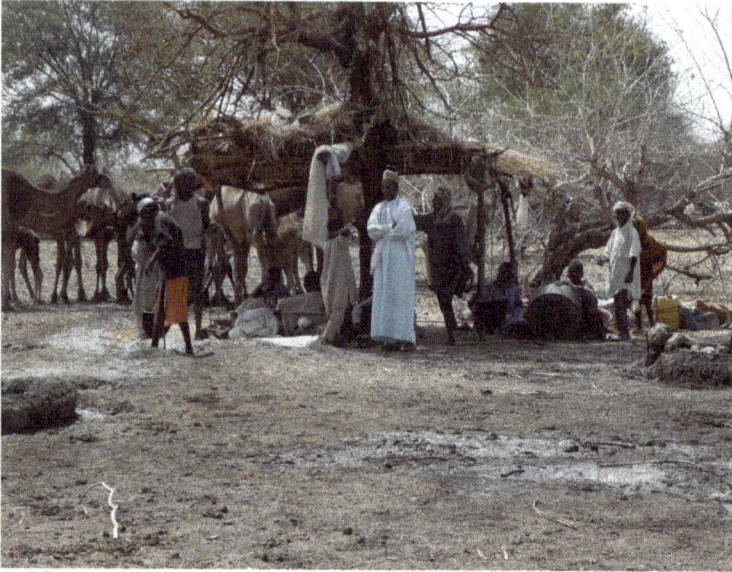

Photo 4.3: Hanging out at the *'eidd*, March 2012. The young men and boys often arrive at the 'eidd in the late morning or early afternoon, having spent the night en brousse with the cattle. They spend a few hours resting and eating in the shade before heading off again to let the cattle graze. How many hours they spend walking depends on how far away the best pasture is.

Photo 4.4: Men working the *'eidd*, March 2012.

Photo 4.5: Young herders eating their meal, March 2013.

Photo 4.6: A woman giving camels water at the *'eidd*, March 2014.

Photo 4.7: Women come to collect water at the *'eidd*, March 2014.

visiting the *'eidd* every day. This situation was the result of the inheritance coming from Moussa and Hadj Saleh's elder brother, Muhammad, who had passed away a few years earlier. This brother had built up a commercial business in the Central African Republic (CAR). With his passing, his inheritance was to be distributed among the family, with one-third going to his direct male relatives and two-thirds to his only daughter.[3] Hadj Saleh was in charge of selling off the capital found in CAR. This capital took the form of cattle, herded by a group of Mbororo,[4] land, and some shops. The cash this raised was transferred to Chad and re-invested in camels.

---

3 According to Islamic custom, there are three classes of inheritors: (A) *'fard'* which means individual, or a full member of the immediate family. (B) *'aceb'*: members of the MAIN group, which means the males. (C) *'ahl alrahim'*: the people of the womb, or who come from the mother's side (Brahim 1988: 65).

4 The Mbororo are a group of nomadic pastoralists (Fulani), commonly found in the CAR–Cameroon region but many of whom fled into eastern Cameroon following the outbreak(s) of violence after the 2013 coup and the increased presence of armed groups in general on their pasture lands. When we visited Nour in the village in CAR (December 2012), among the women and children gathered in her household were several Mbororo. See Amadou (2012, 2015); Amadou et al. (2016); de Vries (2018) for a more in-depth view of the Mbororo's situation, discussing such issues as political inclusion, social exclusion, gaining refugee status in a 'home' country, and the role of the mobile phone in a context of immobility.

Why Hadj Saleh decided to invest in camels instead of in cattle, a type of livestock which they were already herding, is most probably linked to their 'retail value' – the possible profit to be made between buying, rearing, and then selling the camel again. Already in 2012, the influx of camels into their camp had led to a necessary split. From one day to the other, Hadj Saleh had moved his wife and five young children to a terrain known as Al-Berekeh. This terrains was some three days' walk away, and located about 21 km to the south of Mongo but along the same *wādi* (see Map 3). The move had caused an upheaval among the family members left behind and also with the *ferīkh conseil*, whom he had not consulted. 'Al-Hadj is like the weather', Yaya commented. 'You never know what he will do.'

Khadidja, Hadj Saleh's wife, suffered greatly on the journey; and in the days after the move, every one of the children was brought to the hospital on different occasions. As the move was made in such haste, little was prepared in advance. In addition, day-time temperatures in this period (early April 2012) can easily rise over 40 C. Khadidja and the children suffered from dehydration symptoms (headache, fever) and were all at different times placed on a drip. The youngest of nine months had a bad infection of the ear and throat glands. The eldest son of twelve was treated for a skin disease on the head involving huge welts of puss. On such occasions, when a camp is displaced, time is not taken to prepare a warm meal; instead, left-overs are eaten, sometimes with milk.

Usually, when the camps are spaced fairly closely together around an *'eidd*, women have easier access to their social and supportive networks. When the camps disperse or, as in the case of Khadidja, her nuclear family moves to a more remote area, the resources and support/advice others could offer are lacking and health issues tend to be left unaddressed (for too long). It is a combination of access to health care, as well as the support of other women when it comes to household tasks, which can affect how easily a woman recovers (Hampshire 2002). At the new camp Khadidja only had one other woman, her half-sister, to look to for support, and she herself had young children. Under the circumstances Khadidja was lucky in that Hadj Saleh acknowledged the health issues and transported them to the hospital in Mongo. It is, in fact, his duty as a father and husband.

Hadj Saleh had moved his family's camp because the camels needed more space. As Khadidja's half-sister and her husband were already camel herders, he relocated to be with them. This placed a strain on those that now had to take care of Hadj Saleh's cattle herd, which he had left behind. When, a few weeks later, in mid-May 2012, Hadj Saleh left for CAR, Moussa was put in charge of the camels and sent to Al-Berekeh to replace him. This placed an added strain on those that now had to take care of both Hadj Saleh and Moussa's herds, as Moussa had always been an active worker. When Hadj Saleh returned from CAR in December 2013, he regrouped the camp to encompass both his and Moussa's cattle, along with the herd of camels. By

February 2014, we found Moussa and family living on the east side of the road to Ati and at a distance from the *'eidd* on the terrain known as Fadjé. Although they were not as isolated as Khadidja had been in Al-Berekeh, the women complained that they disliked being left 'home alone' while the men were away herding for nights on end. The nearest camp was that of Khadidja's half-sister and her husband, who also still had camels, and together with whom Moussa herded. But the distance was too great for a woman in need of help to be heard.

Photo 4.8: Khadidja and Khachana working together to crush grains, March 2012. Shortly after this photograph was taken, Hadj Saleh decided to move his family and their camels further south, to al-Berekeh. The whole tent was taken apart and all their belongings packed onto camels and cows. It took the better part of the morning, with many hands helping, and the women visibly emotional.

Shifts in strategies

The foregoing account serves to show how, on the one hand, decisions involving the social organization of the camps are strongly related to the composition of the herds and require a level of flexibility from those involved. Camels need more space and thus lead to a certain isolation. Cattle, in contrast, due to their watering and grazing needs, are best tended to by numerous hands. As herds are passed on from parents to children, the preferred marriage is between direct cousins, keeping the herd

Photo 4.9: Khadidja cooking at their new camp in al-Berekeh, March 2012. There were just two tents in this camp, hers and that of her sister, who was in charge of a large group of camels, together with her husband. It was fairly isolated and hard work. In March 2013, we met Khadidja again, this time reunited with the others. She seemed to have more energy again, despite her new pregnancy causing her a lot of heartburn and headaches – symptoms many of the pregnant women were dealing with.

within the family.[5] At times when the herds are too large to be taken care of by the number of men available in the ferīkh, the herd and their owners will split. In the previous chapter, we also discussed such processes of fission and fusion yet added a dimension – namely, the reasons *and* results in light of socio-political relations and the creation of opportunities through the destabilization of existing hierarchies.

On the other hand, kin relations and herd compositions are not the only factors informing nomadic flexibility. The semi-sedentary status of the Walad Djifir has its roots in the years after the cattle disease and droughts of the 1970s and 1980s. The remaining livestock were too weak to continue making the long journeys. In addition, the transhumance is costly, as little profit is made from selling the tired animals, profit with which material necessities are met. While, in one way, settling in camps along a *wādi* near Mongo for longer periods of time has provided a certain rest for the Walad Djifir, it has also brought more work. Women used to make and sell products at the market such as churned milk, butter, woven mats, and baskets.[6] The

---

5 It must be noted here that women from other nomadic groups do marry into the Walad Djifir.
6 See Brahim (1988) on economic activities of the Misseria Rouges.

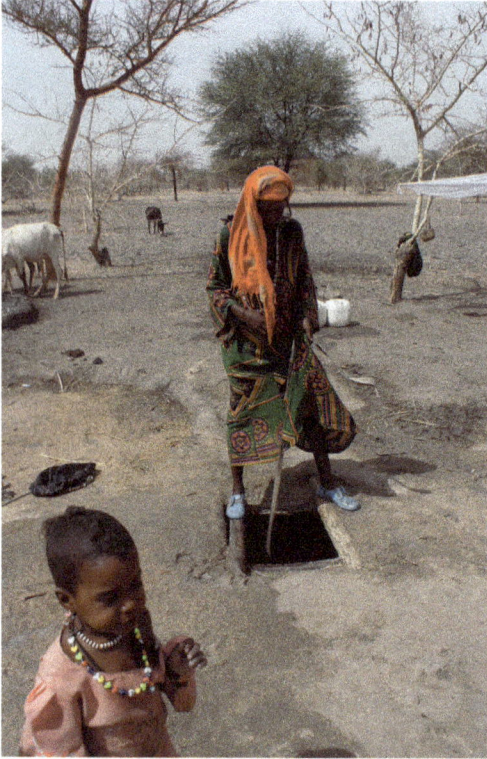

Photo 4.10: Birémê and Farina hauling water at the 'eidd, March 2013.

money earned went toward the daily nourishment of them and their children, with men joining in these meals. Nowadays, at least among this sub-group of the Walad Djifir, there are not many women left who earn some money of their own. During conversations held in March 2012 and 2014, both men and women claimed it was due to the changes in their transhumance patterns that they no longer had time to engage in these kinds of activities. Men in turn take care of the cattle and trade with other men.[7] Traditionally, men did not take part in trade; it was only the women.

---

7 Conversation with Hadj Saleh, fieldnotes, 2 March 2012. De Bruijn (1995) (Fulbe in Central Mali), Casciarri (1995) (Ahamda pastoralists Central Sudan), and Hodgson (1999) (on Kisongo Maasai) describe how the market economy and commodification of cattle contribute to this phenomenon of men taking over what used to be traditional methods of income for women. Shehu & Hassan (1995) (Fulbe of north-west Nigeria) discern a different trend, in which access to cash through participating in the dairy industry has given women leverage in terms of counterbalancing their control in the household, increased regular contact with current events through market trips, and stimulated the daily integration of rural areas with urban markets.

Photo 4.11: Camp of Moussa and Birémé in the distance, March 2014. You can just make out the tent of Moussa's son Bechir (to the left), who lived there with his new wife. Bechir was tending to the goats and sheep at this time, while Moussa and another family looked after the camels. The women felt isolated. It was a long walk to get water at the *'eidd*, and there was no one to hear you if you needed help.

Photo 4.12: Moussa making tea with his camp in the background in an old millet field, March 2014.

Women would, and some still do, trade in vegetables, milk, butter, peanuts, and so on with each other at the markets. At Banda's weekly Thursday market and Mongo's daily market, one can indeed see a divide with women selling vegetables, fruit, and other fresh produce such as eggs, baked items, dried tomatoes, and garlic at one side of the market and goods such as tea, sugar, rice, and clothes being sold primarily by men in a different section.

Now that much of the year they stay put, the women spend most of their time collecting wood and water, preparing food, and taking care of their youngest children. During transhumance fewer meals are cooked, saving time. The wood that is needed is collected en route, as is water. When sedentary, women spend several hours every two to three days gathering wood, having to go further and further the longer they stay in the area. Most women in charge of their own *barsh* (tent) make two trips to the 'eidd per day, using their donkey to fetch about 80 litres – which equals two full jerrycans – each time. Traditionally, these tents used to be made from woven mats (palm leaves) and wooden poles. Nowadays the wooden structures are still the same, but the covering itself has often been replaced by a heavier tarp. People explained that the tents used to be high enough for a person to stand up in. Due to the weight of the material now used, one has to partly bend over while inside.

Photo 4.13: Inside a *barsh*, March 2014. Shells decorating strips of leather woven together. They are often given to women upon marriage and proudly displayed inside their tents or draped over camels while on transhumance.

Photo 4.14: Close up of the inside of a woman's tent, March 2013.

Photo 4.15: Storage of a woman's belongings inside a tent, March 2013.

Throughout the various fieldwork periods I did observe younger women get together to weave mats or baskets, but there seems to be some truth in statements that the majority of the weavers are older women. One man even claimed that many younger women do not have the knowledge or techniques required. I am unsure that this is entirely true, as some women were still selling their woven products within

Photo 4.16: Shells decorating the inside of a tent, March 2014.

Photo 4.17: Outside of a tent, March 2014. Inside one can spot some of the pots and pans used to transport and store possessions.

the ferīkh itself. However, depending on how large the female household is, more hands can do the work, thus leaving more time for other activities. Women with little support are hardly seen 'lazing' around. The direct consequence of women no longer selling their hand-made products at markets is an increased dependence on their male family members. Women own their own livestock through marriage and inheritance. In practice, it is the men who go to market to sell animals – so even if a woman is the owner, she will need a family member to agree it can be sold and to go and sell it. Further study needs to be undertaken in relation to property and gender relations (de Bruijn 1994) among the Walad Djifir. It is unclear to me at

Photo 4.18: A group of women had come together in Birémé's tent to weave baskets and mats, March 2014.

this point to what extent a woman requires her husband's or brothers' agreement when wanting to sell her own animals. Instinctively, I would say this depends on the woman herself, her specific situation, and her relationship with male family members whom she can ask to go to market for her. Even if she feels the need to sell/trade an animal and a husband is unwilling, she could, strictly speaking, find a younger family member (brother, cousin, son) to do it anyway. Changes to women's economies, and the related influence on access to and breadth of social (support) relations require further study.

It is difficult to say in which way each generation has faced economic changes within their daily lives and adopted new patterns as a result. Historical depth is lacking here.[8] What we can discern, however, is that previous nomadic studies on Chadian Misseria Rouges encompass only a fairly limited understanding of what factors constitute or bring about change. Access to pastures and transhumance routes are one such factor; but changes in economic relations, on several levels, have introduced a different type of economy, to which Walad Djifir have been able to adapt and in which they now take part. Due to their relative wealth,[9]

---

[8] De Bruijn et al. (2004: 10) describe how migration by the sedentary population of the Guéra to N'Djaména increased in the last four decades, changing the orientation of the economy. The result has been low remittances and an increase in female-headed households.

[9] The extent of wealth does vary per family and individual, with elderly widowed women seeming to suffer most from a lack of familial support to provide them with basic needs. Through Casciarri's (1995: 110–111) work among the Ahamda pastoralists of central Sudan, we learn how entrepreneurial skills can be informed by socio-economic factors and status. For the Ahamda there is a cer-

we cannot speak of survival or coping strategies *per se*. Instead, this inherent, nomadic flexibility is very much an entrepreneurial skill, a skill which is partly influenced (and regulated) by the workings of a capitalistic market economy and at the same time very much dependent on the motivations and character of the individual.

One of Adoum's maternal uncles, for example, used to be a merchant selling cattle in CAR. When, under Habré's regime (1980s), the situation in Bangui became risky, he decided to quit the business and become a *marabout*. He settled himself and his family in Habilai, their wet-season terrain in Chad's Batha region, and began working the fields. When his extended family saw what he was doing, they were surprised – and even more so when, on their way back from a dry-season period in the Guéra, they found him and his family still alive and well, living on the yield. He had started cultivating sesame, flour (*mil*), and cucumber. When these did well, he added sorghum and *berbéré*. Slowly but surely other people also stayed to pursue agriculture. The maternal uncle has now passed away, but his children still live on the terrain and the previous season's yield had been a good one.[10] From the way Adoum spoke about his uncle, his move back to Habilai to take up agriculture was not the norm. Where this man may have made the decision to move, first to CAR for commerce and then back again only to take up agriculture, another uncle in a similar situation may have made very different choices. In the case of Hadj Saleh's deceased brother Muhammad, who made his move to CAR – and for Adoum for that matter – it seems a certain boredom or dissatisfaction with the status quo of ferīkh life instigated their pursuit of other means of making a living.

Is it possible to understand how these differences in decisions come about? In searching for answers we touch upon the dialectical relationship between flexibility and control (de Bruijn & van Dijk 1997), whereby we not only mean political and cultural control but also the individual's aspirations for their own lives. Lives full of creativity and adaptability in relation to other people, other societies and also in terms of changes in their life's course (Jackson 2013). Jackson argues that we need to be conscious of the spontaneous actions and minor experiences of individuals, which can illuminate such things as chance, luck, contingency, resigna-

---

tain honour linked to women not working outside the domestic domain, restricting the economic activities of women within a context of imposed monetarization and labour diversification. At the same time, there are women who do go out to work, though they often have a particular status in Ahamda society – for example, widows, divorcees, or elderly women from poor households. But what about those non-divorcees, non-widows, and younger women who may still have chosen to go out to work? How can we explain their capability (or need) and choice? Chapter Six delves into some of these dynamics in further detail.

10 Interview with Adoum, N'Djaména, 25 February 2014.

tion, and hope. Apart from the socio-economic and political connections shaping opportunities and people's decision-making processes, there is thus also a person's attitude toward life and ways of making a living – and particularly toward their role in life – which informs their flexibility and shapes their futures, if only to a certain extent. At times a person's will and efforts alone are not enough, and the power of societal, economic, or political constraints are too strong to overcome. The concept of 'duress', as introduced in the edited volume by de Bruijn & Both (2018), provides an analytical lens for understanding such situations of enduring and accumulating hardship, whereby crises have formed numerous layers and have become deeply engrained in a society. The process linked to duress is one in which a certain normalization is discerned, coupled with a form of deeply constrained agency.

In the following section, we highlight how the choices people make are influenced by the structures in which they find themselves and by opportunities, but also by certain 'ideas' – values, norms, aspirations – they may have concerning the taking up of wage labour to supplement the sustenance that dwindling herds can provide.

Cash and cattle: Money for nothing

Ecological circumstances, the development of infrastructure, and an increased security have led to the search for alternative incomes as well as a shift in attitude toward cattle. Walad Djifir work as merchants, with and without cattle, in the capital city and also in countries such as Cameroon, Nigeria, Sudan, Libya, and CAR. In the years of fieldwork the trend among young men was most definitely to go to Libya and work there guarding livestock (goats, camels) or as a compound guard. I even met a young man who had been working in a plastics factory in Tripoli.

How is it that the traditional forms of nomadic mobility and flexibility have come to encompass such non-specifically pastoral activities? A comparable dynamic exists among their neighbouring sedentary populations. Among the latter, shifts are seen in agricultural methods used and the focus of income and food generation altered or diversified as reactions to a long period of drought, famine, and conflict in the region (see van Dijk 2003, unpublished; Alio 2008). Dangbet 2020 describes the sedentarization processes of Batha Arabs, though does not include an analysis of labour migration and wage labour trends. Previous studies on nomadic or pastoral groups often point to a need to supplement incomes or means of living, as livestock are not providing enough – due to drought, disease, mismanagement of the herd, conflict, land reform, or other political dynamics (Azarya et al. 1999; Galvin 2009; Gertel & Le Heron 2016b). Catley & Aklilu (2013) argue that any analysis of people 'leaving' pastoralism must take the variations in their wealth (assets) into account. Some wealth groups are better suited to dealing with the mixed effects of droughts, conflict, and commercialization, while others take much longer to replenish their herds. In certain regions it is easier to find alternative work which is still related to pastoralism (e.g. herding the cattle of wealthier pastoralists); in other regions, the alternatives are very limited and people move out and away into urban centres (Boesen 2007; Boesen & Marfaing 2007; Hashimshony-Yaffe et al. 2023). Instead of seeing these dynamics as 'leaving' a pastoral way of life behind, this chapter shows how they are a reaction to the modernizing world, a continuation of processes of change (Burnham 1999; Fischer & Kohl 2010; Giuffrida 2010; Marfaing 2014; García et al. 2023).

Walad Djifir related how families often have a large number of children and smaller herds to pass down to them. This means that sons are motivated to look for complementary sources of income to grow their herds before and after marriage. Destitution alone is not always the main or only reason for diversification. In fact, the diversification of economic activities does not necessarily constitute a deviation from the norm or a reaction to crisis alone (following van Dijk 1995: 66). In addition, it does not seem like there is a negative connotation related to finding alternative means of providing for your family, as long as a person is willing to put in the work and effort. Among the Fulbe Wodaabe (Niger), it is precisely those who can afford to leave their herds behind that do so, having the right support (social networks) to compensate for their absence from livestock rearing (Köhler 2016a: 205). So what does this response to new economic possibilities look like in relation to the Walad Djifir? There is not much information available on the forms of migrant work and wage labour past generations may have carried out. The stories told suggest a certain continuity in economic diversification and in the fact that attitudes of some individuals have always been open to change.

From cattle as capital to cash in hand

Traditionally, the Walad Djifir did not engage much in commercial activities with their cattle. Cattle were primarily kept as a form of capital in the sense that they provided insurance for the herder and his family. Adoum compared sheep and goats to the money in one's wallet and cattle to that which one has in the bank – safely kept away. 'The sheep are like a bank account. The cows are the savings. You don't touch them, together with the camels – to ensure the children [are provided for].'[11]

---

11 Interview with Adoum, N'Djaména, 25 February 2014.

To keep the herd healthy and growing, cattle were sold and bought strategically. When cattle were beyond their prime, they would be brought to a local market and traded in for commodities. Cows were hardly ever sold while they could still produce calves, while bulls were popular on the market in their prime, fetching a good price. In a way, this strategy is still very much in place, but it has been slightly transformed and is often supplemented with other income-generating activities.

In the past, three or four head of cattle would be sold per year in order to buy grains, tea, sugar, oil, and other necessities. When the cash this had brought finished, other cattle would be sold. When the herds thinned drastically during the droughts and cattle disease of the 1970s and 1980s, the Walad Djifir had to look for alternative ways to earn cash. Some began to work the fields, and people today still use the grains this yields to supplement their diet. By turning to cultivation, they avoided having to sell animals in order to buy certain food commodities at the local market.

Those who had not lost as many cattle turned to a different strategy, investing the money earned from selling livestock into buying other livestock to rear and sell on later. It is the profits made from this livestock fattening that are then used to buy material goods. The trend toward exchanging livestock for cash (instead of livestock for livestock or goods) is a general one among many nomadic/pastoral communities.[12] While in the past one could exchange a particularly nice horse bought in Sudan for three or four cows, nowadays you can buy cattle and horses with money only. 'In the old days a horse from Sudan could fetch you three or four cows, even five if it was a particularly nice horse. Nowadays you can only buy animals with money, 200,000–250,000 CFA. Sometimes even 500,000 to a million CFA.'[13]

The increase in access to cash has come with a few lifestyle changes, in line with advancements in technology (e.g. owning a mobile phone, radio, or memory discs with music or videos on them), clothing (e.g. plastic-based sandals and shoes as opposed to the longer-lasting kind made from leather, factory-made clothes instead of the locally sewn traditional clothing), and transport (e.g. owning a motorbike). Where in the past one may have invested in a horse to travel with from camp to camp or market, some men now opt to buy a motorbike.[14] However, in all the

---

12 See de Bruijn (1995); Casciarri (1995); van Dijk (1995); Shehu & Hassan (1995); Braukämper (1996); Hodgson (1999); Unusa (2012); Holtzman (2009); Elliot (2010); Gertel & Le Heron (2016b); Mahmoud (2013); Manoli et al. (2014); Köhler (2016a).

13 Fieldnotes, Al-Berekeh, 19 April 2012.

14 Djohy et al. (2017: 127) describe the presence of Chinese motorcycles among Fulani pastoralists in northern Benin, explaining how communication costs are managed by using these motorcycles to charge mobile phone batteries.

months we spent in and around the ferīkh, I would argue that only a handful of men purchased a motorbike: Yaya the *khalifa*, who needs to be at the weekly cattle markets to collect taxes on behalf of his *tribu*; a young man working as a merchant trading wares in the region; a friend of Adoum's nephew; and an ex-soldier who had returned to live in the village of Tchoufiou.

On one particular occasion, while visiting the Mongo livestock market in March 2014, we came across one of his nephews and some of this nephew's friends. One friend proudly displayed the side-mirrors he had bought for his motorbike, which he had not come to market with. On seeing the side-mirrors, Adoum jokingly asked him why he had invested in such a thing, implying that such a commodity was more relevant to have in a town or city with actual traffic – what did he expect to see in them when riding his motorbike *en brousse*?[15] The young man replied that he had bought them because they were pretty. The nephew Moustapha, in turn, had sold his horse at the market and bought a baby camel, keeping a profit of 5000 CFA. He did not say what he meant to do with the money.

In a conversation one afternoon with Nour, her aunt Arafa, and Khadidja's mother, we talked about the changes to their way of life throughout the years. Hadji and Khadidja's mother claimed that everything was better in the past. In the past, there was no sugar or pretty clothes to buy. By which she meant: to waste your money on. Later on, when we talked about what we would do if we had a lot of money to spend, they both immediately said: 'Buy sugar, tea and nice clothes!'[16] This idea of 'wasting' money on such luxuries as tea, sugar, and clothing is also reflected in the stories of those sending money back to family in the ferīkh. The variety of goods to be bought are more easily accessed with cash in hand, cash which is often still gained through the selling of smaller livestock. Do Walad Djifir then perceive a difference between the various ways to earn cash?

---

15 Fieldnotes, Mongo, 5 March 2014.

16 Conversation on a visit to Arafa at Khadidja's mother's tent, where the elderly Hadji had been forced to prolong her own visit, as she had broken her lower arm and could not comfortably be transported back to her own tent. Fieldnotes, 2 May 2012. Hadji, Nour, and I shared a tent in the months I was with them in 2012.

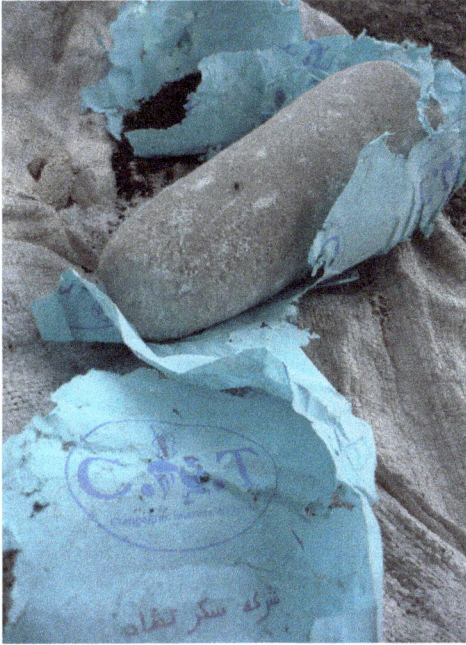

Photo 4.19: The much-loved sugar and tea, March 2012. These blocks of sugar are made by a Chadian company and cost CFA 2250 a piece at a market in town.

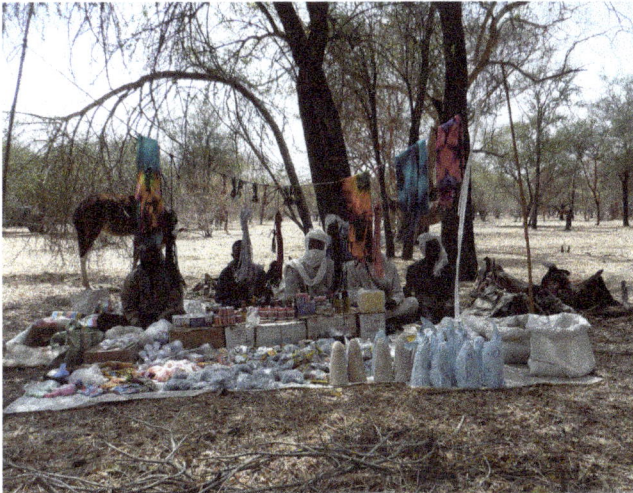

Photo 4.20: *Souq* at a ferīkh gathering, March 2014. One of the young men running the *souq* had recently come back from Libya, having worked in a plastics factory in Tripoli.

Photo 4.21: Soap, toothbrush twigs, Omo sachets, flashlights, and sweets at a ferīkh *souq*, March 2014.

Photo 4.22: Bags of red, green, and black tea sold at a ferīkh *souq*, March 2014. Each town in the region has a different market day. Mongo's large market (with livestock) is held on Wednesdays. The village of Banda holds theirs on a Thursday. Whenever we frequented one of the market days we almost always met Walad Djifir we knew or that knew (had heard of) us.

Attitudes toward wage labour and cattle herding

Rearing cattle is hard work. Every member of the family participates in at least one activity of sustenance or another. Men and boys take care of the livestock, while the women's domain is that of the household. Every animal requires a different form of care, the one more intensive than the other. The hours of walking that the herders do to bring the livestock to suitable grazing land is tiring at best. The young men or boys that sleep with the cattle, camels, and goats or sheep bring only a certain amount of food with them, and there are usually no warm blankets for those cold nights. One man explained to me that, compared with the hard physical labour involved in tending to the animals, working as a merchant was like a rest or holiday. *'Quand tu fais le commerce, c'est le repos.'*[17] In this section I would like to explore what lies behind this statement, returning to the opening of the chapter: how ingrained nomadic livelihood is.

Muhammad Saaleh was the man who referred to doing commerce as a period of rest. When we met, he was temporarily working in N'Djaména.[18] He had initially started working in the cattle trade to supplement his family's income but left it when he could not make enough profit. In the 1980s they had lost a lot of their herds during the periods of drought and cattle disease. The first time he had travelled to N'Djaména was in 2001 or 2002. Before this he had been working for a cattle merchant, accompanying cattle from the market in Mongo. When prices at the N'Djaména market were not high enough, they would travel on to Nigeria. As of 2011 he has been selling blocks of ice along the roadside in N'Djaména. He usually does this in the dry season, spending four to six months in the capital, depending on the income he is able to earn. With the coming of the rainy season, he returns to help work the fields. While he is away, his cattle are herded by his father and his younger brother (same father, different mother), and the goats and sheep are herded by his young children. The money he earns in N'Djaména allows Moustapha Saaleh to buy clothes and a few things to eat for the children, a new *djallabeya* for his father, and such things as sugar, tea, and flour. In Fadjé there was not much work for him to do during the dry season, as his brother and father were helping out with the cattle and the children were taking care of the smaller livestock. This motivated him to look for a way to earn some extra cash. Like many Walad Djifir, he prefers not to sell the animals unless it is absolutely necessary. As he explains himself, Mongo is not so populated, and there is little work to be found. The first time he had visited N'Djaména as a cattle merchant, he had noticed how the selling of ice blocks was a

---

17 'When you do commerce, it's like taking a break.'
18 Interview with Moustapha Saaleh Yakhoub, N'Djaména, 23 May 2012.

lucrative business. Only last week he had sent 20,000 CFA to his father and another 20,000 CFA to his wife and children. He prefers to stay just until the rainy season starts, as he is afraid that if he returns to the ferīkh earlier the money he has earned will not last as long, the temptation to buy cows or sugar being too great.

Before leaving for N'Djaména, he had discussed it with his father (Yakhoub of Chapter Two) and received his permission, promising him he would be away only for a few months and would return straight afterward – not leaving for Libya as so many others were doing. His wife and brother also agreed. While working in N'Djaména, Moustapha Saaleh stays at the house one of his family members has built,[19] along with several others temporarily working in the city. He would never consider moving his family to the city – how can they ever sell their animals? He considers going to Libya one day, but it is hard as his children are still very young; and as his mother has already passed away, there is no one to help his wife take care of their children and his elderly father. In reality, however, he dreams of alternatives to the temporary work he finds in N'Djaména. In the future, he hopes to either travel to Libya or find work which is not seasonal. If he had had more cattle, he would have sold them all and bought a piece of land in Mongo on which he would have built a shop. If there was any money left, say three to four million CFA, he would bring his wife, young children, and brother to live with him.

As Moustapha Saaleh puts it, when one can earn money without selling one's own animals, it is money you have earned for free – '*quand tu trouves les choses gratuit*',[20] you should do it. Working with your hands does not cost anything; you do not lose anything physical.[21] Yet when you sell an animal, you lose it; and finding another one of similar value to replace it is difficult. His explanation illustrates the importance that cattle still have as a form of capital and insurance. At the same time, it also says something about the motivations behind searching for other forms of cash. Work is seen as something anyone can do at any time. Cattle, on the other hand, cannot be sold at any moment if one wants to preserve the herd. When compared to selling one's own cattle for cash, wage labour is an opportunity to create

---

19 This is the house of Abbakr Hissein, the son of the Walad Djifir's former *chef de khashim beyt* and the one who grew up with the *chef de canton* (see previous chapter). Abbakr was sent to veterinary school in Ukraine and has had several ministerial posts under the past two regimes. He is now relieved of his post in the *conseiller de president*. There is a seasonal aspect to the number of visitors lodged in the compound, with the busiest time being during the dry season.

20 'When you find the things for free [. . .].'

21 Interestingly, people working in Chad's oil sector make a link between 'easy' money and the devil. Yorbana (2017: 77) writes: 'Some oilmen consider oil to bring about easy money and consumer goods, with the devil acting as a guiding force. So if you buy a piece of paradise with oil money, you will discover that it is just a mirage.' I did not encounter similar manners of speaking among the Walad Djifir about money earned by not working with cattle.

cash from nothing. This attitude toward wage labour as directly informed by the attitude toward the value of cattle reveals a perception of money and wealth. There does not seem to be a negative connotation related to employing other means to supplement or make an income. People take pity on the poorer members of the community, often the widows and elderly, and respect those that put in the effort to change their circumstances. Some people, like Adoum, leave nomadic life behind completely, though never really losing touch.

Moving away but not 'out', and the investment in land

Upon seeing sixty of their cattle succumb in one season during one of the bovine epidemics in the 1980s (1984–1985), Adoum had decided that it was time for nomads to start thinking about other livelihoods. He did not see a future in 'walking behind one's animals'. After having tried his hand as a rebel at first, he soon realized that that was not the life for him. He returned from his rebel-hood only for a few months before leaving his parents once again, this time for good. Suffice to say that he left without cattle, only to take up a position as a cattle herder for a merchant in N'Djaména. Leaving this position after a few months, he travelled on to Cameroon, where he was employed by a group of Fulani (Mbororo). Although he bought live-stock with the money he earned in the years with the Fulani, upon returning to Chad he did not return to the ferīkh with his cattle. Instead, he stayed on in N'Djaména with his paternal cousin, Abbakr Hissein, much like Moustapha Saaleh had done many years later. Abbakr's father had been *chef de khashim beyt* of the Walad Djifir before Adoum's father in the time of the French (see previous chapter). In N'Djaména Adoum pursued a primary education, which he was forced to stop when the city was attacked heavily in Déby's bid for power in 1990. As a restless man and one eager to provide for himself, he started taking driving lessons. During his later career as a driver for various organizations, and especially for the Ministry of Pastoralism, he was able to make enough money to invest it. While he did invest some of his savings in cattle, now reared by his eldest brother in Fané, most of his money was invested in the buying of land in N'Djaména. At the time, he owned four plots of land and had built and was living on one of them. In 2017 this changed upon his marrying a second wife and selling one plot of land to help pay for the marriage. His first wife was entitled to half of the proceeds from selling the land.

The investment in land is not yet a very common trend among the Walad Djifir, yet it does take place. The preference is still for investment in livestock – as Hadj Saleh's case shows – but one or two family members do now own land in and around Mongo. Hadj Saleh's deceased brother Moustapha was one of the first to buy land in Mongo, but also in Moundou in Southern Chad, and of course in CAR.

The land in Moundou lies vacant, and on the plot in Mongo five rooms have been built. So how can we understand these developments, framed by the general trends of cattle commodification, the increased presence and use of cash, and developing infrastructures? Is Adoum changing or modernizing his nomadic flexibility? Is it part of a sedentarization process, economic diversification strategies, or is it more a matter of a 'walk of life' specific to each individual?

I would argue that these developments reinforce existing values, even if the means to do so have changed. Adoum will never not value the ownership of livestock. It is too ingrained in him and is a way to mediate kin and other relationships. Adoum's cattle help provide the brother tending them with milk and some income, even if Adoum thinks they could be tended more efficiently – claiming his brother does not sell and buy cattle at the right times, often leaving them to become too old to sell well at market. When I asked him why he then did not place the cattle with another brother better at managing herds, Adoum replied that as it was his eldest brother, he could not just take them away. It would be a sign of disrespect. Instead, in the event of his acquiring any new cattle, his tactic would be to place these with someone else (brother or cousin). Adoum also sees the value in investing in other forms of capital – in his case land and housing. He believes that cattle are too risky as insurance. Land holds its value in the sense that it is something his children can inherit and live on. Money earned from herding or selling the cattle he would leave behind for his children would be fleeting and not nearly enough to sustain all of them.[22]

This mediating and maintaining of kin relationships is also very important for those young men carrying out wage labour elsewhere. They depend on the social networks within the ferīkh for help in tending any animals left behind, and for ensuring that female relatives (wives, mothers) are provided for when cash cannot immediately be sent home. At the same time, part of the motivation to travel away for work is to earn enough to marry, to have some 'loose change' for spending without having to sell livestock, or to buy more livestock (increase their wealth) in order to secure the future for themselves and their families.

Apart from keeping cattle as capital and engaging in wage labour, Walad Djifir also take part in the national and regional cattle trade. In the next section, I examine other ways in which developments in economic diversification reveal specific attitudes to the ways of making a living and building/holding on to wealth. The conti-

---

22 This is a trend which Roitman (2005) too observes amongst sedentary Cameroonians when discussing tax as price, though for perhaps different reasons (pp. 67–68). She links it to the legacy of *la politique des prix* which constitutes an attempt to regulate prices by the French and the introduction of the French franc (later CFA), which continues to be associated with instability. Money is seen as something that can disappear, while cloth and pots are items which will remain and can be returned if need be.

nuities and changes involved in the taking up of commercial activities outside of the ferīkh setting are explored in relation to insecurity or crises faced – and ultimately to decisions made.

Cattle and commerce: Politics and economic changes

While it is certainly true that the search for alternative incomes is not merely destitution driven, at times it has been. The ecological insecurity which was at its most extreme in the early 1970s and 1980s continues until today and has been one of the major incentives for complementing a traditional 'walk of life'. At the same time, a changing politico-economic situation has provided a context in which such incentives could take place and were formed. During the period in which Hissein Habré was president (1982–1990), the Walad Djifir refer to there being a lot of insecurity in the country. Travel and thus also commerce were almost impossible. Rebel groups looted and killed, while military troops robbed travellers of their possessions. Following Habré's persecution of Arabs, many fled the area, settling in CAR or further afield.[23] With the relative peace that Déby's presidency brought from the early 1990s onwards, commerce and travel picked up.[24] Improvements to roads and the more recent arrival of Toyota pickup trucks around the year 2000 have contributed to facilitating the movement of people and goods. As one informant said so aptly: '*C'est grace a Dieu que les petites Toyota sont venues.*'[25] Infrastructure – whether in terms of physical local markets or communication technologies for the sending of information or money – has historically gone, and continues to go, hand in hand with socio-political and economic contexts. Walad Djifir, like many other pastoral-nomadic communities, not only found their way into the national and regional export of cattle but also started importing Chadian cattle when conditions to do so became right.

---

23 It is not yet clear (to me) when and where the Arabs of the Guéra and Batha were threatened, but colleague Souleymane (Historian, PhD) and I encountered several of their stories while in Bangui. See Kilembe (2015) on general movements of Chadians to CAR; Hicks (2018) on the prosecution of Habré and crimes committed.

24 As Azevedo notes (2004: 112–113), Déby's presidency was able to build on that which Habré had left behind, a government which was able to function again. In the early 1990s, however, he did not restrain himself from persecuting those loyal to Habré, sending 3000 troops to attack towns around Lake Chad (December 1991), and admitting to the massacre of southerners in April 1994 by government troops. The rebels that came through Mongo on their way to N'Djaména from the east in 2006–2007 do not seem to have disturbed the Walad Djifir. Perhaps their herds and camps were too far from the main roads to be of much use to the rebel forces.

25 'It is with thanks to God that the little Toyotas [pickup trucks] have arrived.'

The Chadian cattle trade

The cattle trade has once again become one of Chad's main domains of export. Unfortunately for the state, it does not bring in an equivalent in revenue. For several years (since 2003), oil was the main source of revenue, but the decline in world-wide oil prices – and a general mismanagement of the oil production process and revenue – has left the state's treasury with a large deficit.[26] On the comparison between the oil and livestock economies, Martin Wiese (2011: 59) writes:

> The direct contribution of the oil production accounted for 33.4 per cent of the GDP in 2004 (1.16 out of 3.47 billion Euro). It provided 163 million Euro in national revenues, covering 32.1 per cent of the national budget in 2004 (106 out of 331 million Euro). However, only 3,600 Chadian citizens were directly employed on the oil fields with six people placed in positions of higher responsibility. Indeed, contrary to the growing GDP, which includes values repatriated by foreign petrol companies, the gross national product, GNP, has actually decreased by 2 per cent with the start of petrol exploitation in 2003. Consequently, the direct benefits of the oil-economy are rather imperceptible for most of the Chadian population which depends essentially on the redistribution of petrol-dollars via government spending. Such redistribution mechanisms are actually weak, fragile and biased towards the elites and the urban centre of N'Djaména. The preset political-institutional crisis of the country is particularly unfavourable to any effective redistribution of the national oil revenues into social welfare and poverty reduction. In contrast to the oil-economy, agriculture and livestock breeding constitute the livelihood for 80 per cent of the population, accounting for 24 per cent of GDP in 2004. Livestock breeding alone produces 38 per cent of the agricultural GDP (i.e. 320 million Euro) and supports the subsistence of 40 per cent of the active rural population in Chad.

Many Walad Djifir take part in the cattle trade in some way or other. The animals they rear and bring to market are bought up by merchants, who sell them nationally or herd them to the markets of Nigeria. Several men work for these merchants, transporting the cattle on foot to the market in N'Djaména or further afield. In some cases, herders are hired to rear cattle for large cattle merchants. While I did not encounter this practice among the Walad Djifir themselves, it most probably does exist. In a conversation with Hadj Allaramadji, a member of the Guéra's sedentary population, in Mongo in March 2014, he explained how the price of cattle is discussed in both Nigeria and Chad's local markets. An open line of communication exists nowadays due to the mobile phone, and merchants hearing that the price for cattle has gone up in Nigeria will be quick to buy up livestock in Mongo. He related how the cattle market in Mongo was established in 1983 at a time when Mongo itself was in ruins. The proposal was made by the population in the hope that it

---

26 For ethnographic studies on oil in Chad, see Behrends (2011); Reyna (2011); Hoinathy (2013); Behrends & Hoinathy (2014); Yorbana (2017).

would help rebuild the economy.[27] It was communicated by drum (*tam tam*) to the surrounding villages that, from then on, a livestock market would be held every Wednesday. With its establishment, the government and *khalifa*'s were able to profit from the taxes levied when an animal was sold, and merchants were able to sell other goods alongside. When asked how the rebels roaming the region affected the market, Hadj Allaramadji said they were primarily after money and not cattle themselves and therefore robbed merchants. Nowadays, the mobile phone allows merchants to warn each other of *coupeurs de route* being active in certain locations. Robbers do not steal as many as before, he said; they are local bandits who will take one, two, or three head of cattle instead of the hundreds looted in the past. Sometimes, these stolen cattle will be recovered, unless they have been slaughtered for consumption.

Currently, the slaughterhouse at N'Djaména's Farcha (L'Abbatoire Frigorifique de Farcha), created in 1958, remains the only one in the country, despite plans for building others which will qualify to export meat to the international market (Mravili et al. 2013). The main means of exporting livestock is on foot, with Nigeria the largest market for Chadian cattle. In the past, Sarh used to house a large slaughterhouse, known as Société Industrielle de Viande du Tchad (SIVIT), which distributed meat to Congo, Gabon, Zaire, and CAR. It was established by Tombalbaye in the mid-1960s as part of his plan to make his own southern region Chad's economic centre. It was shut down after only four years, having made a substantial loss, but its activities were taken up again in 1974 by Climatat.[28] Around the events of 1979, during which Habré's Forces Armées du Nord (FAN) and Goukouni's Forces Armées Populaires (FAP) battled for N'Djaména against government forces which in turn were joined by part of Kamougoue's Forces Armées Tchadiennes (FAT), the slaughterhouse in Sarh was closed. Following the battle, Goukouni was named head of a coalition government and the country became divided into four almost autonomous regions, signalling the demise of the Chadian state (Azevedo 2004).

---

27 According to the Tchad edition of *Atlas de l'Afrique*, many cattle markets were created after the dry period of the 1970s and 1980s, when several nomadic groups moved further south and certain regions became more populated. Before that time only the city of Sarh had a regular cattle market (Ben Yahmed 2006: 46–47).

28 Koussou (2013) explains how the slaughterhouse in Sarh was opened and shut several times. He writes [translated from French]: 'In 1968, SIVIT (the Industrial Meat Company of Chad) was founded in Sarh in the south of the country. The company had an integrated beef-processing complex to supply all of Central Africa. Due to the narrowness of the local market, these facilities were almost entirely devoted to exports. The bankruptcy of this public company after four years of operation put an end to these exports. The installations were taken over in 1998 by a private company with French and Chadian capital: Africa Viande. Yet activities ceased as early as 2001' (p. 5).

In general, the export of cattle remains an expensive and risky business. Taxes make up 25 per cent of the final commercial value (Wiese 2011: 63), and there are more informal payments to be made along the way.[29] The fluctuating value of the Nigerian naira is another source of risk. A trend which has continued into the present day is the investing of profits made from cattle export into Nigerian consumer goods, which are then transported back into Chad and sold locally. Hadj Allaramadji recounted how, in the past, merchants would travel to and fro with large sums of money hidden on their person. When I asked where and how exactly, he grinned and said: 'That is a secret.' Nowadays, merchants are able to transport or wire money to Maiduguri – 'You leave your money there, and it is either transferred on to Nigeria or back to Chad.'

Walad Djifir and CAR

While several Walad Djifir involve themselves in aspects of the Chadian cattle trade, others have commercial ties to CAR. This next section introduces the impact of political insecurity and crisis as a context of economic change, through a focus on decisions surrounding cattle and commerce.

Hadj Tchoudja, one of Hadj Saleh's maternal uncles (see Family Tree in Figure 3), began doing business in CAR as early as the 1960s, bringing Chadian cattle into the country and selling them at local markets. According to a researcher at Farcha's veterinary department, CAR did not have its own herds of cattle before 1973, partly explaining the relative success Hadj Tchoudja had, which allowed him to later diversify into other commercial activities (more in Chapter Six).[30] CAR used to mostly be a transfer zone for Fulani herders (Archambaud et al. 2020). When drought hit Chad in the early 1970s, the cattle had to move further south than normal. Another drought in 1983–1984 and a period of cattle disease further incentivized herders to travel into CAR. To help the herds survive, strategies were developed in order to make space for the cattle by moving sedentary villages. CAR agreed to this policy as cattle provided an interesting source of economy for the country – they had no cattle of their own.

By 1960 and 1970, one could find Sudanese, Nigerians, and Lebanese carrying out commerce, manufacturing products, textiles, and dealing in meat in CAR. For a long time, the largest butcher in Bangui was a Nigerian. Then, during the turmoil of

---

29 For more details on the Chadian cattle trade and the official and non-official processes, people, networks, routes, and amounts involved, see Abderamane & Halley des Fontaines (2011); Koussou & Aubague (2011); Wiese (2011); and Koussou (2013).
30 Interview with a researcher at Farscha, N'Djaména, 20 February 2014.

1979 – which included clashes between students and government troops in Bangui, the arrest and killing of around one hundred civilians by Bokassa's government troops, the consequent imposing of military and economic sanctions by the French, and the eventual deposing of Emperor Bokassa I – many foreigners lost everything and left.[31] The vacuum they left was, to a large extent, filled by Chadians escaping Chad's civil war. Already at the time of French Equatorial Africa (AEF), most traders found in Bangui, Bambari, and other large cities were of Chadian origin. CAR itself had very few native long-distance traders (Kilembe 2015; Marchal 2015: 170). For several years afterward and throughout many more mutinies, changes of state heads, French backing, and Libyan and Chadian support, Chadians in CAR were generally able to prosper.

At the same time, Chad's political arm could still be felt. In the Bangui of the early 1980s, Hadj Tchoudja was assassinated, supposedly under Habré's orders. During Habré's reign, many Chadians fled to CAR and became small traders or shopkeepers. Among them were not only southerners, whose ethnic homeland often crossed the national Chad–CAR border, but also Arabs. Marchal (2015: 173) describes these Arabs as being primarily from the Salamat region and belonging to a faction opposed to Habré. It is not unlikely that other Arabic groups may also have joined this opposition group. Tchoudja belonged to the Sulmani group and was a brother of Hadj Saleh's mother. As a popular businessman, Hadj Tchoudja would receive many Chadian visitors at his home. Habré, in his mission to suppress any form of dissent, targeted Arabs within Chad but also in the wider region. Tchoudja's daughter, who was five at the time of his death, claims he did not have any political motivations and that it was merely his harbouring of those who did which sealed his fate. He was killed in broad daylight while crossing one of Bangui's smaller canal bridges in his car.

In the 1990s a new wave of livestock breeders from Chad arrived in CAR (Archambaud et al. 2020). These herders were well-armed and soon known as being violent toward local populations.[32] In Bangui's market district of PK 5, they disrupted the prior peaceful status quo by inserting themselves into the cattle business and small-scale trade. Those entering the cattle sector clashed with the long-standing Central African Association of Cattle Merchants (ACCB), which was composed of mostly Fulani and others of Chadian origin. This was the birth of a new association, the Association of Cattle Merchants of Central Africa (ACOBECA) (Kilembe 2015: 90–91). The enmity toward Muslims in general increased from the mid-1990s

---

31 For a more elaborate and deeper understanding, see Carayannis & Lombard (2015); Marchal (2015); Smith (2015); Lombard (2016).
32 See Kilembe (2015); Marchal (2015) on these dynamics. Chapter Six elaborates on how it was not only Chadian livestock breeders that caused tensions to rise; there were other factors which contributed to the escalation.

onward, especially when Bozizé came to power in March 2003 with the support of young Muslim merchants from the PK 5 district. These victorious 'liberators' were responsible for much violence and plundering among civilians (primarily Christian) (ibid.: 96). With the upheaval following the overthrow of Bozizé in March 2013, and the role of the Séléka (many of Chadian origin), tensions again rose even further. The political situation has impacted inter-community relations, as well as changing the economic context in which the cattle trade and other commercial actives in CAR are carried out. Physical spaces, such as the PK 5 district, have been altered and 'trust' has become an issue.

Following the coup, cattle herders have fled back into Chad and market prices have gone up.[33] One informant, referring to livestock, claimed that what used to cost 300,000 CFA now costs 900,000 CFA. The Chadian merchant Hadj Allaramadji corroborated this by saying that in March 2014 a bull would sell for 300,000–350,000 CFA and a cow for 160,000–175,000 CFA at Mongo's market, compared with one million (bull) and 500,000 CFA (cow) in Bangui. Even with the costs incurred on the way from Chad's local markets to the markets in Bangui, the normal price would not have been doubled. By 2014 it had become difficult to find meat at the markets in Bangui. According to a researcher at Farsha, herders will eventually return to CAR when things have calmed down.[34] This might, however, create new conflicts around space and resources between newcomers and those who had already been there but temporarily fled.

Insecurity and decisions

One such Walad Djifir family that fled CAR after the coup was that of Nour, Hadj Saleh's cousin. Nour's father Moustapha, the deceased elder brother of Hadj Saleh and Moussa, had joined Hadj Tchoudja in Bangui many years prior. Nour was born and raised in Bangui, marrying and divorcing Tchoudja's son. She later remarried Youssouf, a first cousin and the son of Moussa and Khachana. Together they lived in a village about a day's drive from Bangui.

In the initial few months after the March 2013 coup, Nour and her family had not felt threatened in their village in south-west CAR. By December of the same year, the situation had drastically changed and the Chadian families living in the area

33 Adamou Amadou (2012, 2015) describes the dynamics surrounding Mbororo previously based in CAR, fleeing and 'returning' to Cameroon. See also de Vries (2018) and Chapter 7 in Schouten (2022). Archambaud et al. (2020) describe the future of pastoral-nomads in the Batangafo region of CAR after the 2013 violence.
34 Interviewd at Farsha, N'Djaména, 20 February 2014.

were forced to flee. Youssouf, who had taken over Nour's father's business after his death, refused to leave behind the cattle they still had with the Mbororo. While his wife and two young children made their way across the border and into the Cameroonian refugee camp at Kentzouh, he decided to safeguard their cattle.

The evening before the village they had travelled to was attacked, Youssouf and several others who had come to the same decision made their way south toward the border with Congo. In the following weeks, they made their way through the thick bush, only occasionally hearing evidence of other people's presence. They carried only non-automatic weapons. From the southern border, they turned west toward Cameroon in order to change direction again and follow the border north into Chad. Youssouf called his uncle (Adoum) in N'Djaména from southern Chad on Sunday, 23 March 2014. Three days later, he made his way to the capital with the money that was transferred and was reunited with Nour and their children, who had by that time already been transported to N'Djaména by the Chadian government. Youssouf and his companion were exhausted when we collected them from the bus station in N'Djaména.[35] Relief was visible in both their faces. As the evening passed, they recounted how they had safely made it to the north of CAR. On approaching the Chadian border, they had been attacked and robbed of all their cattle. The journey had been in vain. Adoum criticized Youssouf for having decided to protect his cattle over protecting his wife and children. His family in the ferīkh, however, understood. The fact that the cattle Youssouf had tried to protect were only a part of what was left of his wife's father's inheritance did not factor into his thinking. Hadj Saleh had after all been selling off capital and re-investing it in the form of camels as a way of dividing up the inheritance among family in the ferīkh.

The cases of those living in CAR and that of Adoum are somewhat special when compared with the choices other Walad Djifir have made. Not everyone has a successful uncle to join or such a stubborn and inventive nature as to decide to make oneself a different life. Between 2011 and 2017 the most common form of economic activity outside of the ferīkh was that of agriculture, small commerce, and temporary wage labour – either in Chad itself or in Libya. Among some nomadic communities, such as the Wodaabe of Niger (Köhler 2016a: 206–207) and Dazagada of Chad (Wiese 2011: 69), it is a source of shame to admit that one has to look for alternative means of sustenance. For the Walad Djifir this does not seem to be the case, as so many of them were affected in the 1970s and 1980s, forcing a majority to complement their otherwise primarily pastoral lifestyle. This trend has continued into the

---

35 Adoum, his eldest son Abbakr, and I drove to the Express Sud Voyage bus station in Dembé to pick them up around four o'clock in the afternoon on 26 March 2014.

present and is accentuated by the improvements made in infrastructure (transport, communication), while still also influenced by national and regional insecurities and subsequent economic changes.

The walk of life and modernizing economies

Just as the paths animals and humans make around wells reveal patterns and traces of movement, making visible 'the social relations and contacts of people coming together, meeting and again separating, and defining a particular place by their inter- action' (Köhler 2016a: 162), cattle as a connector embody the economic, social, and at times political relations within Walad Djifir society (Granovetter 1985; van Dijk 1994). The various cases and descriptions above reveal patterns and traces which link back to the ferīkh setting and a 'nomadic way' of doing things. In a way, such an analysis echoes the words of Khazanov: 'Pastoralism is not only a way of *making a living*; it is also a *way of living*' (1994: xxxiii). So what changes and continuities exist in the way Walad Djifir adhere to a 'nomadic way' of life, in light of economic devel- opments, political and ecological insecurity, and regional mobility?

The patterns revealed point to flexibility, wealth, and family as cornerstones (layers) of 'the Walad Djifir way' (connectivity). If one follows the money, many find a way to invest it 'back' into the ferīkh setting – cattle or land within Chad itself – making use of social ties or networks in doing so. Where in the past Hadj Tchoudja and Nour's father's assets had primarily been in CAR, the explosive situ- ation, especially vis-à-vis Chadians, has forced them to continue their affairs else- where. In Nour's case, most of her father's assets had already been liquidated, as is the custom under Islamic law after a death. Tchoudja's own daughter still seems to be running some business in CAR but was also looking for places and means that would give her more security (see Chapter Six).

Examining Walad Djifir's moves and motivations when faced with insecurity or crisis, through an analytical focus on cattle or livestock, reveals a certain ground- edness amidst possible disruption – a groundedness linked to security in wealth (through livestock, land, social networks) and a flexibility vis-à-vis economic diver- sification. It is a groundedness which is also reflected in the 'walks of life' of those not necessarily faced with the more 'extraordinary' moments in life. This walk of life is not only the very literal transhumance and herding of livestock which still forms the day-to-day occupation of a large part of the group; it also refers to mobil- ity and flexibility as engrained in the Walad Djifir way of life. But for what reasons, in this day and age, will the Walad Djifir 'walk'? Economic incentives – primarily related to ideas about livestock, wealth, and family – are embedded not only in their livelihood as pastoral nomads but also in the historical context in which they find themselves. Within a continuing process of navigating changing bureaucracies and state structures, Walad Djifir find ways to supplement incomes, make use of increasing possibilities in terms of transport and communication infrastructures, and link up to cattle trade networks which continue to be hard for the state to control. This moving in and out of state control is necessary when creating social security through economic security. The state is not able to provide for those at risk of poverty and subsequent illness. Instead, people find their own ways, within the networks and infrastructures available.

Returning to the beginning of this chapter: each Walad Djifir has an idea about what his or her livestock (assets) mean to them. Even the young Farina has ideas about the future, linked to transhumance and a preference for what animal she will ride or what milk she prefers. In the case of the increase in camels as a result of Nour's father's inheritance, the situation put added strain on several members of the family. At the same time, we see that circumstances and the composition of herds change continuously – owing to drought or disease or through an inheritance – with people learning (and choosing) to be flexible to accommodate the changes in their daily tasks or work load. The attitudes of such men as Moustapha Saaleh toward wage labour, or indeed Youssouf's guarding of livestock in the face of danger, are grounded exactly in the way they perceive and value 'wage labour' and 'livestock' themselves. Cattle as capital are not easily replaced. More importantly, cattle as capital (wealth) provide a safety net for the future of one's family.

At the same time, the exact value of cattle differs per person and has changed over time. The modernizing dynamics surrounding cattle, and thereby also the 'control' over their potential value, are defined not only by the Walad Djifir or the local market, but also by N'Djaména's market dynamics and state-determined export regulations. In addition, choices vis-à-vis (dis)continuing with cattle as a primary livelihood have been influenced by ecological circumstances, infrastructural advances, and the improvement in or lack of security, among other factors. Walad Djifir such as Adoum, living and working in urban N'Djaména, have chosen to invest any surplus into the purchase of land. While he does still own cattle, herded by a brother, this is more of a symbolic investment than one meant to help secure the future of his children.

While changes are most definitely perceived, they continue to be formulated within a specific 'nomadic' connectivity which is flexible and always has been. Is this the 'primitive humanity' that Jackson (2013) speaks of? It is the idea of an inherentness (or primitiveness) of contradictory characteristics which I find intriguing in Jackson's work – an inherentness which is often overlooked. Within the varying contexts of economic change (commodification of cattle, diversification of economic activities) and insecurity (ecological, political), the importance of wealth (whether in the form of livestock or land, or even a formal education in Adoum's case) and social relations (family) provide a certain groundedness to people's lives, an 'anchoring' in which both the more mundane and extraordinary events are embedded and by which they may be given meaning. This anchoring provides a connection within which even the most spontaneous actions and minor experiences (Jackson 2013) of individuals are lived, and it also shapes this ever-shifting and fluid network of connectivity.

✳✳✳

So how is the CAR inheritance, or money earned selling blocks of ice in N'Djaména moved and passed on to family members in the ferīkh? What existing networks are used and how do individuals position themselves toward them? Hadj Allaramadji already hinted at certain more traditional and contemporary ways of moving money when it comes to Nigeria and the cattle trade. The next chapter follows the money Adoum was receiving during our fieldwork periods, most of which was coming in from Libya.

Chapter 5
New mobilities and old mistrusts

In the time we got to know each other while living in the ferīkh in February–May 2012, it had never really registered that Adoum was being used as a middleman for the sending and receiving of money from family abroad. In hindsight, it explains the random shouted phone calls in which the main message being repeated over and over was, '*Ana barra. Barra!*' (I'm outside, not in N'Djaména). Try again later.' Sometimes he would tell them within which time period he would be back; other times the person would call back every other day, hoping he had returned to the capital. The two countries from which Adoum received the most transactions were Libya and CAR. Of the two, Libya definitely had the highest frequency. The cases described in this chapter are based on observations and interviews carried out between February 2012 and March 2014 among various actors in the 'money chain'.

The digital sending of money is a relatively new technology, only recently reaching Chad's interior, a reflection of the present economic and financial systems. In terms of formal financial institutions, banks have a limited inland radius, while Money Transfer Operators (MTOs) have been able to gain access in some town centres, and the telecom industry has been most successful in cornering the market of money transfers. In terms of informal or unregulated financial transactions, old systems of sending money through merchants and family members are still in place and often even preferred. In the specific context of economic or monetary transfers, a meaningful use of 'informal' involves acknowledging that formal and informal boundaries shift over time and space (Lindley 2010: 42), as transactions cross national boundaries (jurisdictions) and as regulatory environments themselves also evolve (see de Bruijn et al. 2017). I have chosen to use the term 'mixed methods' here to describe the use of regulated and non-regulated monetary transactions systems by the Walad Djifir, as a way to include the different economic realities, or realms, involved in such transactions.

Should these mixed methods be seen as a reaction to ongoing insecurity in the region ('creativity in crisis', as per Appadurai 1986), as a strategy or tactic to navigate (Vigh 2009) duress, enhanced by the use of technological developments? Or should the 'unbanked' Walad Djifir's tactics be seen in light of interlacing displacement economies (see Hammar & Rodgers 2008; Hammar et al. 2010; Hammar 2014). While those Walad Djifir opting for migrant work in Libya cannot be classified as (forcibly) 'displaced', their movements and the context in which they find themselves are part of intertwined displacement processes, creating interlinked displacement economies – economies affected by the fall of Qaddafi, the increased presence of Boko Haram in Nigeria making it a less safe destination, and the ongoing conflicts

https://doi.org/10.1515/9783110714685-005

in both Sudans. At the same time, local socio-economic and political dynamics too affect the choices Walad Djifir make when it comes to sending money.

The financial systems of a country, those regulated and unregulated by a governmental or financial institution, are thus a reflection of its specific situation. Roitman (2001, 2005) goes as far as stating that, in Central Africa, both state and non-state practices of governing refer to a common 'ethic of illegality', an understanding of mutual needs and benefits. She describes how the exact unregulated networks that have established themselves within the gaps of a state's system allow the same state to reconstruct its authority. In other words, 'unregulated economic exchanges and financial relations' function alongside the activities of road robbers and the state (Roitman 2005: 15), having become part of the political logics of this state (Roitman 2001: 253). This entanglement of the formal and informal has developed in specific ways in specific areas, whether along national borders or more inland, and comes with specific codes of conduct, rules, and norms. In Cameroon, for example, the state has fixed the prices of the beef retail market, limiting free economy and ultimately encouraging cattle traders to move to the Nigerian cattle markets (Unusa 2012: 132). Along the Cameroonian border, Roitman (2001, 2005) focuses on such techniques of fiscal regulation such as 'tax-price', avoiding the legal–illegal or formal–informal dichotomies in examining the regional networks of accumulation. The state's regulatory bodies often levy more than just taxes and are of course not the only ones with enough power to request payments. An example of this latter dynamic is given for Central Africa in Peer Schouten's (2022) extensive research into what he calls roadblock politics by rebel groups. The actors may change over time, but the logics of power and accumulation do not seem to change as much, especially as long as officials and rebels remain underpaid, relying on other tactics to supplement their income.

The informal or illegal is thus not synonymous with being chaotic, disorderly, or even unregulated. Instead, alternative forms of regulatory authority can be observed. Merchants, customs officers, robbers, soldiers, rebel groups, the local village chief – they all make use of specific logics of exchange, whereby at times an 'ethic of illegality' prevails. The point here is not to delve into the exact functioning of the Chadian political-economic system, nor to place an emphasis on the workings of the state or the various informal and formal regulators. Instead, it sketches a context in which the Walad Djifir too make decisions.

This chapter examines the entanglement of networks involved in the movement of Walad Djifir remittances, attempting to understand the logics of exchange involved. Exploring the modern ways of transferring money reveals new mobilities and the means of exchange that come with them. In the previous chapter, livestock were shown to play an important role in processes of economic exchange and social relating. As such, they function as a connecting technology. Money plays a similar role, yet it has the potential to create connections where livestock no longer can – it offers a way to connect in times of rupture, as well as a way of binding the ferīkh to the globalizing world of digital technologies. Money and its exchange incorporate a different type of mobility and flexibility than that of livestock, especially when it comes to remittances. Remittances involve a way of relating to one another, opening up opportunities which may not have been possible in the past but may be so in the future (Lindley 2010). At the same time, remittances seem to close off specific ways of doing things, such as a type of economy which is much more related to livestock. Within a context of historical intra-regional mobility, where currencies tend to differ per monetary region or country, how then does the everyday civilian Walad Djifir receive money from a family member living abroad?

Technologies, networks, and transactions

On another occasion, Adoum and I were on our way to drop off a money transfer at the *marché à mil* when Adoum received a call. He parked the car, telling the person on the other end to give him two seconds, reaching for his agenda and pen to write down any details.

> Five, six, zero, zero, two, eight! Yes, yes, another five! Seven, four, two, four! Okay, okay; got it! Yes, I have ten numbers! Amount?! Amount?! Three-hundred-and-twenty-five-thousand. Okay, okay. Name?! Name?! Muhammed Hamdaan . . . beepbeepbeep . . .
>
> Did you get it?
>
> Yes, I got it. Libya.
>> – Based on video footage, N'Djaména, 26 February 2013

The numbers shouted over the phone and carefully noted down in his agenda, correspond to a Western Union transaction, one of the most common ways money is sent from Libya to Chad. The number of the Western Union transfer is fictional, as is the name and amount; however, it does represent how the conversation went. The sender in question actually had two money transfers to pass on to Adoum. If we understood correctly, the caller was sending money from a place called Al-Masrab in Libya.

In the period February 2011 to February 2013, roughly 14,000,000 FCFA (approx. 21,374 EUR) was sent from Libya through Adoum in N'Djaména and on to family members in the ferīkh. Adoum's records indicated that from February 2013 to February 2014, roughly 14,700,000 FCFA (approx. 22,443 EUR) were received by him from Libya.[1] For the first set of transactions (2011–2013), thirty-nine were docu-

---

1 The transaction documentation is based on MoneyGram and Western Union forms of cash received by Adoum. Fieldnotes, 22 January 2013 and 28 February 2014.

mented, of which the average transaction amount was 358,886 FCFA (approx. 548 EUR). The smallest amount sent was 54,000 FCFA (approx. 82 EUR), with 535,518 FCFA (approx. 818 EUR) being the largest. The second set of transactions documented (2013–2014) also coincidentally included exactly thirty-nine transactions, with an average amount of 376,838 FCFA (approx. 575 EUR). The smallest amount received was 59,362 FCFA (approx. 91 EUR), the largest amount 578,616 FCFA (approx. 883 EUR). The amounts mentioned do not account for the handful of transactions which are conducted between merchants in Libya and merchants in Chad, with Adoum acting as middleman to ensure the money reached family in the ferīkh.

The transfer of money involves networks. These networks in turn make use of technologies such as those provided by banks, Mobile Network Operators (MNOs), and MTOs, as well as familial and commercial (social) networks. Both technologies and networks, as trajectories of people themselves moving and needing to move money, have an historical aspect. In fact, the historical roots of monetary transactions are directly linked to the perceptions and experiences of financial institutions, as well as to the historical reliance on social networks (de Bruijn et al. 2017).

Transactions in the past and continuing insecurities

How then was money sent in the past, one might ask? Money was sent through merchants or travellers, though often in the form of merchandise so as to avoid currency issues (Roitman 2005; Lydon 2009). This took a long time and involved a high risk, both for the one doing the transporting as well as for the sender. In the previous chapter, the cattle merchant Hadj Allaramadji recounted how he would travel with large sums of money hidden away on his person. Like other merchants and even travellers he preferred to buy goods with the money he had made in Nigeria, selling them on in Chad. Doing so avoided the possible loss when exchanging naira for CFA and meant there was a chance of additional profit being made. In the time that Adoum was working with Fulani in Cameroon, he would occasionally buy a cow, which, over time, he sent on to be reared by his brother south of Mongo. In both cases – of merchandise and of livestock as investments of money earned across borders – the risks of being robbed were great.

A present-day example sketches a picture of what it could have been like in the past. Early in 2013 a story circulated in N'Djaména about a government official travelling from N'Djaména to a town in central Chad, when he happened on a group of *coupeurs de route* (road robbers). The story goes that the robbers ended up going through all their victim's receipts with him until they were satisfied that he had indeed already spent the money they had been told he would be carrying. They even escorted him past the next *coupeurs de route* further up the road, saying they would be horrible and less likely to be able to read the receipts. This was one of the more 'humouristic' stories of *coupeurs de route* circulating in N'Djaména in early 2013. Only a few weeks later, a more serious version would be added, involving the murder of a government official and his young family. The official had been travelling with the salaries of civil servants. No one understood why the children too had to die – fear of recognition? On top of that, why had the government not opted to send the money through Express Union? Perhaps this had not been an option?

Another example of how money was being sent to family members within Chad involves a group of Walad Djifir who had been arrested and imprisoned on their way to Libya, in mid-2012. Due to the political situation in Libya and Chad's suspicion of nationals moving toward Libya to enrol in mercenary activities, the Chad–Libya border was under strict control.[2] These men happened to be passing through the wrong checkpoint at the wrong time. They were on their way to Libya to take up a job in livestock herding. The road through northern Chad is rough, hot, and dry. People usually travel on large lorries. The men were arrested on suspicion of heading to Libya under false pretences. It is highly likely that none of them were carrying any form of national identification and that this was the primary reason for their arrest. What is clear is that these men spent several days in prison, being robbed of the money they had been carrying. After a few days they were released. In Dutch we say, 'You can't pluck a bald chicken.' They had been released as no one really knew what to do with them, and they obviously would not provide the prison staff with much of an income. After their release, they found a safe location in which to take apart the seams of their clothes. This point in the story is usually told with much gesture and laughter, imitating the men prying open each and every seam. With the money they recuperated in this way, they would be able to send only one of them on to Libya. It was at this point that Adoum was called. He was requested to contact their family members in the ferīkh, asking them to send him a certain amount of CFA. Adoum was then to send this money on through a call box. Amazingly enough, this is what happened. More amazingly, the call box operator in this small village in the middle of northern Chad had the full amount in cash. The men were now able to continue their journey, running the same risks as before.

---

2 On Libya's unchecked southern borders and people-smuggling as one of the only viable businesses left for the economically devastated south: http://www.irinnews.org/special-report/2018/09/06/libya-s-unchecked-southern-borders-key-easing-migration-crisis, accessed 7 September 2018. In this article (dated September 2018), smugglers estimate 4800 migrants enter Libya through Niger each month. It remains a question what figures exist from across the Chadian border, and/or how many of those migrants may be of Chadian origin. During the time of fieldwork, it seemed that most Walad Djifir making their way into Libya did so directly by crossing the border with Chad and did not have the added intention of migrating onward to Europe.

These examples show the way insecurity factors into the 'simple' practice of travelling overland. The last example also shows the impact of the mobile phone, through which the men travelling to Libya were able to contact and alert their family members. In addition, it allowed them to ask for help, which was given to them rather efficiently. Past experiences of having sent money through a far-off family member or merchant and having lost it has driven the choice to send it through call boxes or MTOs. How, though, is that different from what was being done before? The sender still needs to trust someone to pick it up at the other end? This is true, but now there is the mobile phone with which one can stay connected and involved in the whole process from beginning to end. I cannot count the number of times a person, having sent money from Libya, would call to make sure everything was going well. Of course, there is always the option of not answering a phone, delaying the process as a whole.

The remittance infrastructure: Availability and affordability

Throughout many African countries there is a lack of banking penetration, mostly in terms of personnel and sufficient cash flow. In addition to banks, there are less than one hundred MTOs in Africa, all of which together are responsible for 90 per cent of all remittance service providers (RSPs), according to an IFAD report published in November 2009 (IFAD 2009). Western Union and MoneyGram remain the two most dominant MTOs on the African market, having required banks and other remittance-paying agents to sign an exclusivity agreement. This means that banks make up half of the businesses making payments (41 per cent) and providing a location for pay-out (65 per cent) (ibid.: 6). Some African countries categorize remittances as foreign exchange transactions, which allows only banks and foreign exchange bureaus to handle this business. This prohibits micro-finance institutions (MFIs) from paying out or, in the case of Uganda, from carrying out any kind of electronic commerce. In such countries, with a low percentage of banks or other financial institutions such as MTOs, and a high level of intra-regional migration, the demand for more informal means of sending or receiving money is created (see also de Bruijn et al. 2017 for case studies in Cameroon, DRC, Senegal, and Zambia). The restrictions on outbound money transfers – namely, on the amount – have strengthened the role of the informal financial sector. Apart from regulatory hurdles, there are also the often steep transaction fees to consider.

Chad itself hosts a mixture of national and commercial banks, of which most, at the time of fieldwork, were located in the capital and several major cities and towns – namely, Abéché, Moundou, Sarh, and Doba (see Map 1 to get a sense of the spread). Both Moundou and Abéché had relatively large business and humanitarian activities, corresponding with a higher percentage of commercial banks. Up to November 2013, no bank branches or Western Union facility existed in Mongo, the closest main town for the Walad Djifir. The MTO Express Union has been in town since 2009. Next to this a Caisse Urbaine exists, as well as a handful of community micro-finance programmes. As of 15 and 20 November 2013, both Orabank and the Societé General (SGTchad) respectively have set up a *dependence* in Mongo. With the opening of the branches in Mongo came a sensitizing campaign: both banks invested in educating the local community in terms of what it meant to open a bank account as well as lowering the restrictions and fees associated with opening an account. In March 2014, both banks had attracted primarily government employees and the larger cattle and gum arabic merchants.[3] SGTchad works together with Western Union, while Orabank is in partnership with the MTOs Coinstar, Money Express, and Oryx. Western Union was originally a telegram-sending service, based in the US, which evolved into incorporating postal services and has more recently used its existing infrastructure to provide monetary transfers. Coinstar is part of the Sigue money transfer network, which has its origins in Latin America and the US. Orabank Chad is a private bank and has been doing business in Chad since 1992. It has branches in Gabon, Togo, Guinea, Mauritania, and Benin (Orabank website).

The outreach of the mobile phone has seen much greater efficiency (de Bruijn et al. 2009; Chéneau-Loquay 2012; de Bruijn 2013, 2015; Djohy et al. 2017). It is thus only common sense that mobile phone companies and financial institutions have looked to combine the infrastructure of mobile networks, already in place, with financial transactions, within the scope of a country's financial regulations (de Bruijn et al. 2017). Of the three mobile network companies present in Chad – namely, MOOV, Airtel, and Tigo – the latter two now also provide mobile banking services and have offices in Mongo. Airtel Money was launched in partnership with Ecobank from June 2012 onwards. Ecobank is a pan-African bank and the largest independent regional banking group in West and Central Africa, covering thirty African countries. It was founded in the 1980s to fill the vacuum of commercial banks in West Africa. In an article on the website of *Mobile Payments Today*, dated 18 June 2012, Airtel claimed to be the first of its kind to offer such a service to its Chadian clientele. Tigo Chad partnered with Orabank and Millicom International Cellular (MIC) to set up mobile financial services, announcing this service in January 2013. Tigo also claimed to be

---

3 Sources: interview with bank manager Orabank, Mongo, 18 March 2014; interview with SGTchad bank manager, Mongo, 19 March 2014.

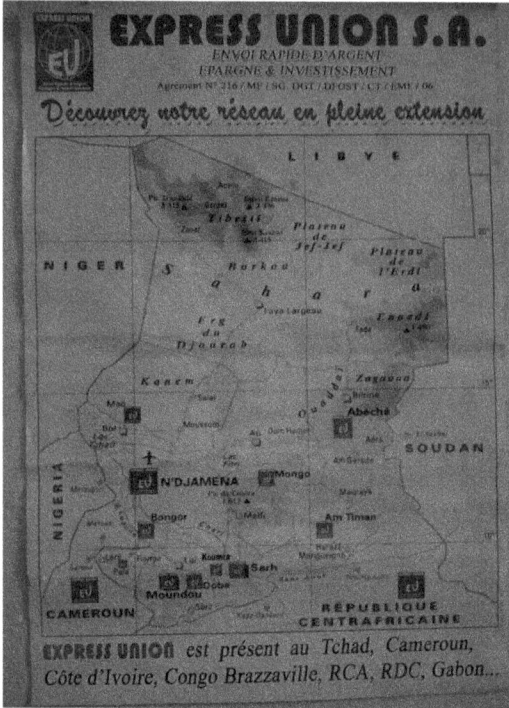

Photo 5.1: Map of Express Union locations within Chad, February 2014.

the first, in an article published on the website of *Telegeography.com* on 14 January 2013, then planning to make their service available to agents in N'Djaména, Mao, Moundou, and Abéché. Mobile banking refers to monetary transactions which are made from a mobile phone via a bank account. This differs from those transactions which are carried out through a mobile network provider only – that is, via the use of a call box. When using a call box, the client does not need to own a mobile bank account to send money. Instead, they give the mobile phone agent cash, which is then transferred to e-money and sent to another agent, where it is collected as cash by the end-recipient.

On a visit to N'Djaména in October 2017, both Airtel and Tigo could be seen advertising their mobile money services. In fact, on purchasing a SIM card, I was advised to open a TigoCash account, which would allow me to top up my own airtime from the credit deposited in it and, theoretically, allow me to pay at various shops. As we were only there for a week, I declined; but it was interesting to see how these types of products had developed. At the same time, the reactions of various colleagues also in N'Djaména that week to the prices of phone calls, text messages, and Internet use, compared with neighbouring countries, were a good reminder of how expensive mobile phone use still is for the average Chadian.[4]

Thus, aside from infrastructural availability, an important driver behind choosing the means to send money is the cost involved. Apart from Adoum, the other intermediaries along the transaction chain stand to benefit, making it a potentially costly endeavour. In the sending of money via MTOs, fixed commissions and exchange rates are paid. Merchants have their own prices, which are not that transparent – more often than not basing their exchange rates on the black market and charging a fee for their services. In N'Djaména, for example, changing euros for CFAs at a local MTO could be done at a rate of 665 CFA/euro, while the official exchange rate is 655 CFA/euro.

Mixed methods: A chain of transactions

There were various ways in which money was being sent from Libya to Chad, involving numerous middlemen (see Figure 5 for two examples). In all cases, the mobile phone played an important role. Over the past few years, Adoum had become one of the main actors in the transaction chain for his extended family. Based in N'Djaména and literate in the institutional ways of the city, his trustworthy reputation had made him an ideal candidate. He was continually receiving phone calls from Libya.

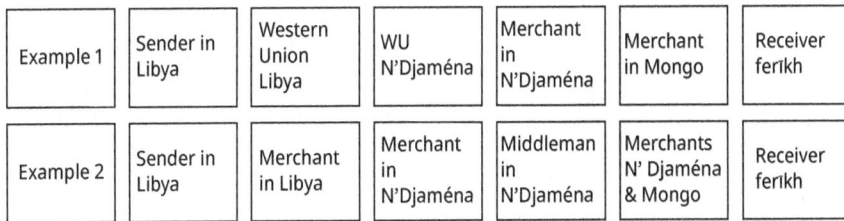

| Example 1 | Sender in Libya | Western Union Libya | WU N'Djaména | Merchant in N'Djaména | Merchant in Mongo | Receiver ferîkh |

| Example 2 | Sender in Libya | Merchant in Libya | Merchant in N'Djaména | Middleman in N'Djaména | Merchants N' Djaména & Mongo | Receiver ferîkh |

Figure 5: Typical money transfer schematics.

---

4 The Ivorian blogger and conference participant Emmanuel wrote a blog on his astonishment regarding the costs of megabytes in Chad and how it makes social activism via social media tricky: http://emmanueldabo.com/portrait-de-deuhb-zizou-cyberactiviste-blogueur-tcahdien/, accessed 18 December 2017. At the same time, we need to remark that Facebook and Tigo, for example, offer the Internet user the free use of Facebook Messenger and a version of Facebook without images on their mobile phone. For more on Internet-use prices in Chad, see http://tchadinfos.com/societes/tchad-internet-luxe-majorit-de-population/, accessed 14 May 2018.

Step one: Across national boundaries
Due to an often bad phone connection, or perhaps due to the caller's credit running out, these conversations were loud and held at a fast pace. They began with a much shortened version of the extensive greeting ceremony and would launch right into transmitting the number of the Western Union transaction. Sometimes a call would come in at an inconvenient moment, when the caller would be asked to call back at a later time. Adoum would never call back – too expensive, he was not the one wanting something, and the phone numbers often came up as 'unknown' on his screen.

Once the Western Union number and amount had been taken down with pen and paper, Adoum was sure to pick up the cash as soon as possible, wishing to be rid of the responsibility. In some cases, the sender in Libya opted to transfer money via a merchant. This entailed the sender giving cash to a merchant in Libya with commercial ties in Chad. In such a case, Adoum would receive a phone call indicating to which merchant he should go to retrieve the money. These merchants varied from being importers of Libyan clothes or rugs to dealers in foreign currency. There are many cases in which such a middleman proved untrustworthy, first investing the money into his own business and waiting for the return, before sending it on to Adoum. One can imagine the phone costs this led to, not to mention the frustration on both the Libyan and Chadian side, since those on the ferīkh side had already been notified about the money transfer.

Step two: National transactions
The next step in the chain was for the money to be sent on to the family member in the ferīkh. Sometimes this was done using Express Union. More often than not, the money was sent on through a merchant. In Adoum's case, he had developed a rapport with a Kanembu merchant in N'Djaména, who imported such goods as rice, tea, and sugar. This Hadj Ali[5] had commercial ties to a relative in Mongo. When Adoum handed over his cash to Hadj Ali, the latter documented the sum in his notebook and made a phone call to his counterpart in Mongo, informing him of the impending transaction and asking him whether he had the amount in cash available. Hadj Ali now owed his Mongo counterpart a certain amount in wares, cutting down on the transportation of cash between N'Djaména and Mongo. In a country like Chad, where *coupeurs de route* (road robbers) still make an appearance from

5 Name has been changed. Similar processes of trader networks adapting to new technologies (mobile phone) and specializing as money transfer agencies can be found in a variety of countries. See Beuving (2006) for an example of Lebanese traders in Cotonou. In Chad it is the Kanembu who are well-known for their trade networks.

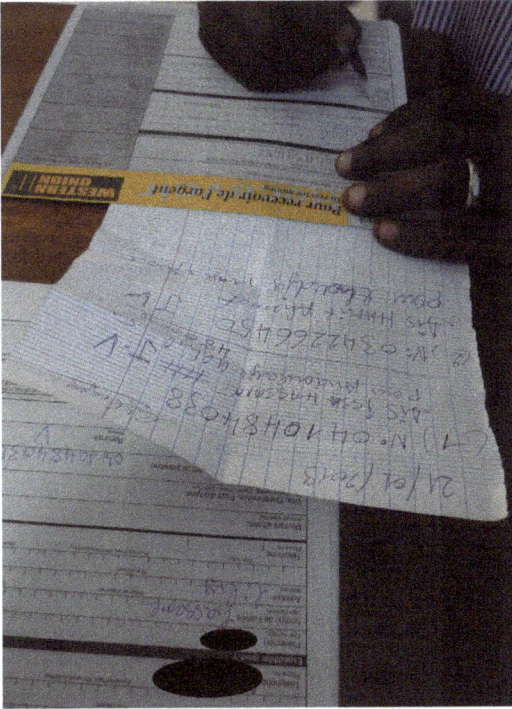

Photo 5.2: Adoum filling out a Western Union reception form at a bank branch in N'Djaména, January 2013. The larger monetary transfer operators such as Western Union and Express Union have both independent offices and counters within the premises of some banks.

time to time (Dangbet 2020: 116), this was one of the safest ways to do business. One of the consequences of money hardly ever circulating between cities was that the money found in Mongo was impossibly old. With the coming of Express Union and the two banks, old notes have slowly started to be exchanged for newer versions. When the merchant in Mongo was asked whether he would consider opening a bank account now that both Orabank and SGTchad were in town, he responded: 'With what? What should I put in the bank? This [these goods] is all I have. I buy and sell them, from which I can feed my family and children. What is left to put into a bank?'[6] Hadj Ali in N'Djaména did make use of a bank account. Depending on the amount Adoum sends through Hadj Ali, a transaction fee is paid.

---

6 Interview with merchant in Mongo, 18 March 2014, translated from Chadian Arabic.

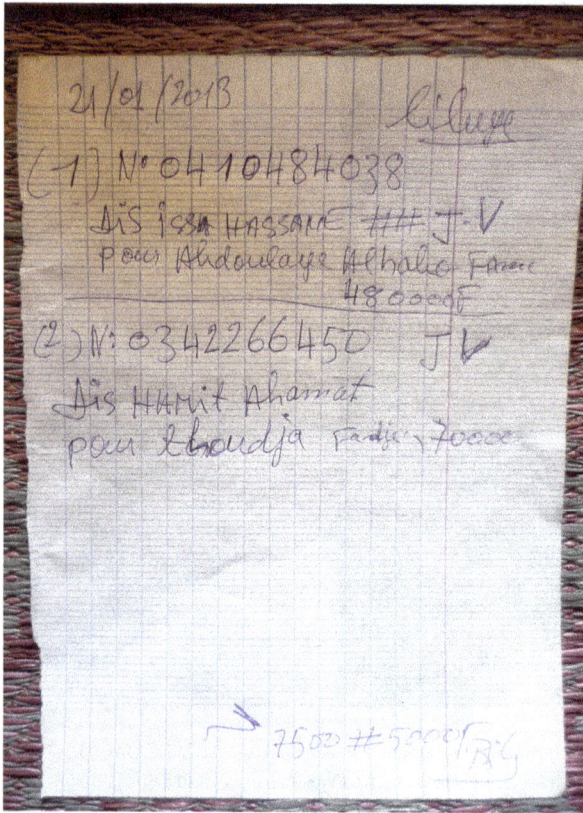

Photo 5.3: Notes after a phone call from Libya, January 2013. Adoum was very meticulous in noting down details of transactions and would also retain these documents.

Step three: The local pickup

The transaction chain is a system with many checkpoints, a phone call being the method to ensure money has been correctly sent or received. Hadj Ali will have passed on the name of the Walad Djifir picking up the money, mentioning when he should be expected. This is usually on a Wednesday, Mongo's weekly market day and the day on which several Walad Djifir will come into town on business. Adoum in turn will phone the ferīkh relative responsible for collecting the money, stating the amount he is to receive, that he should not forget to go as soon as possible, and often giving instructions as to how the money should be divided among the Libyan sender's relatives. Adoum often decides whom to contact in the ferīkh, basing his decision on the person's relation to the one in Libya, the frequency with which he can be reached by mobile phone, and his general trustworthiness. Many younger men in the ferīkh possess a mobile phone; however, the two national net-

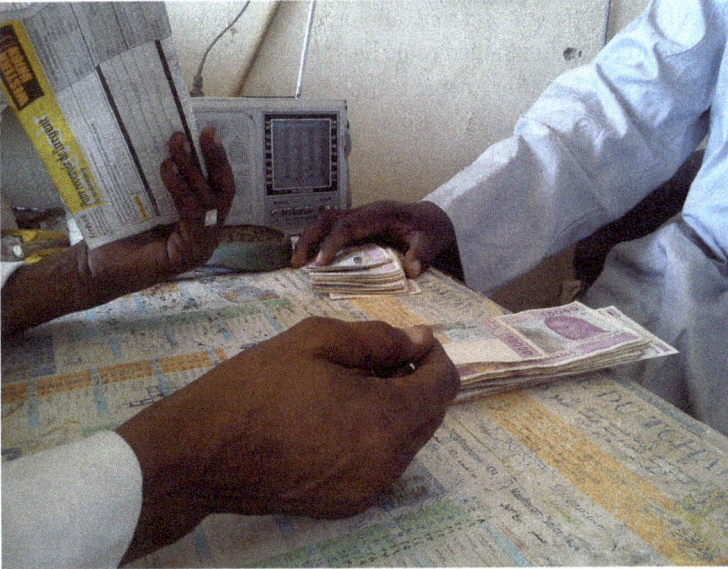

Photo 5.4: Adoum handing over cash to a merchant in N'Djaména, February 2014. This money had been sent to Adoum from Libya and needed to be sent on to someone in a ferīkh near Mongo. The merchant kept a record of the transactions he carried out. This paper money (cash) would stay with the merchant, acting as credit for a trade partner in Mongo. The trade partner / shopkeeper in Mongo would then distribute cash to the person who came to collect it.

works available do not yet cover every inch of Chad, and charging batteries can be an issue.

As soon as the exchange has been made, Adoum will receive a phone call from Hadj Ali. Adoum will then call the ferīkh relative to confirm. The contact between Adoum and the ferīkh is often somewhat one-directional. Relatives in the ferīkh will *beep* his mobile phone or hold very short conversations, but in general Adoum is in the position to buy phone credit more readily. Depending on the one sending the money from Libya, Adoum will be allowed to keep 5000–10,000 CFA (approx. 7–15 EUR). This fee goes toward the costs of the many phone calls with actors in the chain and toward providing petrol for the motorbike with which he makes the trips to the various MTOs and merchants. It is a source of income, albeit not large.

Merchants are also used to send money transnationally, as another example of sending money from Libya to a ferīkh in Chad shows. In this case, Adoum was informed that a specific amount of money was to be picked up from the merchant Muhammed. The merchant Muhammed could be found among those buying and selling foreign currency at the capital's large market. On approaching the place where foreign currency is bought and sold, Adoum asked a seemingly random merchant where this merchant Muhammed could be found. Said merchant Muhammed was at first a bit reluctant, but after Adoum mentioned the right names and amount, handed over the money. The next step was now to send the money on to the ferīkh, a process performed as described above, through a merchant with commercial ties in the closest large town (to the ferīkh). The money had been sent via a merchant in Libya with commercial, and probably familial, ties to Chad. The merchant Muhammed in N'Djaména, in turn, had thus provided credit to this merchant in Libya. Whether they would even out the score with another monetary transaction or goods was unclear but probable.

Contexts of sending money

The communications technology revolution has not only benefitted the more formal financial (transaction) system but also the older, traditional systems based on sending money via merchants. Apart from the technical improvements surrounding the sending of money, the various intermediaries use mobile phones to stay connected and involved. Nevertheless, such new technologies as the mobile phone, and products related to it, are used within a certain context – a specific context shaped in interaction with individuals and by the economic, political, and social environment which is Chad. This section will discuss the reasons for sending money – namely, everyday economic life in the ferīkh and the need to supplement income; the role of infrastructures available in relation to insecurity and mistrust; and the place of technology in creating security and regulation.

Remittances and everyday economic life in the ferīkh

For the Walad Djifir, as for many nomadic populations, their livestock function like a bank (Unusa 2012: 86). Their cattle are their main source of credit and insurance. Once the credit runs low and there are no obvious ways of replenishing the stock, many men turn to forms of labour migration, whether within the country or regionally. In terms of a means of saving, investment in more livestock and the buying of land play this role. Through the natural reproduction of livestock and by selling and buying them at the right times, wealth is accumulated. Typically, cattle will be bought during the dry season, fattened up, and then sold after the wet season. Asking about livestock numbers among nomads is as taboo as asking about their number of children; they will hardly ever give you an exact figure. Instead of dealing with mortgages half of their lives, the average urban Chadian invests in land and housing for their children throughout his or her life, saving up to buy a plot of land and then slowly building on it as money trickles in. There are not many Walad Djifir who have bought land, but those family members who are more urban-oriented and carry out large-scale commercial activities have done so – often with money earned abroad. For those in the ferīkh, remittances go a long way toward replenishing livestock and providing a source of income in other areas of daily life.

Take the case of Yakhoub (introduced in Chapter Two), who, as a young, unmarried man in the early 1970s, set out for Sudan. The herd of his father and uncles was not large enough to be divided among his brothers, and so he went in search of work in order to earn enough money to enlarge the herd. He describes Chad as being poor at that time; there was little work to be found and no security due to an ongoing civil war. In comparison, the situation in Sudan provided more opportunities for employment, and the added benefit of a shared language in the north (Arabic) made it an appealing place to go. Yakhoub did not know anyone on leaving Chad, but he says Chadians and Sudanese are '*ahl wahid bass*' (all one family).[7] He was able to find work guarding sheep and goats. In those days, money (or news for that matter) was not sent back regularly; instead, on return to the family, Yakhoub brought back money and a horse. The horse he sold in exchange for three or four cows.

Yakhoub's story is not unique; and come the early 2000s, members of his extended family are active as second- or third-generation merchants in CAR; as seasonal factory workers, guards, and goat herders in Libya; and as long-term cattle merchants travelling to Nigeria and Cameroon. The context of economic exchange in each of these countries is a different one – Chad, Cameroon, and CAR are part of the Communauté Économique des États de l'Afrique Centrale (CEMAC), a monetary union officially facilitating the movement of people, goods, and money across national borders. In reality, being part of the CEMAC does not necessarily benefit the regular traveller or sender of goods. Libya and Nigeria do not share such an economic unity with Chad; and with the fall of Qaddafi in 2011, politico-economic relations changed.

Infrastructures, insecurity, and mistrust

Within Libya and Chad's political context, using the infrastructure in place, the Walad Djifir have formed a transaction network. Insecurity has an ambiguous posi-

---

7 Apart from ethno-linguistic similarities (Manfredi & Roset 2021), there are socio-cultural and religious aspects which would have felt familiar for a semi-nomadic Chadian in Sudan.

tion as push and pull factor in the movement of people. Throughout 2011–2013, Walad Djifir could be seen fleeing Libya as a result of the revolution and the consequent persecution of Chadians, accused of being mercenaries in Qaddafi's forces. At the same time, the continuous stress of life in the ferīkh and the availability of herders' jobs in remote Libya have resulted in various Walad Djifir leaving for Libya. In a conversation with Adoum, he explained how young men from the ferīkh leave for Libya with trucks from the town of Moussoro.

> The *khalifa* [representative of a specific sub-group] will get information about whether the merchant has space to transport people. They will pay up to 300,000 CFA per person. The truck will leave without much merchandise or with camels. With the camels, the Chadians and merchant can pretend they have been hired to take care of them, but they will still usually avoid the big roads (*c'est la fraude*). The same when travelling without a lot of merchandise and several Chadians. On the way down from Libya, the trucks are heavily charged [with merchandise] and they can't risk taking the fraud routes. There is less problem for Chadians leaving Libya. (Fieldnotes, 28 February 2014)

Apart from the explicit post-revolution violence, a more implicit insecurity exists. Walad Djifir working in Libya are frequently harassed, news of which is passed on in their phone conversations with Adoum and other family members. Their Libyan employer is often asked to accompany them to the Western Union branch as a form of protection. Apart from this, the clandestine nature of their presence in Libya implies that they may not have the necessary credentials to send money through official channels. The choices they are then faced with are to entrust the transaction to someone who can make use of an MTO, or to entrust it to a merchant with ties to Chad. The fees asked by the different money operators (MTO or merchant) also factor into this calculation.

Lately, Adoum has been receiving requests from non-relatives to act as a middleman. This is a development he is not pleased with. 'It invites trouble. I have told them to stop giving my number to people whose families we don't know.' He is worried that if something happens to the money, or if one of the relatives of the sender is not honest, issues will arise that cannot be resolved within the group, as usually happens among the Walad Djifir.

There is, then, a role for trust when it comes to making decisions about sending money.[8] Infrastructures have to be available but also trusted. Social networks need

---

8 Carey & Pedersen (2017) provide a lens with which to interpret the ethnographic observations of daily handlings (Jackson 2004), namely by examining the 'infrastructures' underpinning or enabling certainty and doubt, as opposed to merely the 'technologies' (22) – in the case of the Walad Djifir, for example, the underlying logic (infrastructure) involved in decisions as to how money should be sent. For an analysis of trust in relation to money transfer infrastructures and networks used in Cameroon, CAR, DRC, and Senegal, see de Bruijn et al. (2017).

to be accessible and trustworthy. Observations and conversations indicate that the focus of decisions on whether or not to make use of a certain network or infrastructure is based on *mistrust*. Adoum does not trust that the non-relatives will not take advantage of the situation and create some kind of problem for him and his family. When dealing with a misbehaving relative, even if a distant one, his family members can be called upon to put things right. Carey (2017) suggests using mistrust as an explanatory model of everyday social relations,[9] within which actions and decisions of Walad Djifir are formed. Carey posits that trust is (a) not merely a matter of choice but also a way of viewing the world; and (b) that 'this way of viewing the world is one that relies on familiarity as a basis for simplification' (ibid.: 5–6). Trust helps us to foresee future consequences of choices made. Adoum's reluctance to receive money from a non-family member is because he cannot oversee the risks. He would rather not give up the control he would otherwise have and risk becoming dependent on the good-will of those involved in the money chain. These reservations are based on experience: in 2013 Adoum had received money from the friend of a family member working with him in Libya. This friend had sent money to a merchant in N'Djaména, from whom Adoum was supposed to collect before sending it on via Express Union to the friend's family elsewhere. The merchant had decided to invest the money into his business before passing it on. It took Adoum many phone calls and trips by motorbike, meanwhile dealing with both the sender and end-recipients' anxiety about where the money had gone, before it was in his hands and he could send it on. If it had been someone from his own *tribu*, it would have been easier for him to manage the different parties.

The place of technology in creating security and regulation

One may argue that future use of only formally institutionalized means (e.g. MTOs, mobile banking, banks) will contribute to creating a feeling of security around the sending of money. Apart from providing security, formalization and technological developments may also go toward cutting down the costs of sending money. Pres-

---

9 'Simmel describes trust as "a hypothesis regarding future behavior, a hypothesis certain enough to serve as a basis for practical conduct" and suggests that people, eras, and societies differ by the particular admixture of knowledge and ignorance that suffices to generate trust (1950: 318–19). In other words, the morphology of the trust hypothesis shapes and produces particular social forms. I [Carey] argue that just the same is true of mistrust. It is an alternative hypothesis and one that gives rise to social forms of its own. These are not merely the photographic negative of those produced by trust, but interesting and occasionally admirable constructs in their own right' (Carey 2017: 3).

ently, due to the remoteness of senders' and receivers' geographical locations, often multiple 'handlers' have to be used, making transfers a costly process. An MTO or merchant is needed for money to cross Chadian–Libyan national boundaries, while merchants and mobile networks can be used for intra-national transfers. Throughout these transactions, the trust placed in whatever system is chosen is intricately linked to the trust placed in the individuals involved.

Recent developments, such as Express Union's alliance with MoneyGram, opens up the possibility to bypass the capital when making transactions from remote Libya (via MoneyGram) to remote Chad (via Express Union), also eliminating several middlemen. Elsewhere, Western Union has partnered with mobile operators to offer a mobile money-sending product, enabling international money transfers with the MTO through mobile phones. In 2015, Chad was not yet a country with which they had partnered. Since November 2013, the setting up of a bank account in Mongo and the possibility to transfer money internationally through it are now possible. Whether or not these banks are partnered with banks located in Libya is another question. I am unsure of the situation on the ground in remote Libya and the feasibility of sending money through a bank branch, also considering the often illegal status of Chadians working in Libya. While mobile banking can grow to become a viable alternative, in Chad it currently functions only within the country – more specifically, within one mobile network, making the sending of money between two providers impossible.

Insecurity, in its many forms, presents itself as one of the main reasons for the movement of Walad Djifir and their money. The current reasons for, and means of, remittance sending are being kept in place by a combination of economic necessity, resulting in the need and demand for labour migration, and the availability of infrastructure. While the Walad Djifir need to supplement their income, Libyans need their livestock tended. The available transport routes for merchandise provide the Walad Djifir with a means of getting across the border. The infrastructure in place, in terms of money-sending opportunities and mobile phone networks, informs part of the connections maintained with their family in the ferīkh. While families in the past would not hear from those abroad for years at a time, not reaping the benefits of income made, in recent years the transfer of money and news has become more frequent. Of course, there are always cases of family abroad 'disappearing' and not 'checking in', for whatever reasons.

What then is the result of these developments? The up-and-coming opportunities for the sending of money mentioned above may alter the scene again. In an interview with a large-scale cattle merchant based in Mongo, Al-Hadj Allaramadji, he explained how Chadian merchants trading with Nigeria, for example, use both the older system of exchanging goods and only occasionally the sending of money.[10] For the cattle Al-Hadj Allaramadji sells in Nigeria, a Nigerian merchant sends him products which he then sells in Chad. He does own a bank account in which he deposits money, but the bulk of his trading activities are still conducted in kind.

Based on my stays with the Walad Djifir and on talks with representatives of the local community and bank branches, it might be quite a while before the major-ity of the semi-sedentary Walad Djifir start opening bank accounts. Chadians in general, especially those in remote areas, are concerned about what will happen to their hard-earned money when another wave of rebels loot the city. Those already involved in trade, local and international, or with official positions in the local market – that is, those owning national IDs and handling large amounts of cash – may be among the first to make the switch. Although remittances are not yet widely used to invest in the buying of land, this change from cattle-as-capital to land-as-capital could in the future be followed by the keeping-of-capital in a bank account[11] – assuming there is enough capital to be put away.

New mobilities, new exchanges, and old mistrusts?

Chad has an extensive history of internal and external political unrest in combi-nation with ecological strains. The politico-military history of Chad, Libya, Sudan, and CAR especially are intricately intertwined.[12] Since 2011, Chad has taken up an active military role in Mali as well as an official and unofficial role in CAR. Other political events taking place in the region around the time of fieldwork were Libya's ongoing post-revolutionary scene, the Boko Haram insurgency in Nigeria and northern Cameroon, and West Darfur's continued unrest. In relation to Libya, the International Organization for Migration (IOM) alone had helped 150,000 Chadian migrants fleeing Libya to reintegrate since July 2011 (IOM 2013). Within this setting, there were always people who left the Walad Djifir community to go out and work,

---

10 Interview with Al-Hadj Allaramadji, together with colleague Souleymane, Mongo, 19 March 2014.

11 Something to consider may be Islam's stance toward the earning of interest: it is forbidden. Whether the Walad Djifir make the comparison between the keeping of capital as livestock or land, which can potentially make a return, and the keeping of capital in a bank account with no interest is a question I have yet to ask. Both methods have pros and cons.

12 See Debos (2008) on the cross-border activities of Chadian fighters in CAR, which seem to have become a structural pattern since the 1970s and should be seen in relation to regional migrations; see Azevedo (2004 [1998]) on Qaddafi's long-term meddling in Chadian politics; Boggero (2009) on the complex causes and implications of the crisis in Darfur and Chad. See Berg (2008) for an over-view of the interconnectedness of the conflicts in Chad, Sudan, and CAR.

earning cash to supplement their dwindling livestock numbers (see Chapters Four and Six). This movement has not changed. It is the world around this movement that has changed, as Adoum put it, thus also affecting, in different ways from before, those moving out and staying. So what changes, if any, do we see in terms of the social processes linked to remittance sending?

Various nomadic studies show a common trend in pastoral modernization with individuals moving out of their communities in search of economic alternatives (Casciarri 1995; Catley & Aklilu 2013; Catley et al. 2013; Unusa 2012; Chapter Four).[13] In the case of the Walad Djifir leaving for Libya, there is a certain temporariness to this 'opting out' of pastoral life, with most returning home eventually. Where in the past an uncle or nephew would leave the ferīkh to spend years in Sudan, ideally returning with a horse and some nice extras – money for clothes, sheep, or cattle – nowadays remittances are sent back home throughout the stay. The main reasons for this are not only technological and infrastructural developments in relation to the sending of money (e.g. Western Union and MoneyGram); it is also safer to send money back in parts, enabling family members to buy livestock which will keep until their return. Travelling overland with large sums of money between Libya and Chad still carries a high risk. In the past, partly to circumvent the difference in valuta between Libya and Chad, returnees would import Libyan goods to be sold in Chad. A contemporary alternative would be to open a bank account, relying less on the help of family – yet general illiteracy, financial illiteracy, ID issues, and the lack of banks in remote regions still impede this development. Many Walad Djifir working in Libya report being harassed and require the assistance of their Libyan employer when sending money. A related issue is not being in possession of an ID card, which most agencies require.

There is a much more immediate effect, and benefit, to people working abroad now than in the past. People even complain when they have not heard from a family member abroad, worrying about their safety or health, or merely expectantly awaiting a sum of money.[14] Most of the money is invested in livestock, while small amounts are used for the more luxurious needs of direct family. Here one should think of tea, sugar, and clothing. Some will refer to family members as *voleurs* or robbers, claiming they do not spend the money as the sender in Libya has requested,

---

13 For studies on, for example, changes in nomadic livelihood strategies within a context of economic, environmental, or other global changes, see de Bruijn (1995); Casciarri (1995); van Dijk (1995); Shehu & Hassan (1995); Braukämper (1996); Hodgson (1999); Holtzman (2009); Elliot (2010); Unusa (2012); Mahmoud (2013); Manoli et al. (2014); Gertel & Le Heron (2016b); Köhler (2016a).

14 See Lindley (2010) for similar stories from among the Somalian diaspora residing in the UK, explaining the difficult situation this sometimes puts them in. Similar dynamics were encountered in Senegal (de Bruijn et al. 2017).

instead 'drinking' more than their share through numerous cups of sugared tea, or buying themselves a new radio, watch, or mobile phone. Remittances from Libya are also used to pay for weddings of a direct family member (i.e. brother or uncle). Women, such as Khachana's daughter Zaynebah, showed me the carpets and pillowcases her husband had brought back for her on his last trip to Libya.

At this point it is uncertain (to me) how long the Walad Djifir have been going away to work in Libya. Their transhumance routes did not go that far north – travels to northern Chad were usually to buy salt for the cattle and camels – and Sudan and CAR are named more commonly when speaking of labour migration or commerce in the past. During the first fieldwork period (October 2011), family members who had clearly been living in Libya for several years were now returning, fleeing the violence. Those returning consisted of complete families, with children born and raised in Libya, as well as single men. The men in these families had often worked as guards in Libyan cities. In three cases, returned single men had been soldiers in Qaddafi's national army, bearing passport-sized photographs of themselves in uniform as proof. They all struggled to find their place again in Chadian society and within their family. One man in particular was extremely dissatisfied with the lack of support he felt he was receiving from family members, complaining loudly and emotionally during evening talks in the ferīkh.[15] He had worked as a guard, proudly proclaiming he used to cook for himself. Back in the ferīkh setting he had no cattle of his own and accused his family of not helping him.

On another occasion, on 7 March 2014, Souleymane, James, and I interviewed a retired solider[16] who had spent some time in Libya in the late 1980s and early 1990s – the time of the battle around the Aouzou strip under Habré – and returned to live in the sedentary village of Tchoufiou. At the time his friend and he joined the army, neither of them knew anything other than the tending of cattle. They went to Mongo to join the army during the period of problems between Goukouni and Habré (ca. 1979). During the interview, he mentioned being in Faya (northern Chad) in 1983 and in Abéché, Oum Hadjer, and Am Timam in 1984. In 1992 he returned to N'Djaména with Déby's MPS. His leg was injured as a gendarme under Déby, but he was able to get around on a motorcycle. He receives a pension from the state, although it is not particularly regular. His family had helped him build a *kouzi*, a round mud-house with dried grass roof. He was thankful and looking for ways to make himself a living. In N'Djaména, Adoum and I also met several Libyan returnees, one or two of them camped out at the house of Adoum's cousin, the ex-minister.

---

15 Fieldnotes, on a visit to the ferīkh of Adjidei at Fané, 17 March 2012.
16 Fieldnotes and interview (film and voice recording), at the village of Tchoufiou II Arabe, 7 March 2014.

One hoped to be integrated into the Chadian army, but Adoum was sceptical of the possibility, as the man's past in the Libyan army might come up and not be in his favour.

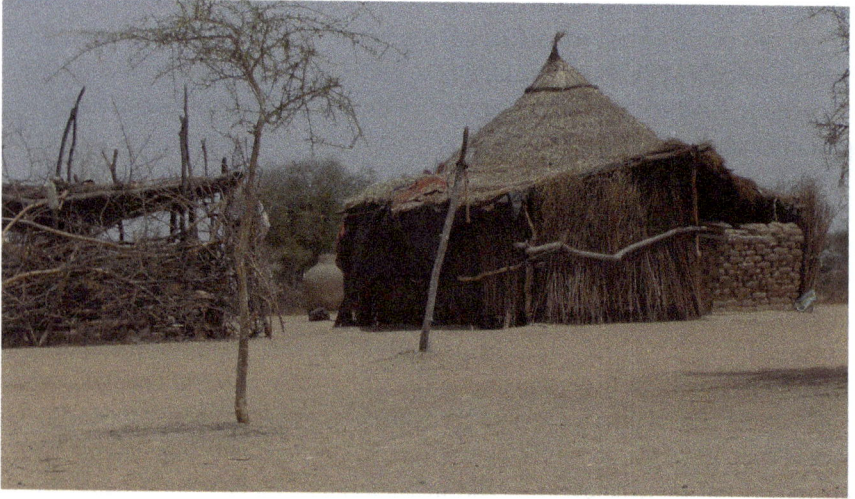

Photo 5.5: Kouzi of a man returned to the village after having finished his military service, March 2014. His family members had pulled together to help him build this home in the Walad Djifir's sedentary village. The man had spent some time in Libya, and had returned to the village after his pension. He was still adjusting to life in the rural village but was fairly positively minded. He received a pension from the Chadian state and helped with his family's agricultural fields insofar as his injured leg would permit. Having been away from the Guéra and his family for many years, he noticed a number of positive changes to their 'mentality' [his words] – though there were certain areas which could do with improving. His focus for the future of the Walad Djifir was education, not only of the children but also in relation to adult literacy.

During the course of the fieldwork in 2012, many men were leaving to go to Libya again. In most cases, family members in the ferīkh said they were going to work as herders for Libyans. There is seemingly a great demand for livestock herding in Libya, and it is popular due to how well it pays.[17] These men often leave with the intention of returning after a few months – ideally after 'enough' money has been made. In February 2014 I met several younger and older men who had already returned from Libya. Having left Libya voluntarily, as opposed to those who fled

---

17 Livestock here refers to goats, sheep, and camels. Although this remains to be researched, one might suggest that the increase in jobs (and pay) for herders in Libya is directly related to the post-Qaddafi disorder.

post-2011, their return to ferīkh life was relatively smooth. One man in his early twenties had worked in a plastics factory in Tripoli. He now helped out running a *souq* in the ferīkh, laying out their wares wherever there were gatherings.

So what can we ascertain from all these stories about social processes in general and the mobilities in which the Walad Djifir are involved? We have seen that the sending of money, namely remittances, connects family members but also geographical regions, cities, and villages. In addition, it seems to connect the formal/regulated and informal/unregulated networks of money transfer. There is a certain continuity in the way the newer methods have been appropriated by the Walad Djifir: the processes of moving away for whatever reasons are ongoing, but the means of staying in touch and thus also the sending back of money have become easier, safer. Not everyone makes use of this, however, and there are other issues as the cases show. Nevertheless, Walad Djifir mobility (and connectivity) persevere and have a place within the present-day contexts of a departed Qaddafi, a disrupted CAR, or even within the context of Chad's modernizing economy.

***

How is it that the Walad Djifir seem to embrace such a technology as the digital transfer of money fairly easily? Can this embracing be seen as creating a new social fabric, or is it merely a continuation of earlier patterns but in a new guise, so to speak?[18] The answer lies somewhere in the way the Walad Djifir deal with risk in general. They live in an environment strongly informed by an insecurity fed by the general, frequent occurrence of crises and the oppressive character of the Chadian state.[19] Such an environment, coupled with a certain type of behaviour when making decisions, reveals the importance of trust and mistrust – namely, a trust which is based on the evaluation of risk and which is closely demarcated along familial lines.[20]

As Chapter Two has shown, the politics in which the majority of the sub-group are involved are more often than not of the more immediate and local kind, involving leadership rivalries at the level of the familial and tribal *chefferie*. However, in

---

18 See de Bruijn et al. (2010) on the directions of social change linked to the appropriation of the mobile phone in Cameroon's Bamenda Grassfields – power relations were affected while at the same time people were shaped by and shaping the mobile phone; Elliot (2010) on social ties not being lost but changed and adapted in the context of camel milk commodification in Eastleigh, Kenya among the Somali diaspora.

19 See Roitman (2005); Seli (2012).

20 See Debos (2016) on the ethnicization of men under arms during colonial rule and the general hardening of formerly fluid ethnic and religious identities, including the polarization of the north–south divide. The reinvention and fixing of identities was continued during the civil war (1979–1982) and continues up until today.

making adaptations to their livelihood, Walad Djifir seem to have a certain knack for finding economic niches in otherwise dangerously insecure environments, such as the one in Libya – thus taking part, however indirectly, in resulting displacement economies. Their approach to sending money may be seen as an extension of these strategies, making use of the technologies and networks at hand while basing decisions on experiences and perceptions of mistrust. The Walad Djifir are flexible in their adaptation to changes such as those brought on by technological developments, which in turn is a continuity of former ways of doing and being.

These factors combined mean that the technology of sending money digitally, over distances and in contexts of insecurity, has been adopted relatively easily by the Walad Djifir. It fits within their nomadic-pastoral 'walk of life' (Chapter Four), building on networks of (mis)trust and an inherent need to be flexible. They have adopted the technology, however, in their own specific way, incorporating aspects such as the use of merchants and family members – revealing again the centrality of (mis)trust which, in Chad, often translates into the use of one's own networks. Remittances as connector thus seem to strengthen relations, and ensuing actions, of trust and mistrust – and in so doing, also strengthen that which the ferīkh embodies. One could argue that a certain groundedness in this way of dealing with the 'outside' world, based on both trust and mistrust, is key.

Chapter 6
Family and belonging in times of crisis

The first encounter with Bangui-born Nour was a somewhat casual one in October 2011. On our arrival in the ferīkh toward the late afternoon, I had accompanied Adoum in giving our best wishes to a sick woman. She had been lying in the shade of a tent, covered by a heavy blanket. Later in the evening, it was this same woman that accompanied me to empty my bladder *en brousse*. It was only when I came to live in Nour's tent in February 2012 that I was able to connect the dots and realize those women had been one and the same – namely, Nour. At the first encounter in 2011, she had been with the family in the ferīkh for about a year, and she was often feeling poorly. By February 2012, she was doing a lot better, taking a more active part in the household duties while at times still suffering from bad days. She would often recount the types of food one could eat in CAR, laughing aloud at the questions asked by the other women. She would exclaim, 'Uh! There is so much choice every day. Fresh fruit like papaya, corn . . . .' In private conversation she explained that in the beginning she had tried to change the mentality of the women she lived with in terms of hygiene and methods of cooking. Her attempts had been unsuccessful, as the women's responses were, more often than not, to listen, shrug their shoulders, and continue as they always had. 'I might have been able to "teach" them a few things,' she said, 'but not much.' The best way to try to change this, according to Nour, is to talk to the young men. Even if it is just to one or two of them, it might change things slowly.[1]

***

Nour Moustapha was born and raised in urban Bangui to a Chadian mother and father. Upon the death of her father, which followed the passing of her mother two years previously, she was sent to live with her father's family in a ferīkh just north of Mongo. She arrived in this rural Chadian setting in September 2010, with two young sons in tow. In the ferīkh she would stay with her husband's father and paternal uncle Moussa (see Chapter Four), her paternal uncle Hadj Saleh, and their wives Khachana and Khadidja respectively (see Family Tree in Figure 1). Her husband,

---

1 From fieldnotes, 3 March 2012.

Note: Parts of this chapter have been adapted from a piece written for the 'Connecting in Times of Duress' website, published in the form of a web dossier on CAR on 14 January 2015 and comprising pieces by myself and colleagues Catherina Wilson and Adamou Amadou; http://www.connecting-in-times-of-duress.nl/wd-car-unexpected-forces-that-shape-chadian-citizenship-from-fluid-to-fixed-belonging/, accessed 12 January 2018.

https://doi.org/10.1515/9783110714685-006

Youssouf, stayed behind in a village in south-eastern CAR, running the business her father had left behind. In the course of 2012, Nour would return to the village in CAR, only to flee again in the spring of 2013. Nour's story is somehow always linked to the solidarity with – and adherence to – family. Despite initially finding the women's ferīkh-ways unlike her own, being in the ferīkh with her family helped her get through a depression following the death of her father. Unfortunately, she was to encounter more personal hardship in the years to follow. This chapter is an attempt to unravel what lies behind a certain groundedness people like Nour seem to feel despite and amid periods of disruption. Where do connectivity, family, and belonging play a role? And what is overlooked when framing these situations as crisis?

Mobility, disruption, and family

The Walad Djifir's socio-economic network reveals historical patterns of change and continuity within the connectors through which it spreads and is made use of. Building on the idea of the ferīkh as embodying such networks and thus personifying space within a transnational setting, through the various connectors, this chapter both takes us away from and returns us to the physical setting of the ferīkh and Chad in general, through the narratives of three Chadian women born and raised in CAR: Nour, Howwa, and Raouda. Due to the many similarities and differences in their stories, these three women provide an ideal analytical entrance into dynamics related to family, belonging, and crisis. The stories of the men in Nour's life – Hadj Saleh, Youssouf, Adoum, Moussa – have to a large extent been told in the previous chapters. It is now 'her turn', as my four-year-old would say. At the same time, this chapter questions what could be a fairly linear way of thinking by comparing Nour's story with that of two other female family members born and raised in Bangui: Howwa and Raouda (see the Family Tree in Figure 4). Setting her story next to those of these two other women provides context and reflective insights related to the role of family and (economic and social) wealth (Bonfiglioli 1988), vis-à-vis gendered flexibility.

Crisis narratives?

In their introduction, Graw and Schielke (2012) suggest turning toward the personal and existential dimensions – that is, the expectations and experiences of migration – in order to understand 'what makes migration such a compelling path'. They explain how more existentially sensitive ways of researching and analysing migratory processes may be crucial to perceiving and understanding what is most central about migration to the individuals and societies involved. In our view, such a more existentially sensitive perspective is helpful in understanding that houses (and the family ties they represent) may be more central to migration than boats, people more central than money, expectations more, or at least equally, important than regulations and border regimes. (p. 9)

Recognizing that these propositions are made within a context of primarily 'voluntary' migration – even if determining to what extent we can speak of there really being a choice is complicated – they can be extended to other forms of mobility, such as not only to the forced migration observed after the CAR coup of 2013, but also to the idea of groundedness, whereby 'houses', people, and expectations play a crucial role. The search for what is central to forms of mobility can also be applied to other explanatory narratives of contemporary situations: narratives of diverse insecurities in the Lac Chad basin (Chauvin et al. 2020), the (non)violence of youth in CAR (Both et al. 2022), and narratives describing the nature of social responses to pastoral poverty and illness (de Bruijn 1999). Examining these three women's daily life choices, decisions, and expectations in the context of the CAR coup's aftermath – vis-à-vis mobility, disruption, and social relations – ultimately raises questions related to the position of agency and structure.

Social relations are shaped by external factors, while also shaping the interpretations of these same factors. This chapter's connector of focus is 'family', which it approaches in its function as both technology of connecting various people over distances and in terms of the networks it embodies (Strathern 1996). To Walad Djifir, family is kin – that is, the blood relatives and their intricate family trees which exist through a preference for cross-cousin marriages.[2] Analytically, family is interpreted as a social construct that enforces or strengthens the bond among and within kin.

For each of the three women, the diverse natures of the relations with their kin have had different implications in terms of the degree to which they are 'bounded' by family, as a source of support and constraint. 'Family' as a resource thus seems to create and recreate forms of compartmentalization in society,[3]

---

[2] See Holy (1974: 49–70) on the distinction between different social groups among the Berti of Darfur, i.e. of kinship and territorial groups, with membership of one or the other entailing different rights and duties vis-à-vis social reproduction and economic production, as well as within political and ritual spheres. Holy distinguishes further between different groups of relatives, a distinction which I did not explore in the context of the Walad Djifir. Such further study would be interesting, adding a level of detail to the analysis of this chapter. At the same time, such specificity would most probably not alter its main argument.

[3] See de Bruijn & van Dijk (2012) on connectors as resource.

informed by gender hierarchies and wealth. But when can such compartmentalization be interpreted as entailing 'constraint', or perhaps even 'duress', for those individuals undergoing it? One of the underlying queries of this chapter is the wish to understand to what extent narratives of mobility, disruption, and family – within a context of the CAR coup's aftermath – can be framed or interpreted in reference to 'crisis'? This touches upon debates about the family as a violent institution (Scheper-Hughes 1993, 2008); enduring forms of constrained agency (duress, de Bruijn & Both 2018; conflict mobiles, Wilson Janssens 2019); social relations, security, intentional action, and crisis (von Benda-Beckmann & von Benda-Beckmann 1994; de Bruijn 1994; Johnson-Hanks 2005; Both 2017); and ordinary or everyday violence (Bouju & de Bruijn 2014; Das 2007). In choosing such an approach, what lines of enquiry are assumed, and which lines then become discarded or overlooked (Roitman 2013)?

This chapter sketches how three women have navigated through changing and continuous insecurities, within the context of the CAR coup's aftermath, and the role of family as a possible factor of disruption and solidarity – ultimately acting as both a connector and disconnector in relation to their Chadian origins. By narrating the stories of three extended family members born and raised in CAR – namely those of Nour, Raouda, and Howwa – this chapter addresses whether particular situations of distress work as a type of amplifier of the way social relations are structured and thus also as an amplifier of the duress (or solidarity) they can create?

The angle with which this period in history is approached is from the perspective of the Walad Djifir. Nevertheless, some context is necessary to understand the nature of Chadian presence in CAR, before delving into the stories of the three women. Who are these people that have become both victims and perpetrators in an immensely complicated conflict – what are their stories of belonging, in relation to nationality, citizenship, and familial roots?

The nature of Chadian presence in CAR

Chad and CAR are linked not only through various forms of conflict and political support; between the two territories there is a long relationship of exchange in the form of cross-border family ties, trade networks, and resource exploitation. In pre-colonial times, different empires united or divided the region, with slave raids greatly impacting the demographic make-up of current-day CAR (Marchal 2015). Under the reign of the French as the Afrique Equatoriale Française (AEF), established in 1910, the territory was governed as one military region. The division between

Chad and CAR in 1958[4] started a period in which questions of nationality gained meaning, and categories of strangers and migrants were increasingly part of the social landscape. Nevertheless, when colleague Souleymane[5] and I visited Bangui in 2012, the capital city came across as a cosmopolitan town housing people of various roots and nationalities. Chauvin (2009) describes this cosmopolitanism as existing prior to the inter-ethnic tensions which erupted in 1996. Under this cosmopolitan appearance, imbalances between ethnic groups could be perceived in terms of the distribution of staff at the neighbourhood and city levels.

The information presented here is based on interviews and conversations with Chadians living in Bangui in October and November 2012. An open question-naire was also carried out among ninety men and women of Chadian origin. The oldest woman who answered the questions was in her nineties and had come to CAR around 1940, having been adopted by her aunt at the time. She later moved to Bangui upon her marriage. The youngest were students in their early twenties who had moved to Bangui for their studies at the University of Bangui. The survey was carried out by myself, Souleymane, and four Chadian students of Bangui University: a linguist, sociologist, anthropologist, and medical student. As the students had been born or raised in Bangui, they had connections with Chadians of various generations within their neighbourhoods, family networks, and at the university. Souleymane and I targeted specific people we had heard about or met through others, as well as in areas known to host Chadians, such as specific groups of *forgerons* (metalworkers) in the Sara neighbourhood. Souleymane was also able to approach elderly men, many of them ex-soldiers, frequenting a mosque close to where he was lodged in Miskeen.

Past and recent reasons for migrating to CAR

In the case of those of Chadian origin, we met people with ties to various regions and ethnic groups – Sara, Kanembu, Salamat, Oudaiian – and whose travel histories had begun in the twentieth century. Some Chadians came as soldiers, forced labourers, or merchants in the time of the AEF. Men came looking to set up trade in the time of Bokassa, while one woman remembers coming into CAR, following her new

---

4 The Oubangui-Chari (Central African Republic) as independent from France came into being under Boganda in December 1958.
5 Dr. Souleymane Adoum Abdoulaye is an historian who, at the time, was working on his PhD (Souleymane 2017). We carried out fieldwork together at different times between 2012 and 2014 in Bangui, and in and around Mongo.

husband, on the day Habré became president (1982).[6] In the more recent context of CEMAC, travel and commerce are (officially) made easier over national boundaries. In practice, it is still considered an expensive challenge to travel overland between Chad, Cameroon, and CAR, and many we spoke to in Bangui mentioned the discrimination toward those of Chadian origin and the large number of roadblocks (*formalités*) where one always has to pay a certain amount to get through.[7] Nevertheless, and over time, the relative openness and permeability of the border have helped people to make a living and to feel both Chadian and Centrafricain. What, then, happened to these 'cosmopolites' when in 2013 the Séléka alliance descended on the capital[8] and when, in the following months, national origins and boundaries seemed to become more pertinent?

When I was visiting in 2012, Chadian merchants from all walks of life seemed to have found a niche importing all sorts of wares in bulk. In a corner shop in the neighbourhood Cinq Kilo, also known as Kilometre Cinq (KM5), you would find a former Chadian rebel soldier selling hardware – screws, bolts, any sort of iron, paints; another 'common' man selling jerrycans of cooking oils and construction materials; young men outside, their stalls filled with medicines; individual entrepreneurs importing jewellery from as far away as Nigeria; and both men and women selling spices and produce such as onions and garlic. The latter are grown in Chad itself. In a special side section of Cinq Kilo, one could find the Souq Soudanais, which is in fact run predominantly by Chadian women and some men. Here you would find colourful scarves, the perfumes which Chadian women love, a large array of spices such as cardamom, cloves, and cinnamon, and coffee, dates, and other dried goods. Some women sell honey, a typical Centrafricain product. The area seemed to thrive and bustle with sellers and buyers milling around each other. However, Chadian merchants and vendors complained that it had become more difficult to get by, saying that over the years competition had grown and there were now more locals taking up commercial activities.[9]

---

6 Conversation with an elderly woman, of Misseria origins, working as a merchant at the Souq Soudanais in Bangui, 30 November 2012.

7 For an IPIS study on the presence of roadblocks in DRC and CAR, see: http://ipisresearch.be/2017/12/roadblock-rebels-ipis-maps-important-mechanism-conflict-funding-central-africa/, accessed 16 January 2018. 'IPIS puts roadblocks on the map as key mechanism of conflict funding besides natural resources, revealing its devastating scope in funding armed actors in Democratic Republic of Congo and Central African Republic'. See also Peer Schouten's book *Roadblock Politics* (2022).

8 For an overview and background of CAR political history leading up to the coup and its aftermath, see Lombard (2014); Carayannis & Lombard (2015); Lombard (2016); Chauvin (2018).

9 Based on separate conversations with Espérance, Ahmed, and Howwa (fieldnotes, 29 October 2012 and 9 November 2012). For an historical view of the evolution of commercial practices in the Oubangui and Bangui between 1930 and 1945 specifically, see the Master's thesis by Michel Azou-

Apart from reasons of economic migration (see Chapter Four), many young Chadians came to Bangui to continue their higher education.[10] The reasons given were several: the level of education is higher than in Chad; the cost of living is relatively cheap; there is less corruption at the level of the university; and there are more possibilities for students to succeed. A distinction must, however, be made between male and female students. Espérance, a woman in her forties who had first come to Bangui to study sociology and who has since stayed and made her life there, recounted the sexual intimidation by professors in return for good grades. Among the students who answered the questionnaire, a number of them stated that they were grateful for the opportunity the University of Bangui offered to them in terms of furthering their studies and receiving a diploma. They hoped it would increase their chances of finding work. Several would like to become integrated in Chad so as to secure a position as a civil servant. Others were hoping to work as either teachers or in the profession they were studying – ranging from geography, to modern languages, history, sociology, anthropology, and medicine. Students mentioned it being difficult to be away from family, with some not receiving much financial support. They also referred to the harassment of mostly those of Chadian origin by police, who ask them to pay 'fines' even when they possess the correct papers for staying in CAR.

Mixed sentiments: The duality of national identity and belonging

In a conversation with Howwa's little brother, a student in computer science at the time, he spoke of the discrimination toward Chadian students at the university. According to him, Chadians always get graded down. His Centrafricain friend said he was exaggerating, while another Chadian friend said, 'We Chadians all know it's true.' These young men are second-generation Chadians in CAR and often feel harassed. Following my questions, a discussion on adopting the CAR national identity ensued. Their parents had chosen to keep their Chadian ID papers. They themselves now had the choice of what to do. Howwa's little brother had not applied for CAR ID papers and his friends wondered why. 'No,' he said, 'I'm a Chadian.' 'Yes,' said the others, 'but you have a right to them because you were born here.' He did not

zou (1999), in which he asks why CAR has neither purely Centrafricain commercial companies or enterprises nor large local merchants but instead relies heavily on foreigners.
10 See Chauvin (2018) for a study of economic, political, and social relations between Chad and CAR and the escalation into outright violence. Chapter 3 of his report discusses the contemporary migration of Chadians into CAR.

agree with this logic, saying that even though he may officially have a right to these papers, he did not want them. 'I am Chadian. At birth, my father went to register me at the Chadian embassy [here in Bangui].'[11]

During these and other conversations held in Bangui in October and November 2012, and based on the questionnaire, a few themes surfaced which touch upon belonging, (national) identity, and being strangers. Those of Chadian origin, who had spent most of their adulthood in CAR, complained about the recent waves of Chadians coming in. 'They don't respect the Centrafricain ways; they act like they are still in Chad and that this is okay. They should adapt; they need to adapt to their host country.' Most Chadians who have spent a considerable amount of their life in CAR, many being born and raised there, have a double nationality and speak fluent Sango. 'Things are a bit better now than before. Before we would get harassed and stopped on the street all the time [by the authorities]. If you don't speak Sango, it is very hard. And even with a Centrafricain identity [card], if they see your name is Muhammed or Mahammed – you know, a Muslim name – they will make it more difficult for you.'[12] This I also heard from those travelling through CAR from Chad when they encountered the many roadblocks. Despite these sentiments, most did also have strong feelings of Bangui and CAR being their home. As Espérance, who came to Bangui in 1994 from southern Chad, put it, 'I have lived through a lot in CAR and given it a lot. The country owes me.' She will not leave, not after everything she has invested and lost in CAR. Espérance is referring here to the times she was caught under French fire when still studying to become a nun in 1996; to the numerous times her possessions were looted when she took up a study in sociology after quitting the nunnery, her schoolbooks being burnt following the harassments during another wave of attacks on Chadian university students in the late 1990s (Chauvin 2018); and to the other harassments against those of Sara origin (a group found primarily in southern Chad) at the time that Patassé (president of CAR between 1993 and 2003) had to ask the Congolese rebel leader Jean-Pierre Bemba for help in 2002.[13]

It was rumoured that Patassé had Sara origins, speaking the same language and belonging to the same ethnic group. This made it dangerous for Sara to be living in

---

11 Conversations recorded in fieldnotes, 15 November 2012.

12 Conversations with Chadian students and shop owners born and raised in Bangui (fieldnotes, 9 and 15 November 2012).

13 Based on numerous conversations with Espérance (fieldnotes, 14 November 2012). See Carayannis (2008: 9) and Chauvin (2018: 34) for more on Patassé and Bemba's alliance. In the summer of 2018, Bemba was liberated. Catherina Wilson wrote a blog on this surprise liberation on 8 June 2018, http://rumoursontheubangui.tumblr.com/post/175025198512/the-bemba-surprise-version-20, accessed 19 June 2018.

Bangui at the time.[14] Simultaneously, in these early 2000s, Chadians predominantly working in the cattle industry were being violently targeted by Abdoulaye Miskine's militias, on behalf of Patassé. These Chadian merchants and pastoralists were accused of helping road robbers (*coupeurs de route*) and of supporting Bozizé's rebellion (Chauvin 2018: 58). Over time, Chadians of mixed backgrounds – whether Christian, Muslim, from the south, or from the north of Chad – have been targeted from various angles, depending on the current political alliances (Marchal 2015). In 2003 Bozizé was helped to power by Chadian president Déby, probably contributing to the more recent experiences of Chadians – like those students above – finding CAR authorities a little easier to deal with. Nevertheless, the stories of people such as Espérance and others we spoke to reveal how many long-time Chadians in CAR continue to feel some form of belonging with the country and its people.

This duality of belonging and identifying with both CAR and Chad was put to the test in an extreme way following the ousting of Bozizé in March 2013. It is said that a few months before the coup – while Souleymane and I were still in Bangui, in fact (October 2012) – numerous jeeps and trucks containing Chadian forces had been seen leaving the city, forces that had been put in place by Déby to protect and maintain Bozizé in power. Their departure paved the way for rebel advancement on and ultimately capture of Bangui. The coup itself was relatively non-violent. Its aftermath, unfortunately, was not, with waves of violence escalating between several different parties.[15] In the media, this was often attributed to the anti-Balaka ('*les fils du pays*') protecting the population from the Séléka forces responsible for the coup.[16] It did not help that among the Séléka were many of Chadian origin. Nor did it help that the Chadian government had played, and still does play, such an ambiguous role in CAR (Marchal 2015; Chauvin 2018). Déby had helped Bozizé into power in March 2003 and subsequently let him fall upon removing his security forces stationed in

---

14 Sara-Kaba, according to Chauvin (2009). Chauvin further mentions the Karako as one of the four militias Patassé armed and which were all located in Bangui's northern neighbourhoods. These groups were often a mixture of civilians and military and belonged to ethnic groups close to the president. In Bangui, groundnuts (*karako* in Sango) are associated with people coming from the north of CAR (i.e. southern Chad).

15 For context on the violence that evolved between Séléka, anti-Balaka, and peace forces, see Käihkö & Utas (2014); Mayneri (2014); Weyns et al. (2014); de Vries & Glawion (2015); Chauvin (2018). See also the chapter by Kilembe (2015) on 'Local dynamics in the PK5 district of Bangui' and Wilson's (forthcoming) detailed description and analysis of events leading up to and after the coup from the perspective of people in Bangui itself.

16 See Wilson Janssens (2019: 86) for more on possible origins of other such movements historically.

Bangui in late 2012.[17] Déby then sent in Chadian troops as part of the MISCA[18] to help stabilize the country, together with Rwandan and Burundi forces. After much under-standable protest from within CAR and the international community, the Chadian peace-keepers were withdrawn at the beginning of 2014 (Chauvin 2018). Aside from the complicated political role Chadians have played in CAR, the economic positions of civilians of Chadian origin may also have aggravated the population (see Chapter Four this volume, 'Cattle and commerce: politics and economic changes').

The lives of Howwa, Raouda, and Nour have evolved within the contexts de-scribed above. Howwa's primary address was in Miskeen, and she worked in the middle of Cinq Kilo – which would later become an almost impregnable space within Bangui. From conversations with colleague Catherina Wilson, who visited Bangui in the spring of 2018, I understand that since 2014 it has become impossible, as a foreigner, to arrive in Cinq Kilo. Many Muslims and Chadians left, especially at the beginning of 2014 after Djotodia left his post and the Chadian contingent of the MISCA was sent away (Chauvin 2018: 37). In fact, even the Chadian embassy in Bangui was closed for a couple of years.

Raouda lived along one of the main roads leading up to Cinq Kilo, her business and relative wealth giving her access to certain levels of political protection while at the same time making her very vulnerable. The murder of her father (described in Chapter Four) was said to have been done on Habré's orders. Like Raouda, Nour's life had been crafted by her father's economic endeavours in CAR. At the same time, her socio-economic position was different from that of her cousin, not having the political connections or relative freedom of possessing her own wealth. The stories below show how a variety of mundane and extraordinary aspects of the contexts sketched above surfaced in the everyday lives of the three women, requiring actions and reactions. How these actions and reactions to disruptive events were shaped or anchored[19] to the more mundane parts of life is something this chapter explores.

---

17 Marchal (2015: 184) writes that it was Bozizé himself who sent home 'the few dozens of Chadian soldiers who were his personal guards to prove that whoever was to be blamed, they were Chadi-an'. From about 2006, political relations between CAR and Chad had started unwinding, partly as a result of Sudanese and Chadian insurgencies. See Marchal (2015) for a more detailed analysis.
18 MISCA: Mission Internationale de Soutien à la Centrafrique sous Conduite Africaine. 'MISCA is a Mission set up by the Peace and Security Council (PSC) of the African Union with the full support of the United Nation[s]. It was established on 5 December 2013 by a resolution of the United Na-tions Security Council (Resolution 2127) to stabilize conflict in the country following a coup d'etat in March 2013. The Mission, led by the African Union and backed by the UN, was deployed on 19 December 2013.' Source: MISCA, http://misca.peaceau.org/en/page/110-about-misca, accessed 19 June 2018.
19 See Das (2007) on extraordinary life events having 'tentacles' anchoring them to the more mun-dane aspects of life.

Three women, three stories

Raouda, Nour, and Howwa have spent the largest part of their lives in CAR. They were in their twenties to forties (in 2011–2014) and consider 'Centrafrique' as their home. Raouda and Nour are second-generation immigrants, while Howwa belongs to the third generation of her family living and working in Bangui. All three women are of Chadian Arab origin, hailing from various nomadic groups in central and eastern Chad, with specific familial ties to the Misseria Rouge and its Walad Djifir sub-group. The ways in which they have lived in CAR vary, as do their ties to their country of origin and the way they have navigated familial, local, and regional politics during the ongoing conflict. Their experiences (and futures) are entangled with those of friends and family on both sides of the national border. In this conflict, there is no clear 'good' or 'bad' side, and all members of the Centrafricain population have suffered its consequences.

Nour was born as the first and only child of her father and mother. Her mother would go on to have more children in her second marriage. Her father would never marry again. While Nour was born and raised in Bangui in the late 1980s, her father Moustapha had grown up living as many Walad Djifir do, amidst ferīkh life. Moustapha ʿUmar was one of many siblings, and after having tried his hand at a Qurʾānic school in the town of Ati – and having been denied a girl's acceptance in marriage – he decided to follow in the footsteps of a maternal uncle and try his luck in CAR.[20] This uncle, Tchoudja, had left for CAR in the 1960s and had by now set up a relatively successful business as a merchant. Tchoudja had travelled to Bangui with cattle, first setting up as a livestock trader before moving on to other goods. This Tchoudja is the father of the second woman whose story we tell: Raouda. Tchoudja belonged to the Sulmani group and was a brother of Hadj Saleh's mother (see Family Tree in Figures 3 and 4). In that sense Raouda is not a blood-related cousin of Adoum, except through marriage into the family. Adoum's mother and Hadj Saleh's father were brother and sister. Raouda's aunt, her mother's youngest sister, married Nour's father, with Nour marrying Raouda's brother during her first marriage. Howwa, in turn, is related to Raouda through their fathers' side – their fathers were brothers (Family Tree in Figure 4).

---

20 It is unclear when Nour's father made the move to CAR, but it was probably some time in the 1970s. Tchoudja went to CAR in the 1960s and was assassinated in the early 1980s (see Chapter Four). From the stories I heard, it seems that Nour's father worked with Hadj Tchoudja for some time before the latter's death.

Nour

Nour was raised in urban Bangui in relative luxury compared with life in a ferīkh, living in a house and surrounded by both close and extended family members. As most Arab Chadians in CAR, she grew up speaking Sango, Chadian Arabic, and some French. Her father had married the younger sister of Hadji Fadimatou, the wife of Tchoudja. This younger sister, Zarga, had been a mere child (not even a teenager) when she had begged to accompany Hadji Fadimatou from Chad to CAR. For Hadji Fadimatou, Tchoudja was her second husband. The marriage between Nour's father, Moustapha, and her mother did not last; and even while they were married, Nour lived with her mother in Bangui. She recounted how the first time she met her father she was ten years old. When she speaks of him, it is with great fondness. Her father always told her he would look after her and never denied her anything. Her father conducted business between Bangui and Berberati, only occasionally making the trip into the capital to see his daughter. After her parents divorced, her mother remarried and had several more children, allowing Nour to grow up with four half-sisters and one half-brother, the Benjamin of the family.

At a fairly young age she was married to Tchoudja's son, Ahmed. It must have seemed like an ideal way to strengthen family ties, and Nour and Ahmed had practically grown up together. She bore a son to him who was named after his grandfather, Tchoudja. The marriage, however, ended in divorce.[21] Currently, Nour is married to her first cousin, Youssouf Moussa. He is the son of her father's younger brother Moussa (see Chapter Four) and was born and raised in a Chadian ferīkh. By 2014, they had had three children: Moussa (7), Saleh (5), and a girl named after Nour's mother: Zarga, born in 2013. Upon marrying Youssouf, she moved to the village of Sassileh, a full day's drive west of Bangui where Youssouf was being taught her father's business. Nour's father Moustapha had started out working for his maternal uncle Tchoudja and had, over the years, acquired businesses ranging from 'boutiques' selling an array of goods in several CAR villages to owning and renting out houses. He also owned land in Berberati, CAR and in Moundou, Chad. Unfortunately, only two years after her mother's death, Nour's father became ill. When it became clear his illness was a serious one, he was brought to Fadjé, where he passed away not long afterward in 2009.[22] He lies buried in the common burial grounds next to the village of Tchoufiou II Arabe.

---

21 One cannot help but ask what life Nour would have had if she had stayed with her first husband, the well-to-do, urban-living son of her father's maternal uncle? How different would her life have been? What decisions would she have faced and from what position?

22 It is difficult to put an exact time on events as such, but the reasoning for 2009 is as follows: Her father was alive when she married Youssouf, as it was he who forced her: 'either you marry him or

Photo 6.1: Photo of Nour and her mother Azehera, taken in Bangui (printed 5 February 1985) and kept amongst Nour's possessions.

With Moustapha's passing, his brother Hadj Saleh became responsible for the distribution of the inheritance (Introduction and Chapter Four). As her father's only child, and in accordance with Islamic law, Nour was to receive one-third of the inheritance. Hadj Saleh is a younger brother of both Moustapha and Moussa, making him an uncle to Nour and Youssouf. He had been working alongside Moustapha, spending time in Bangui and Sassileh. Over the past few years, Hadj Saleh has been managing the investments Moustapha had made in CAR, selling the majority and keeping others. Apart from shops, land, and property, their capital is in the form of livestock herded by the pastoral-nomadic group known as Mbororo. In order not to

---

you are no longer my daughter', as she recounted to me in one of our many conversations. Assuming they must have had Moussa not too long afterward and he was five in 2012, he would have been born some time in 2008. In 2012 she said her mother had died five years before (2007) and her father three years before, meaning that it would have been some time in 2009. Nour was supposedly about twenty-three when we met in 2011, although later I had the feeling she may have been older.

incur the wrath of these herdsmen by selling all the cattle at once – people believe strongly in witchcraft, especially in relation to the Mbororo – he has been selling a few at a time.[23] In 2010, Nour came to stay with her father's family in the ferīkh, together with her two youngest children.

Photo 6.2: Cooking and living area with Nour's children's laundry hanging out to dry in the distance, Fadjé, March 2012.

Family disruptions

Over the many afternoons and evenings that followed my stay in the ferīkh between February and June 2012, I was slowly able to piece together the story of Nour and to recognize the moments in which she was feeling down. I sometimes felt bad asking her about her past, as I noticed that the next day she would often have one of her bad days, sleeping away most of the day and complaining of a bad headache. It was on one of these bad days that I asked her what was wrong. For weeks we had been

---

23 The reference to witchcraft and the Mbororo was made during a conversation with Raouda and Adoum in N'Djaména, fieldnotes, 26 February 2013. Adoum claimed the Mbororo had put a spell on Nour's father, making him ill. Why they would do so I did not discover. From other conversations it seemed that Nour's father had a good relationship with those herding his cattle, often providing them with shoes and clothes. Adoum said the family had been afraid that they would put a spell on Hadj Saleh once they discovered he was pulling out of business with them.

talking about when she would return to CAR. She desperately wanted to but refused to ask Hadj Saleh about it, preferring to keep silent. Nour felt it was up to him to take the lead and allow her to go home. She had not seen her half-siblings[24] and those she had grown up with for at least three years and missed them dearly, even if she had grown close to her ferīkh family. On this particular day, the conversation once again turned to her departure. It emerged that the family wanted her to leave one of her sons with his grandmother. She was to take only the youngest child back to his father, back to CAR. It was plain that she found this very difficult; nevertheless, once again, she refused to assert her own wishes. If this is what Hadj Saleh and her mother-in-law (Khachana) wanted for her and Moussa, the child, then it was what she would do.[25]

Her mother-in-law – who is simultaneously her aunt, through the latter's marriage to Nour's father's younger brother Moussa (see Family Tree in Figure 1; see also Chapter Four) – is a strong and sincere woman. Khachana wished to keep the child, as her own children had left the nest. The only one that remained was the youngest son Tāhir, about twelve years of age, for whom she would cook meals. As he was taking care of the cattle, however, he was hardly ever at home, sleeping *en brousse* with the herd. She desperately wanted a young child to care for and keep her company – one who could stay and look after the goats. Nour worried because whenever she had left Moussa with his grandmother Khachana before, he had always fallen sick. She believed in the goodness of her intentions but knew that Khachana would not care for him as she would. Nour had always made sure both her sons were scrubbed clean with water and soap at least once a day. She made sure they ate and drank well. Khachana would surely do the same but in a different fashion; she would raise him as she herself had been raised, a much harder way although not with any less love. As babies and toddlers, children are coveted, hugged, and played with. From the age of five, when they take up responsibilities such as taking care of the goats and sheep, a more distant relationship between them and adults begins. At times, they will still be taken onto someone's lap, but more often than not they are treated as young adults, expected to behave accordingly. Another thing that factors into this is that a mother only has so much room in her lap – siblings who cannot walk and need to hang near the breast most of the day end up taking precedence.

In this situation of finally being able to return to the country and family she had longed for, yet being asked to leave a child behind, she was torn. This manifested itself in days of lethargy, sleeping late and spending most of the day in a horizontal

---

24 Howwa and I visited two of Nour's half-sisters while we were in Bangui in October and November 2012. Both were married, one to a businessman/merchant of Chadian origin. I met up with her half-brother, on several occasions, in N'Djaména.
25 From fieldnotes, 17 April 2012.

position. She hardly participated in any of the household chores, complaining of headaches and heartburn while taking numerous doses of paracetamol. In the past seven years, she had lost both her father and mother and been made to give up her first-born child. By now leaving another child behind, not knowing when she would see him again, she was reliving and adding to old sorrows. After the death of her father in 2009 had left her orphaned, she had fallen into what one can only assume was a deep depression – she and others referred to her as being tired (*ta'bān*) and sick (*malade*) – and took to her bed. In this period it was Gallami who had stayed by her side and grieved his old friend with her. At the time of her father's death, she was already living in Sassileh with her second husband Youssouf. She had not seen the son she had borne to her first husband for several years,[26] as he was being raised in Bangui by her ex-husband's elder sister, Raouda. It is the custom for children to stay with their fathers upon a divorce.

The discussions on Nour's return to CAR seemingly went on between Hadj Saleh, Adoum, and Khachana, with Nour herself being called over to be told what was to happen and at times consulted for her opinion. She never made clear what she herself wanted. She did not want to leave Moussa behind, and yet she also did not want to upset his grandmother. She felt obliged to adhere to this custom.[27] It was clear it was taking an effect on her physically. Moussa would have so many more opportunities by going with his mother than if he were to stay in the ferīkh. Even though their nearest sedentary village, Tchoufiou II Arabe (Map 3), had opened a school in early 2012 and his uncle was on the 'board', he had never gone a single day. As a child in Sassileh, he had attended a type of kindergarten; and this is what Nour wanted for her sons – for them to be able to go to school to learn and play, and not for her five-year-old to spend half his day herding goats. I spent a lot of time with Nour, trying to discover what *she* was planning to do about the situation. During the duration of her stay in the ferīkh, she was always kept in the dark about when exactly she could return. This was a decision Hadj Saleh would make. Of course, there were many things involved, and women were often the last to find out about decisions made. In the case of Hadj Saleh, whom one member of the *ferīkh*

---

26 When I met her son in Bangui at Raouda's house in 2012, he seemed close to twelve years old. It may be that she did not return to Bangui after her re-marriage in Sassileh in 2007/8, so it is probable that she had not seen him in five years, with her son being eight at the time she left. This would make him thirteen in 2012 and fifteen when we met in 2014, which seems to fit.

27 I have to admit that I had heated discussions with Adoum at this stage. I mainly tried to understand why they would make her go through such difficult emotions once again. We argued, and he agreed with my interpretation that a child belongs with his mother. He in turn tried to make me see Khachana's perspective. In hindsight, the practicality of travelling to CAR overland with two young children, neither of whom probably had any official paperwork, would have been challenging (and expensive!).

conseil said is like the weather – always changing – the gender aspect here might have been irrelevant. As the *chef de ferīkh*, members of the community rely on Hadj Saleh's presence and opinions. He too had been away from home in CAR on numerous occasions, sometimes even for years at a time and, on finally returning, was not left to depart without any reluctance expressed by the others. Aside from this, there was the financial aspect of the trip. Hadj Saleh kept arguing that now was not the right time. Why exactly this was the case was difficult to determine, though it was probably linked to the care of the livestock (the many camels mentioned in Chapter Three) and to the time of year. He had also just resettled his wife and children in a remote region where they had little community support at hand when he was away. It may have been that he was waiting for more of the inheritance to be transferred from CAR before making the move.

Whatever the reasons, in May 2012 Nour left for CAR with her three-year-old son Saleh, leaving her five-year-old Moussa in the care of his grandparents. She was accompanied by Hadj Saleh. She told me that on her departure Moussa had said, 'Don't cry, mother. This is for the best. Grandmother needs me and I will be fine here.' She could not believe he had been so wise.

The first leg of the journey, from the ferīkh to N'Djaména, we travelled together. Their departure to CAR coincided with the finishing of my fieldwork period and thus with my return to the capital. We left the ferīkh to spend a night in Mongo, before continuing on to N'Djaména and arriving at Adoum's home.

In N'Djaména

Over the next few days, Hadj Saleh and Nour were to prepare for the next part of their trip. They initially stayed with Adoum and his family, but Nour was able to spend a few nights with some of her half-sisters and half-brother, her mother's children. They had been anxious to see her, having had little news about her well-being. In an earlier conversation with Abu Kawsar, her half-brother, he had asked me to show him a few photographs of what Nour looked like now. He was shocked by the physical marks ferīkh life had left on his half-sister. She had already had white spots on her neck and darker ones around her eye sockets where she had had a reaction to a perfume. She now also had a burn mark on her leg and calluses on her ankles from sitting on floor mats. When they met, he asked Nour why she had not been living in Mongo where her father had built a house. She explained she had only been 'in transit' in Mongo. Yes, there is a house there but it has not been completed yet. She had really only transited in Mongo and gone straight through to Fadjé, the local name for the area the ferīkh is in (Map 3). While looking at the photographs of Moussa and Saleh in the ferīkh, he seemed taken aback by the living conditions. He agreed, although not wholeheartedly, that the *barsh* (tent) was a large one. Abu

Kawsar wished she could spend more time with her half-siblings in N'Djaména and felt frustrated at not having a say in her well-being.[28]

Among those visited in N'Djaména was also Gallami. Gallami and Nour's father had met the very first time both were travelling to CAR. They had bonded on the journey, and many years later they remained close friends. The meeting at a large compound near Rue Quarante was clearly emotional for both her and Gallami. Usually living in south-eastern CAR, he was visiting family in Chad and so the house held a gathering of men, women, and young girls who had known Nour and her father. I accompanied Nour on this visit, and in my fieldnotes I wrote the following:

> Two evenings ago we went to visit a good friend of N's father. N tells me they were always together, her father and him. They had met on their way to CAR and were in the same line of work as merchants: cattle trade and boutiques. When her father passed away three years ago it was Gallami that spent four months by her side. When he heard the news of her father's death he says he lost two hours – he can't remember anything. (Fieldnotes, 16 May 2012)

Nour spent the evening chatting with the women while I listened to their conversations, frustrated at their mixed use of Sango and Arabic and not wanting to disturb too much of the reunion by asking for interpretations. Luckily, some of the younger girls spoke French and were patient enough to help when needed. At times they were jubilant and happy; at others the conversations turned to more serious happenings. Nour had brought little Saleh with her, and so all the women were constantly asking her where Moussa was and why she had left him behind. She explained that he was with his grandparents, that it was Hadj Saleh's decision, following with a mumbled phrase about Allah and it all being for the best. They had many questions about where she had lived, as most had origins in the ferīkh but had never grown up in one or even visited. She replied somewhat jokingly yet with a certain pride as well, quick to defend the perceived backward practices of ferīkh

---

28 At the time, Abu Kawsar had been in Chad for ten months and was about to finish his schooling. Like Nour he was raised in urban Bangui and not accustomed to the way of life *en brousse*. Being the Benjamin of four older sisters, he admits to being spoiled at home and being allowed to do as he likes. He had decided for himself that this was no longer good for him, as it was not helping him achieve all he could in school. Abu Kawsar therefore chose to come to N'Djaména to acquire his *bac*, with which he then hoped to study architecture abroad. We have maintained contact via Facebook, and toward the end of 2013 he took up a course in architecture in Guinea Conakry. By 2015 he had returned to Chad; his family could no longer afford his stay in Conakry. Due to the continued troubles in Bangui and CAR in general, his family had lost their business. In 2017, he was studying spatial planning at the university of Ati, followed by an internship for an NGO working in the area of conservation in one of Chad's national parks. The work suited and interested him, causing him to specialize in environmental planning and biodiversity. He is currently working his way through a research master on this subject in Douala, having exhausted the possibilities Chad had to offer.

women. She told them of how sick she had been in the beginning and how the first few months she had been unable to go to the bathroom. It had turned out to be the traditional *boule*,[29] to which her stomach was not accustomed, and so when occasion permitted she preferred *boule de riz* (rice). Cow milk was another product she learned to avoid.

During her stay in N'Djaména, Nour had been promised she would be able to visit a doctor for her heart, an ailment she had had since she was a child and one of the reasons she claims she cannot walk for very long. For a young woman, she is worryingly out of shape and fairly large. In the ferîkh, she often complained of heartburn and palpitations. She had been wanting a check-up because she was worried and wanted to know what was wrong. They had done tests when she was younger in Bangui, but nothing conclusive had been found. She hoped that the medical attention in N'Djaména might be more developed. We dropped them at the hospital early one morning only to be called back a few hours later. They would have to wait nine days before they could be seen. This was time that Hadj Saleh did not want to waste, and so it was decided they would get on with their journey and that Nour would get herself examined in Bangui after Ramadan.

Before returning to CAR, Nour wanted to purchase gifts for friends and family. As she did not possess any money of her own, she asked Hadj Saleh for 100,000 CFA of her father's inheritance. He refused but eventually conceded by giving her 65,000 CFA. Adoum, with whom they were still staying, was upset at the way Hadj Saleh was treating their niece and gave her an extra 24,000 CFA, which she initially refused. Adoum later told me, 'It is her father's money, the work of *her* father's cattle and boutique. Normally these earnings would be shared among family members. He [Hadj Saleh] did this before he left Fadjé, but he refused to give Nour her share – even after I had spoken to him.'[30] Adoum had spoken to Nour the morning before she went to the market, accompanied by his eldest daughter. He had told her he did not agree with Hadj Saleh but that she needed to keep her patience and stay calm. She would soon be reunited with her husband and able to take care of these kinds of business together. The business her father left now belonged to her and her husband, and it should not be the case that Hadj Saleh had a say over everything. Privately, he told me he used to respect Hadj Saleh as a good friend among the *parents*, but now ... '*Ça ne va pas.*' It is not normal. Nour returned from the market completely exhausted and with bags of presents. Among other things (jewellery and clothes), she had bought a thermos can and a stuffed black panther animal for

---

29 *Boule* is cooked like porridge and then rolled into a ball, accompanying different sauces. In this case it was most probably made of a type of sorghum. *Boule* can also be made from maize, millet, rice, cassava, or peanuts, depending on which crop is in season locally.
30 Fieldnotes, 15 May 2012.

little Saleh. Saleh did not take to the animal immediately and regarded it with much suspicion. I do not think he had ever really seen a fake animal before.

Sassileh

In early December 2012, after having spent several weeks in Bangui, I travelled to Nour's home in Sassileh, together with colleagues Souleymane and Mirjam while on our way to Cameroon. Due to a flat tyre and a wrong turn, the planned two nights had turned into one, allowing us only an afternoon and evening there. This was a shame, as we ended up missing Hadj Saleh by one day. He left Sassileh for Chad on the same morning we left Boda for Sassileh. I had tried to call him from Bangui and again from Boda, to let him know we were coming, but Sassileh does not have any mobile reception and I had been unable to reach him. The closest place with mobile phone reception is 50 km away.

The village of Sassileh itself is situated several hours' drive west from Boda, along the road to Gadzi (Map 2). It is spread out along both sides of the road running through it, and along another leading off to the south. A roundabout decorated the main road, with a drawing of a peace dove and the words 'rond-point de la paix'. The village seemed to be made up of a mixture of inhabitants, with people of Chadian origin like Nour and her family, as well as Central Africans.

Not long after our arrival we were asked by the village mayor, whom we went to greet, whether we wanted to see a diamond mine. Our curiosity got the better of us and not long afterward we were off. The two armed men who had been chosen to escort us became one, as both could not fit in the car. This escort directed us to a typical alluvial diamond mine, the car at times having trouble getting past the natural roadblocks, and we ended up walking part of the way. We were allowed to film and take pictures while there, which we did. There were many men and some women working at the site, alongside a handful of women and children to cook meals. The extraction process is labour-intensive, with a generator used to pump out water one of the only motorized tools. After having cleared the land of its many high trees, the miners dig until they reach a light-coloured layer of sand, all the while pumping out the ground water. This sandy layer is where the diamonds can be found. The sand is brought up and sieved in order to reveal any diamonds.

When we returned to Sassileh and asked Nour a bit about the mining process, she admitted that, yes, Youssouf too sometimes did a bit of trade as a *collecteur* (middleman), though not much. Hadj Saleh, however, had not. She laughed at my surprise, as diamonds had never been mentioned before during our times together. This indicates that the diamond business may either be such a common practice in the area – not special enough to mention, especially to those lower down in the production chain – and/or that those who are part of it do not scream it from the rooftops. Diamonds have different supernatural properties associated with them in different areas of CAR (Dalby 2015: 128). While Nour was keen to share what she knew about the business, she also said, 'The diamond is like the devil. If you find one – oof! – you can buy all the things in the world. But the money doesn't last. And if you find nothing even to eat [making a gesture of picking a tooth with her index finger and thumb], you won't find one thing.'[31]

Dalby (2015: 126–127) describes the general production chain in CAR as consisting of an *exploitant artisan* – a head miner – who employs a team of *ouvriers miniers* (diggers). Middlemen, such as Youssouf, in turn buy up diamonds from these head miners – who have a right to sell what their diggers find – and sell them on to *bureaux d'achat* (buying offices). The walls of compounds in the town of Boda, where we had spent the first night, were covered with the logos of various buying offices. Most of the diggers are of local origin, while the middlemen and those in the buying offices are primarily Arabic-speaking Muslims who have immigrated 'from Chad, West African countries such as Mali, Senegal and Mauritania, and Guinea, and also Lebanon' (Dalby 2015: 129). On our way to visit Sassileh, we were pulled across a river at the same time as one such Mauritanian *collecteur*, a young man who proudly showed us his wares. Upon visiting the mine close to Sassileh, however, we met several young men of Chadian origin working as diggers. They had come to the region as labour migrants, earning 2000 CFA a day (approx. 3 EUR). When they find diamonds, the diggers are given a finder's fee. Depending on the relationship with the head miner, they are sometimes allowed to keep and sell some of the diamonds.[32] It is possible that the dynamics Dalby (2015) describes, of primarily Arab Muslim outsiders being higher up the production chain, contributed in some way to the violence directed at them from December 2013 onwards. At the time of our visit, relations seemed amicable enough.

In hindsight, the driver (Sylvestre) had been ill at ease and anxious for us to leave quickly the following morning, perhaps picking up on tensions we did not perceive.[33] Nour, on the other hand, seemed very relaxed and at ease during our presence. She was living in the compound her father had built and which Hadj Saleh had added to in earlier years. She looked well, rested and healthy, the climate obviously agreeing with her more than that of the hot and arid ferîkh setting. Despite Hadj Saleh promising to take her to a doctor in Bangui, they had not passed

---

31 Filmed interview with Nour, Sassileh, 4 December 2012.

32 From conversations with a young Chadian miner, 4 December 2012.

33 He and Souleymane had been hosted across the road from Nour's compound, in what was described as the restaurant – an open hangar. As in Chad, men and women were to have their meals separately. Mirjam and I were invited into Nour and Youssouf's compound. Souleymane and Sylvestre did join us for a while later, when Youssouf returned from his shop and in between meals.

through the capital, instead going straight to Sassileh. She hoped she could make the visit to Bangui after Ramadan. Nour described how it was difficult to find food in Sassileh and that water was expensive to buy. At the time, the cost of one jer-ry-can (*bidon*) of water was 250 CFA, while in Mongo a similar amount cost 75 CFA. Surprisingly, the fairly lush surroundings of Sassileh, compared with the aridity of Mongo, did not mean that water was available close by. Those collecting water had to walk relatively far, while around Mongo it could be found at the surface (ferīkh) or at one of the deep wells.

Photo 6.3: The compound in Sassileh, December 2012. Nour's father built the first few buildings and Hadj Saleh later added to them. She was now living here with her husband and their youngest son. The building on the right housed the kitchen. The one in the middle was where Hadj Saleh stayed when he was there, and the one on the left was used for storage. She and Youssouf occupied the room from which this photograph was taken.

Her cousin Howwa had given us perfume to pass on to Nour to sell. I had bought corn flour from Howwa's grandmother in Bangui, for Nour to use. While showing us around the neighbourhood behind their compound, she was happy to let us film and take photographs, pointing out the variety of mushrooms and other edible veg-etation one could not find in Chad. She introduced us to many friends and neigh-bours, Fulani Mbororo and Chadians. They mostly spoke Sango together. On one occasion we met a man whom she referred to as *deuxième mon père*, 'my second father'. This Chadian man had come to CAR in the 1960s, from Am Timam, finding work in different places before settling down in Sassileh.

Photo 6.4: Youssouf's shop in Sassileh, December 2012. His shop was positioned along the main road going through Sassileh, and opposite their compound. Nour's father had also owned some land and houses which he had rented out. Youssouf bought most of his wares across the border in Cameroon. This was the first time we met each other and he seemed a little wary at first. I had heard his name mentioned so often by his mother Khachana and told him so. I think he was unsure of what I wanted from him and found it bizarre that I had spent time with Nour and his close family in the ferīkh and was now there, in Sassileh.

Youssouf's shop was across the road from their home. We were new to each other, Youssouf and I, even if he had heard about my presence in the ferīkh from Hadj Saleh and Nour. Youssouf was not as outgoing or at ease as Nour was, perhaps not really understanding what we were doing there. In his shop he sold a range of wares, such as fuel for the motorbikes and cars passing through, clothes, and beauty products. He explained how he bought the clothes from a large second-hand market in Cameroon, with the other merchandise also coming mainly from that direction.[34] When we asked him where he thought life was better, here or in the ferīkh, he replied, 'Here.' Later he nuanced this statement by saying that life was better in the ferīkh because of the presence of family there; but that in terms of making a living and the quality of life, it was better here in Sassileh. He would like to go and visit his family in Chad, but he preferred to live in Sassileh. Nour replied that she did not know. She liked life here and wished to visit her half-sisters in

---

34 From a filmed interview with Youssouf, Sassileh, 5 December 2012.

Bangui. If they moved back to Chad, she would want to live in a house in Mongo, as this would allow her children to go to school and not herd the livestock all day.

I could not discover why Nour's father had chosen Sassileh as a home for Youssouf and his daughter. Could it have been its location along one of the main roads in a mining region? He had started his business in Berberati, known to be a hub of buying offices, owning a house there. At one point, he had opened up a shop in Sassileh and, over time, bought up land in the village on which he built houses to rent out. After his death, Hadj Saleh had started selling these, as is the custom when dealing with an inheritance.

After our one night in Sassileh we headed onwards to the border town of Garoua-Boulaï in Cameroon. On the way we made a very brief stop in the middle of the road in the town of Geng to say hello to Gallami, the old friend of Nour's father. He was a jovial man, huge smiles, a right arm already outstretched in greeting – a tall man with an equally long and skinny face. He eagerly passed us a plastic bag with two large bottles of soft drink before waving us off.

Violent disruption

Fast-forward to almost a year later, February 2014, and the situation in CAR had only become worse. I was scheduled to carry out one last 'follow-up' field visit to Chad in February and March. Due to Chad's numerous roles and interests in CAR, the media was full of news about what was happening and the many donations that were being made by all sorts of actors. One local Chadian newspaper, for example, featured an announcement by Airtel of a donation of 10 million CFA, and staff were pictured on the front page, standing alongside the donated goods. One of the repercussions of the CAR violence had been a great influx of people of Chadian descent, whether recently migrated or having lived in CAR for several generations, into Chad.

In January 2014, amidst the bits and pieces of news that were being gathered together about loved ones in CAR, I learned that Gallami had been among the eleven people killed in Geng.[35] Nour had passed through Geng when she fled from Sassileh. They left because they had been warned, by whom is unclear, that it was getting 'hot'. She and her husband, with their two young children, had stayed with Gallami for a few days. It is here that Youssouf, Nour's husband, decided he would stay with their cattle, together with several other men. Nour and her children were

---

35 Geng is one of the villages one passes when travelling along the RN6 between Boda, Gadzi, and Carnot. On a fateful morning in January 2014, the village was attacked and eleven people were killed. It is not clear who the attackers were. What we do know is that they specifically targeted the Chadians living there. A (Muslim) Malian neighbour was spared.

sent on to Cameroon, arriving in a refugee camp in Kentzouh. The morning after Youssouf left Geng, the town was attacked. Gallami had stayed behind with his other guests. He could or did not want to leave them. The news reached family members in N'Djaména by way of a Malian neighbour and friend of Gallami. The Malian neighbour had been left unharmed; and as he had been a figure in the life of Gallami, he knew whom to contact in Chad (or perhaps the news travelled via Bangui first – I do not know). Of the eleven people killed, six were unidentifiable.[36]

When the news reached the ferīkh, it was feared that Youssouf was among the unidentified bodies. As *chef de ferīkh*, Hadj Saleh decided it would be best to hold a *dowtt*, a ceremony held for the deceased. The *dowtt* was carried out as planned, costing the family a lot in capital (cash and livestock). The morning after the ceremony, a phone call came in: Youssouf had been spotted *derrière son bétail*. There was no further explanation of how this had happened and what his status was. Before leaving, Youssouf had said they were planning to head south toward Congo–Zaire, as they call it, before turning and heading north along the Cameroonian border, up toward Chad. Family in Chad worried; they knew Youssouf was not carrying any weapons. They had discussed this over the phone when he was still debating whether or not to leave. The group that left were carrying sticks and the knives all Chadians own. Nothing automatic.

The return to Chad and family reunions
In March 2014, less than two years after her departure to CAR, Nour arrived in N'Djaména. The Chadian state had arranged for transportation to pick up their 'repatriates' and bring them back to their country of origin (see Figure 6). The buses left Kentzou in Cameroon and travelled via Garou-Boulai to Moundou in Chad and eventually on to N'Djaména. On arrival in N'Djaména, the passengers were dropped at a large petrol station not far from where the buses heading east leave. At 11 pm. Nour called her paternal uncle Adoum, who resides in the city. He knew she was on her way, as someone she was with in the refugee camp in Kentzouh had called. For the next few weeks, Nour and her children spent time recovering from the long journey, dealing with the stress of not knowing how her husband was faring. She alternated between living with Adoum and his family and with her cousin Raouda, who had also arrived in N'Djaména. Since Nour's marriage to Youssouf, Raouda had been taking care of her nephew (Nour's son from her first marriage). Nour had not seen her first-born son Tchoudja since he was eight years old. By now he had grown into a boy of fifteen years. Between Raouda and Adoum, decisions were made as to what would be best for Nour. They both felt she should stay in the capital for a

---

36 Phone conversation with Adoum, January 2014.

good few months before heading to the ferīkh. Family in the ferīkh were desperate to have her and her children back.

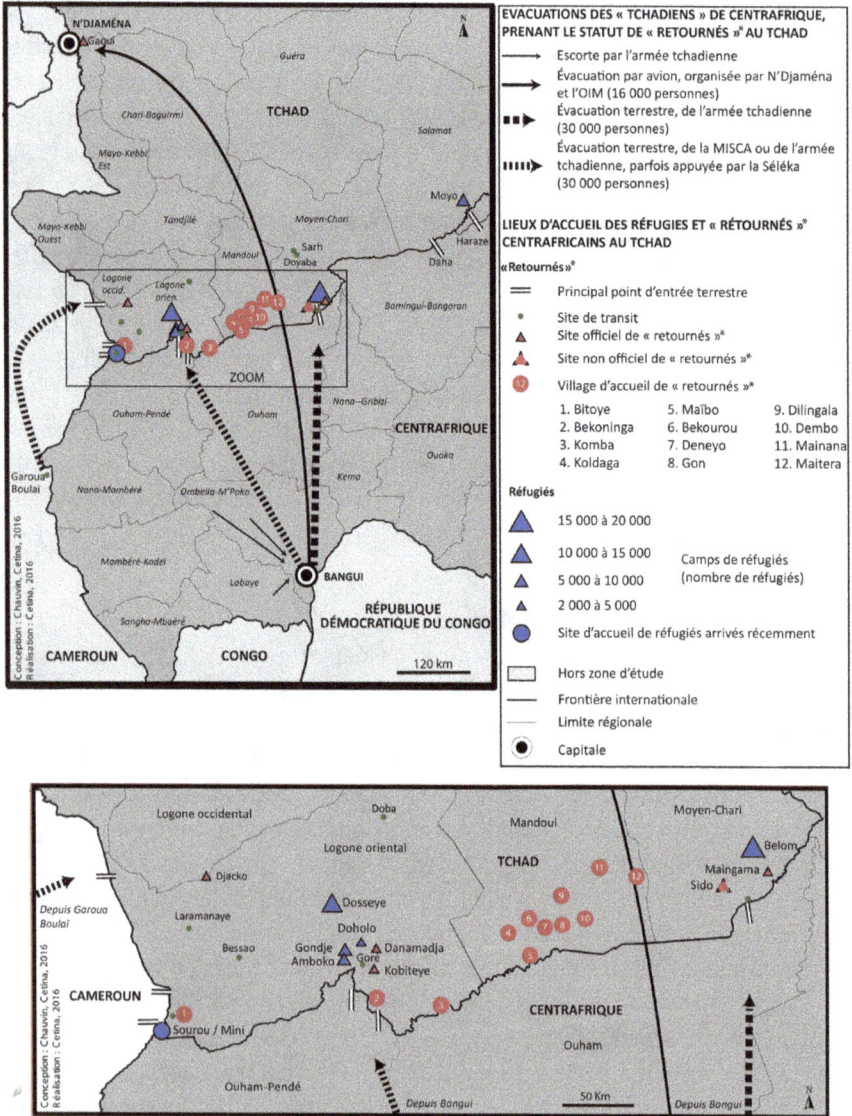

Figure 6: Evacuation routes of Chadians classified as returnees & Location of refugee and returnee camps in CAR and Chad (Source: Chauvin 2018: 73).

Discussions were cut short when on Sunday evening, 23 March 2014, Adoum received a phone call from Youssouf to say he had arrived in the south of Chad, without the cattle. He and those he had been travelling with had lost everything. It was arranged that Hadj Saleh would send money so that Youssouf and his friend could take a bus to N'Djaména. On Wednesday at four in the afternoon, Adoum and I drove to the Express Sud Voyage in Dembé to collect the pair. It was an emotional reunion. Both men were noticeably relieved. They looked tired and thin, each carrying nothing more than the standard *sac* in which groceries are carried. That evening, after a bottle of Coca-Cola and some food, Youssouf and his friend recounted their story.

The morning after Youssouf and the herd left Geng, the town was attacked. Nour and her children had already left for Cameroon a few days earlier. With the herd they travelled south, as was the plan, before heading north along the Cameroonian border. Most of the journey went through dense forest. They never met anyone else, only heard people in the distance. It was a tiring walk of several weeks, and by the time they reached northern CAR the cattle were exhausted. Close to the border, bandits attacked them, firing in all directions and scattering the livestock. Knowing that people were trying to make their way back to Chad with their possessions, bandits had taken up strategic positions along the border region. Youssouf and the others fled for the bushes where they could. Some were successful and the rest were rounded up. Youssouf and his friend were let free for some reason, and they did not think twice. This is how they came to enter Chad with not much more than the clothes on their backs.[37]

Now that Youssouf had returned, Nour could no longer stay on in N'Djaména as planned. She and her children belonged with her husband and, in turn, he belonged with his parents. Youssouf was allowed to recover for a few days while logistics were discussed. Nour's father had bought land in Mongo and built five rooms on it. All were being rented out by Hadj Saleh. The idea was that two of the renters would be given notice so that Nour and Youssouf could occupy these rooms. The other three rooms would remain rentals, at least for the time being. Getting the renters out could not be done in one day, and the rooms would need some work before they were considered suitable. First off, the young couple would stay in the ferīkh until after Ramadan, before moving into the rooms in Mongo. This was not as Nour had envisioned it, nor what Raouda and Adoum wanted for her. She had come to terms with life in the ferīkh before, yet was understandably reluctant to do it again for a longer period of time. Now that her husband was present, there was no real reason to not move into the rooms in Mongo – except for what the family thought best. By

---

37 Based on the time we spent together at Adoum's house on the evening of their arrival in N'Djaména, 23 March 2014. Parts of the conversation about how they fled were recorded on video.

September 2014, the young family was still living with their *parents* in the ferīkh. As expected, the youngest two children had been sick. They ended up staying in the ferīkh for quite some time, but by 2016 they were living in Mongo and the children were going to a Qur'ānic school while Youssouf worked the boutique.

Reflection

Throughout Nour and Youssouf's stories, various themes surface relating to the role of family amidst dynamics of disruption, mobility, and separation. Youssouf's move to CAR is a continuity of Chadian linkages with the country. The specific nature of his move was family-related, with his marrying his direct cousin, who had been born and raised there. It is unclear how he had reacted to the proposition of moving to a new country and life. Meeting him in Sassileh several years later, he had clearly adapted to his new future. Nour, in turn, had gone through an opposite process of belonging. Having been brought up with her mother and half-siblings in Bangui, this is where her initial orientation lay – with urban life, Sango, and Chadian roots. With time, upon marrying Youssouf under her father's will and with the death of her mother, she became more familiar with her father's side of the family. Hadj Saleh had come to work alongside his brother by then, and his eldest sister, Hadji Arafa, joined him when he took too long to return home to his wife. While both were in Sassileh, Nour's father paid for the brother and sister to go on pilgrimage to Mecca together. When Nour came to live in the camp of her father and husband's parents, it was Hadji Arafa with whom she shared a tent, each having their own bed. After the death of her father and subsequent stay with his and her husband's family in the ferīkh, her circle of belonging shifted to include them and their rural nomadic life. At several points throughout her life, her circles of belonging were challenged – whether through the death of a parent or by the aftermath of a violent coup. It is not possible to compare such various levels of disruption and separation (forced mobility), yet we can examine the role of family at such 'extraordinary' moments in time, questioning its role in anchoring one, during disruption, to the 'everyday'.

Howwa

Howwa and Nour know each other from Bangui (see Family Tree in Figure 4)[38] as well as from the ferīkh. Howwa had moved to Mongo for a period of time while Nour was also there. Howwa would come to visit often, bringing her young son Umar along

---

38 Howwa's father Fadoul was a brother to Nour's grandmother (her father's mother), and also a brother to Raouda's father Tchoudja. Howwa's father was thus also a brother to Hadj Saleh's mother.

with her. They would chat in Sango, and it was obvious they got along well.[39] Howwa had married a Walad Djifir and followed him back to Chad, only for him to leave for Libya. By April 2012 she was fed up waiting and made her way back to Bangui with son Umar not long afterward. This is where I encountered her in October and November 2012, visiting her at the Souq Soudanais or at her mother's house in Miskeen.

Life in Bangui and Mongo

Howwa herself was married as a second wife to a Chadian *collecteur*. He would collect diamonds from the different mining sites around Berberati and sell them on to larger companies (the buying offices described earlier). His business was never very successful, and he was not the best in managing his affairs when it did turn lucrative (according to Howwa). In 2010 he decided to try his luck in Libya by engaging in wage labour. He travelled via Chad, leaving his new wife with young child, and his four other children from a first marriage, in the care of his family members in and around Mongo. His eldest son, Moustapha, was lodged with the same *marabout* as the one with whom Howwa came to live. Moustapha was able to attend school in Mongo. His siblings – two sisters and a younger brother – were sent to the ferīkh. It must have been quite a shock for them, adjusting from life in the border town of Berberati to one in a rural nomadic setting. Some family members found especially one of the sisters too outgoing. She definitely did have a lot of energy and a different temperament from most other girls in the ferīkh: less reserved and more outspoken.

Howwa had refused to live in the nomadic ferīkh and instead rented a room from Djibreen, selling perfumes and other beauty products at the local market. She complained that making a living in Mongo from the market was more difficult than in Bangui. In Mongo it was hard to live off the 2500 CFA one might make, while in Bangui this could buy you a lot more, since food is cheaper there: 1000–1500 CFA being sufficient.[40] Retail prices in Chad were already steep, not leaving much margin to make a profit. When, after a year-and-a-half, Howwa's husband had still not returned or sent any money, she decided to head back to Bangui. In total, she had paid 95,000 CFA (approx. 145 EUR) for the four-day journey from N'Djaména to Bangui: 10,000 CFA on each bus ride from N'Djaména to Moundou, and Moundou to Goré, and from Goré she had paid 75,000 CFA (approx. 114 EUR) for a place in the cabin of a truck. She disliked taking the large buses, especially when travelling with a small child. They drove very fast and did not stop often, only for prayer. She had not had to pay at the many roadblocks in CAR, saying that they only asked money

---

39 Fieldnotes and observations, February–April 2012.
40 Conversation with Howwa at her home in Miskeen, Bangui, 30 November 2012. CFA 2500 is not quite 4 euros (3.81 according to the exchange rate in November 2018). CFA 1000 is about 1.5 euros.

from travelling Chadian men. The police had asked her for her ID papers but not for any money. In the past, the journey had been more difficult, with much more harassment by the CAR authorities. Howwa appreciated that things had calmed down now.

When we met again in October 2012, she had picked up her old life in Bangui, selling Chadian products at the Souq Soudanais in Cinq Kilo. Since her return to Bangui, she had not received a dime from her husband, even after Ramadan, and was so angry at this that she had declared a divorce. She wanted her son to grow up in Bangui and was planning on working hard so that she would be able to provide him with an education.[41] Alongside other Chadian and Sudanese women, Howwa was selling perfume in bottles, incense known as *dokhaan* in Chadian Arabic, dates, henna, bed linens, scarves, and a variety of typically 'northern' spices such as cloves and cardamom.[42] Like the other women, she rented her stall from a Chadian merchant who also owned the storage spaces behind them. He would come round at the end of the month to collect their rent. Her colleagues ranged from young women like herself to more elderly women who owned their own boutiques as merchants and made frequent trips to Chad to visit family there.

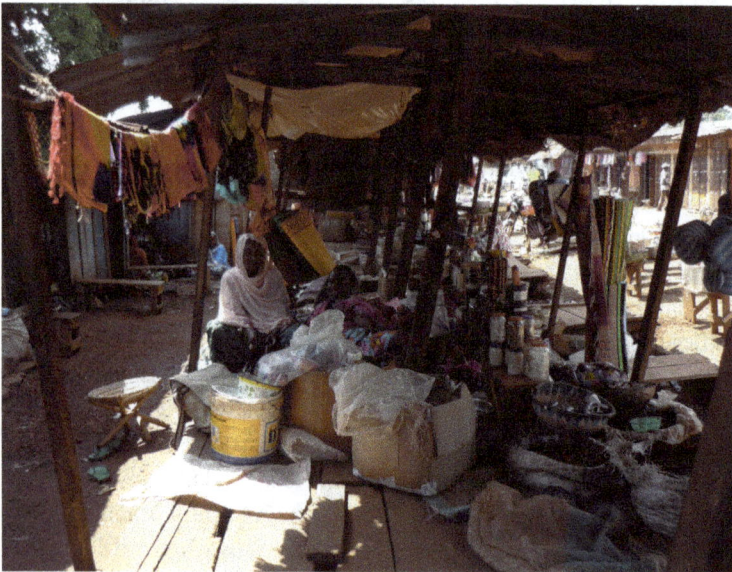

Photo 6.5: Howwa and a Sudanese merchant friend passing time among their wares, Marché Soudanais, Cinq Kilo, November 2012.

---

41 Conversation with Howwa at the Souq Soudanais, Bangui, 9 November 2012.
42 Observations in fieldnotes, 27 October 2012.

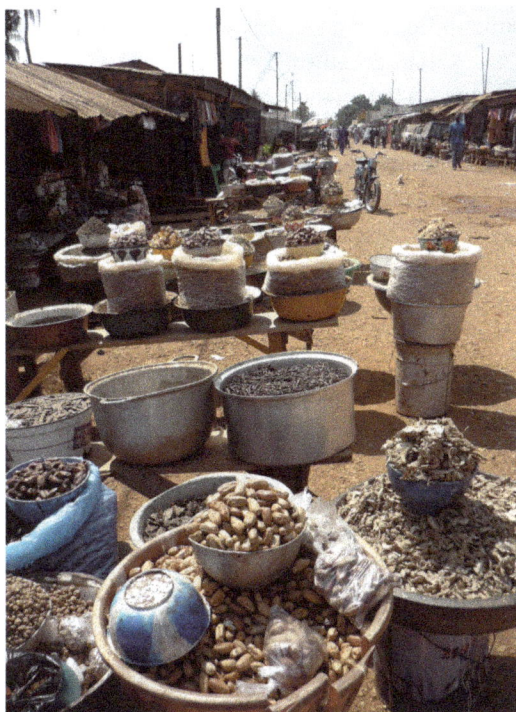

Photo 6.6: Goods at the Marché Soudanais, with a view of the street towards one of Cinq Kilo's main avenues, November 2012. Hadji Fadimatou's shop was just up the road.

In reality, life in Bangui for Howwa and her family had not been ideal. It was tough. Howwa and her two brothers lived with their mother, aunt, and grandmother in two badly built rooms on a relatively small plot of land. Howwa's mother was born and raised in Bangui, with Howwa's grandmother being the one who had accompanied her husband to CAR from Melfi (Chad). Unlike some of the other houses in the neighbourhood, theirs was built in the old-fashioned way, with mud and straw (cob). There was no gate around the compound and the latrine had caved in on itself a while earlier. An improvised latrine had developed right next to it. Howwa's grandmother processed corn into flour, drying the kernels before grinding them and then selling the flour.

In 2013, the husband Howwa had divorced had decided to return from Libya. In February 2013, the wife of the *marabout* Djibreen, in Mongo, with whom Howwa used to stay, recounted a phone conversation she had recently had with Howwa. The plan was for Howwa's husband to return from Libya in March. Howwa would then also leave CAR and move to Mongo permanently. Her husband's son Moustapha would move in with her.[43] Speaking to this son a few days later, it sounded like things had not yet been decided. Once his father returned, plans would be made for them to either stay in Mongo or for Howwa to join them here, or for his father and him to move back to Berberati where they still had a house. Personally, he would prefer to live in CAR.[44] These conversations were going on in the month before Bozizé was overthrown and everything changed, although it was not until the end of 2013 that Howwa and her family actually fled the country.

Flight to Chad

Howwa and her family were among those that were airlifted out of Bangui on 29 December 2013.[45] They had initially taken cover with relatives in Bangui's neighbourhood Cinq Kilo, having left their own unsafe housing in Miskeen. In Cinq Kilo they were eventually rounded up by Burundian MISCA troops and brought to Bangui's international airport refugee camp, where they waited for several days without enough drinking water. Humanitarian agencies were having trouble catering to the needs of the hundreds of people fleeing their *quartiers*. The Chadian government sent several airplanes to pick up its nationals, women and children receiving priority. Even though Howwa and her family had CAR identity, they did not claim this nationality but instead chose to assert themselves as Chadians.[46] It is unclear to me at which stage Howwa and her family claimed Chadian nationality. Was it the moment the Burundian MISCA troops rescued them from Cinq Kilo; was it when they arrived in the camp by the airport, thus getting them onto a plane to Chad; or was it not until they reached Chad itself? It may not even have been a conscious decision they made themselves. It would be interesting to discover more about the way this process unfolded, to understand more about under whose influence and at what stage the allocation of national identities became important. A direct consequence for Howwa and her family was that they became 'repatriates' instead of 'refugees' – which, in the eyes of the UNHCR, meant a different process. Instead of being taken into the care of the UNHCR, they were brought under the responsibility of the Chadian government and settled in a camp set up a few kilo-

---

43 Conversation with Ma'azala, Mongo, 7 February 2013.
44 Conversation with Abdallah, Mongo, 19 February 2013. By 2022 Abdallah had been living in Berberati for several years, after a period of study in Yaoundé.
45 Fieldnotes based on conversation recorded with Howwa and another Chadian woman who had fled and were now living in Camp Gawwi, N'Djaména, 26 February 2014. Howwa and her family totalled twenty-eight people, housed in three tents.
46 Wilson Janssens (2018) describes similar dynamics in her article on CAR refugees in Kinshasa, who sometimes assert their CAR identity while at other times presenting themselves as Kinois. See also Wilson (forthcoming).

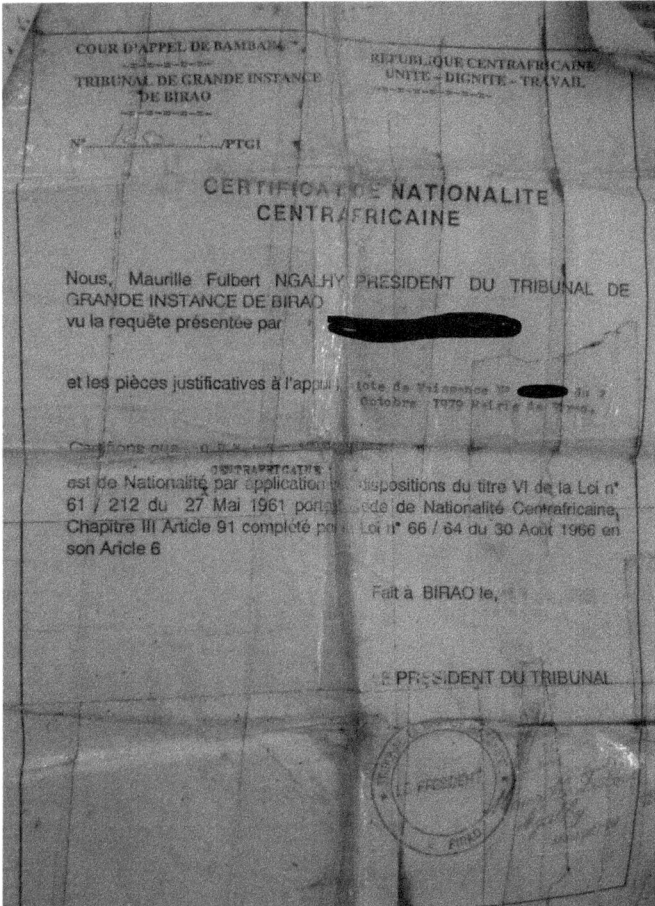

Photo 6.7: Certificate of CAR nationality, Gawwi Camp, March 2014.

metres to the south-east of N'Djaména, near the neighbourhood formerly known as Gawwi and now as Diguel Dingessouh (Kassambara 2021). This is where Adoum and I went to visit Howwa in February 2014. At that time, they had been living in the camp for two months. The day of our visit, Howwa had gone to visit her cousin Raouda, who had suggested she stay with her, but Howwa had been reluctant to leave her mother, aunts, and other family members behind.[47]

---

47 Conversation with Raouda and her mother, Hadji Fadimatou, N'Djaména, 24 February 2014. At that time, the family consisting of twenty-eight members were housed in three tents. Many tents in the Gawwi camp held an average of ten people.

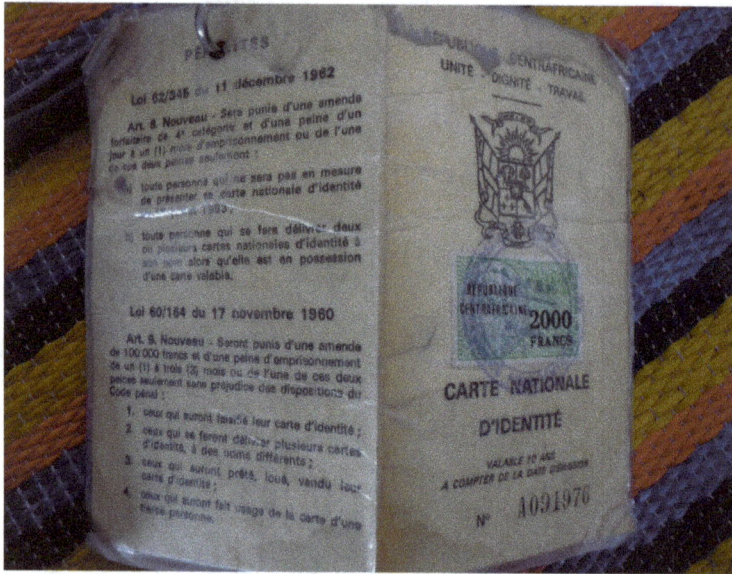

Photo 6.8: CAR ID card, Gawwi camp, March 2014.

The camp had been laid out in an orderly fashion, with occupants knowing to which block and tent they belonged. The tents had been provided by the UNHCR, as had the water supply system.[48] The terrain itself was provided by a private company, which seemed to be in the process of almost completing their own offices. The terrain had a wall around it and military and police guarding the gates. Occupants and visitors, however, were free to come and go as they wished. Visitors were asked to leave their ID at the gate, but, as we found out for ourselves, after our second visit this no longer seemed necessary. In February the weather was just heating up and still pleasant enough, but toward the end of March the sun had become unbearable, and the UNICEF tarpaulin tents provided little relief. With the sun at its highest peak there was no shade, and people were almost forced to sit inside. Over the weeks in which temperatures were rising, occupants had started cutting holes in the tents to allow some air circulation. Howwa's family were hesitant to do so, thinking they would get in trouble as the tent was not theirs. But when I returned in mid-March in the middle of the day to find the women and children sweating profusely inside the tent, they were quick to be convinced and a knife soon sliced two small windows. The effect was instant.

---

48 There was no pump but a large rectangular structure made up of a flexible water-holding material. Attached to it was a faucet from which camp inhabitants could draw water.

Those living in the camp in Gawwi had been provided with floor mats (*birsh*), rice, water, and oil. One of the main things lacking, however, was firewood to cook with. Being an already expensive item to get hold of in N'Djaména, this proved to be an issue for many families. Those who had fled with money were able to buy certain goods or use the money to set up a small business. Others were forced to sell the *birsh* they had been donated in order to buy other much-needed products, such as certain food items. Howwa, being the businesswoman she is, had been quick to set up a little commerce of her own and was selling perfumes as well as tea and coffee from her tent. She would go to the main market in N'Djaména several times a week to buy goods. She would take either one of the mini-buses that passed by the camp or a shared taxi. It would not surprise me if she had the phone number of someone who could take her into town, like a motorcycle taxi (*clando*). It is unclear with what she started the business: with money she had brought with her from Bangui, or with a little start-up capital help from others? It may well have been a mixture of both. Suffice to say that she seemed to have a knack for making the most of a little. Her brother arrived by road in late February, and by March he was selling cigarettes just outside the camp terrain, along with many other vendors of various products (vegetables, wood, soaps).

Howwa's brother had stayed on in Bangui, not wanting to give in to the anti-Balaka aggressors. He had first stayed in Cinq Kilo, bunkering down with other, mostly

Photo 6.9: View into the camp at Gawwi from Howwa and family's tent, March 2014. A few tents down we bumped into one of the ladies I had interviewed at the Marché Soudanais in Bangui.

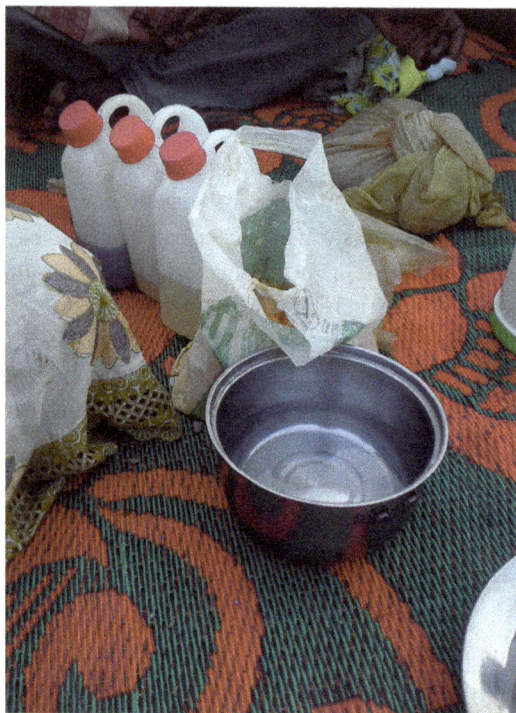

Photo 6.10: Some of Howwa's market wares, Gawwi, February 2014. Howwa would travel to one of N'Djamèna's main markets, purchasing items in bulk to then sell within the camp.

Muslim, Chadians. After a few weeks, he took the opportunity to leave, claiming that those who had decided to stay had no way of leaving nor a way of receiving water or food once their provisions ran out. Even the MISCA was having trouble reaching those that did want to be rescued. Cinq Kilo had been surrounded. Howwa's brother had left all this before it became too bad, staying instead in an old colonial *quartier* close to the Oubangui River. When he was attacked one evening by neighbours he had always been friendly with, he decided it was not worth the risk and made his way to Chad overland. It must have been a tough journey. He came across as being exhausted, very pensive, and without energy. It was good to see him somewhat recovered in March, helping out the rest of the family. In Bangui he had been selling tea in the neighbourhood Miskeen. Unfortunately, he used most of the profit to support his drinking habit.

By March 2014, Howwa and her mainly female relatives and children had been living in the refugee camp for three months. The outlook was unknown. People expected the Chadian state to act like they had when Chadians fled Libya after the fall of Qaddafi and provide repatriates with cash handouts, land, or jobs. In N'Djaména it

Photo 6.11: Talisman for protection inside Howwa's tent at Gawwi camp March 2014.

was said that these repatriates should find a way to return to their origins – the families from which they had come. For some this was an option, but for many more – especially those second- and third-generation Chadians in CAR – this was an impossibility. Take Howwa and her family, who in total consisted of twenty people. Which family member would be able to house them all? Even if they were to provide for their own food, the sheer lack of sleeping space would be an issue. Howwa's grandmother knew the name of her village but not its exact location. Visitors had told her to go back with her daughters and grandchildren. 'Your family in the village will help you build somewhere to live with the grasses, mud, and sticks the land provides.' Even if she could discover where exactly she had grown up, who could say they would be waiting for them with open arms? It had been forty years since she had last set foot in Chad, and she was now an old woman. What would they live off? They had outgrown life *en brousse* and were too well acquainted with urban living, fresh foodstuffs, and more humid temperatures.

Photo 6.12: The inside of Howwa's tent at Gawwi, March 2014. Some of their possessions and provisions are visible in the background. At the time of this visit Howwa's mother, aunt and grandmother were both present, along with three young children. One of the girl's is the daughter of Howwa's sister, who was in hospital in N'Djaména at the time, expecting a baby.

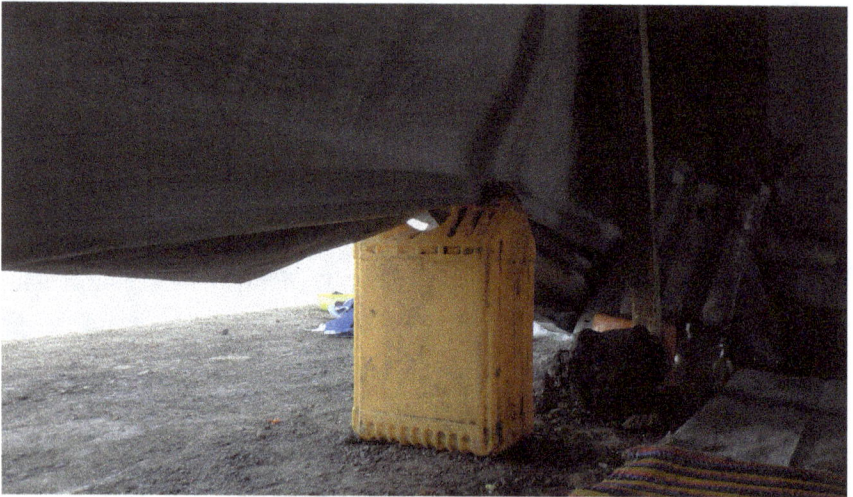

Photo 6.13: Propping up the tent to let in a much needed breeze, March 2014. It was hot inside the tents and the ground itself would flood as soon as the rainy season started. At this time, they were waiting for a solution to come along. Going back to where the grandmother had come from in central Chad, all those years ago, was not an option. She no longer knew anyone there, and there was nothing to go back to.

Postscript

Howwa's story has many more side-stories and layers, showing the complexity of familial relations. In a conversation with her husband on 7 March 2014 in the ferīkh, he described how in the twenty-two years that he had been in CAR, he had never even sent home 500 CFA (not even 1 EUR), while in the one year in Libya he had sent home 1 million CFA (approx. 1524 EUR).[49] His plan was to buy land in Mongo and work his field. With the Libyan money he bought cows, which were being kept by his father's children and brothers. At the time, he had no plans to go anywhere else, though he said with a smile, 'Maybe only within Chad.'

In the time that Howwa's husband had been away, his first-born son Moustapha (by his first wife), had made the journey to the far south of Chad to tell his Centrafricaine mother she needed to come live in Mongo and be there for her daughters. She followed her son, bringing children from later relationships with her. Speaking to one of Moustapha's sisters who had been placed in the ferīkh and who had now rejoined their mother in Mongo, she clarified that she, her sister, and younger brother had spent the first year with a paternal aunt in Mongo. When her father (Howwa's husband) left for Libya, they moved to the ferīkh of their grandfather, known as the *grand marabout* Issa. Moustapha was allowed to stay in Mongo with a different *fakīr* (another name for *marabout*), Djibreen, for his studies. According to the eldest daughter, she had spent four years in the ferīkh. Her mother said it had only been three.[50]

While the family of her husband's first wife seemed to have found a place and means to settle in Mongo, Howwa returned to Bangui fairly soon after I last saw her in 2014, and she was still there in 2017. Her mother, grandmother, and their children were said to have returned as well. It is not clear to me where in Bangui they are living, as Cinq Kilo is still said to be an impregnable enclave, and the neighbourhood where they used to live, Miskeen, saw a lot of destruction. It was Nour's half-brother, Abu Kawsar, who told me that they had returned. When we met each other in October 2017 in N'Djaména, he confirmed that they were still there.

Reflection

Howwa's story reveals a different groundedness and perhaps also belonging from those which we find in Nour's story. The nature of Howwa's mobility has gone hand in hand with personal affairs such as following her husband and the ability to earn

---

49 Souleymane, James, Adoum, and I had a conversation with him on 7 March 2014 at his father's ferīkh in Fadjé (north of Mongo, Chad). Fieldnotes, Fadjé, 7 March 2014. Video recordings by James Chama.

50 Conversation with Moustapha's sisters, Mongo, 13 March 2014.

a living wherever she goes. While Nour's mobility is closely linked to (and relies on) family, Howwa's family seem to have been 'disconnected' from the start, in the sense that its members are relatively free to choose their own paths. Howwa has a prominent caring and providing role, although her own mother and aunts do also contribute. Even her elderly grandmother was bringing in income in Bangui by preparing corn into flour.

This relative independence – as a form of disconnectivity within a family – has resulted in less of a shifting between circles of belonging than in Nour's case. Despite violence uprooting them from their lives, and then living in a camp setting for several months, Howwa and her family members continued their entrepreneurial approach to life – a life which definitely included hunger, an unvaried diet, and the general hardship associated with living in a camp. Is 'groundedness' in Howwa's case then related more to Jackson's (2013) 'wherewithal of life'? It is a groundedness which refers to the more personal characteristics of coping with a crisis – giving the impression of a person being relatively 'grounded'. The role of family, amidst various encounters with the *'extraordinaire'* (disruptions to daily life), shines light on how people like both Nour and Howwa find a way to function amidst so much change. This change includes moments of disruption but also possibilities provided by their expanding socio-economic and familial networks. Growing up and living in a modernizing Bangui they received some schooling and formed ideas vis-à-vis their futures. Howwa is entrepreneurial and independent, while Nour has conformed to the role of depending and following others. At the time Nour did not have her own mobile phone with which to keep in touch with family members. She relied on her uncles for news and direct conversations with Youssouf and her siblings. Howwa did carry a mobile phone and used it to do business and stay in touch with relatives, though she complained that her husband never called while he was in Libya. Raouda's story introduces a third woman's experiences and the role of family relations (or lack thereof) in times of disruption or crisis.

Raouda

Another relative of both Howwa and Nour, Raouda had also made the move to N'Djaména from Bangui. Her father belonged to the Sulmani group and was a brother of Hadj Saleh's mother (see Family Tree in Figure 4). As the eldest daughter of Tchoudja and Hadji Fadimatou, Raouda was in her late thirties or early forties and was born and raised in Bangui along with her two siblings, a sister and brother. Their prosperous father was murdered when she was five years old and her brother Ahmed only a few months. As a popular businessman, Tchoudja received many Chadian visitors at his home. In the 1980s, former Chadian president Hissein Habré, in his mission to suppress any form of dissent, targeted those within Chad and also in the wider region.[51] Raouda claims her father did not have any political motivations, and it was merely his harbouring of those who did which sealed his fate.

Upon reaching adulthood, Raouda was able to take over some of her father's remaining businesses, which an uncle had guarded for her. All this time, and still, her mother Hadji Fadimatou ran her own business, selling products from her boutique in the markets of Cinq Kilo. Raouda's husband had been a well-to-do businessman, who died at a young age leaving her with several young children to steer the family business. Despite her lack of a proper secondary education, she is a successful businesswoman with a lot at stake. She owns land in Bangui[52] and N'Djaména and is continuously occupied with where she should raise her children.

We met for the first time in Bangui in October 2012 when Howwa took me to her house. It was Hadj Saleh who had given me instructions on how to ask around for the house, but it was with Howwa that I ended up going. Howwa would occasionally spend the night at Raouda's, and although socio-economically the two women live very different lives, they seemed very concerned with each other's well-being – emphasizing their familial ties (their fathers were brothers). Raouda lived in a large, high-walled compound encompassing two buildings. In the one she lived with her family, and the other she rented out as office space to a well-known aid organization. The income this provided was enough for her and her extended household to live off. Whatever her various businesses, and that of her mother, were bringing in was extra.

In February 2014 Raouda had been living in N'Djaména for less than a year. She had made the move in July 2013 after returning from a medical operation in Khartoum and finding Bangui too 'hot'. As a wealthy businesswoman, she belongs to the elite and has 'friends' with close ties to Bozizé's former government. She admitted once that she kept these acquaintances as a form of protection. She felt insecure

51 During Habré's reign, many Chadians fled to CAR and became small traders or shopkeepers. Among them were not only southerners, whose ethnic homeland often crossed the national Chadian–CAR border, but also Arabs. Marchal (2015: 173) describes these Arabs as mostly being from the Salamat region and belonging to a faction opposed to Habré. It is not unlikely that other Arabic groups may also have joined this opposition group. Tchoudja belonged to the Sulmani group.
52 On updating this chapter in 2018, I was no longer sure whether she had been able to keep hold of the land in Bangui – whether she had sold it or whether it was confiscated. Further below, I describe how she had tried to protect these assets by renting them out to international organizations involved in the peace-keeping mission.

driving in Bangui at night and preferred to be accompanied by such an acquaint-ance. It helped when harassed by police checks and added an extra layer of safety.

She had kept her familial ties to Chad alive, visiting on occasion with and without the children. Upon the death of her husband, his family had given her the choice: his business selling veterinarian pharmaceuticals, or the land he owned in N'Djaména. Her husband's children from an earlier marriage had been eager to take over a business which produced a ready flow of capital. His brother, however, was reluctant to give Raouda and her children the plots of land. In the end, her *parents* came to talk to the brother and he quickly agreed. She and Adoum laughed over this; apparently the Misseria have quite a reputation for being strong-willed and able to get what they want. She is still grateful for her decision to fight for the plots of land. The business is hard work, but the land just sits there and increases in value. Land prices in N'Djaména have gone up considerably in the past years. Raouda owns three such plots of land. When Adoum and I met up with her in N'Djaména toward the end of February 2013, she was planning to build on the first two smaller plots – one for her children to live on and the other for herself. The third and largest plot, worth at least 150 million CFA (almost 230,000 EUR), she planned to sell. She calculated that she could get the construction work done for about 60 million CFA (approx. 92,000 EUR), and with the remaining money she would buy a new plot a little outside the centre, investing whatever was left into her business. On leaving Bangui, she had decided to rent out her own house as well, which is situated in the same compound as the other building she was already renting out. A smart move as it turned out. Besides bringing in a large sum of income, it would secure the compound against looting, as the international organizations renting there are part of the peace-keeping missions. In terms of daily expenses while in Chad, she and her children could live off the 4 million CFA (approx. 6000 EUR) in rent she was receiving each month.

In February 2013 Raouda had not yet decided where she would let her chil-dren grow up. We visited her in the home of her half-sister, a woman married to the imam of the large mosque in N'Djaména at the time. Raouda did not like the mentality found in N'Djaména. She said it was one of mistrust, intrigue, and corrup-tion.[53] In Bangui the educational system had been sliding backward for some time, and in N'Djaména she had found a Turkish-backed school in which it would be easy to enrol the children. This school would teach them Turkish, French, and English – languages she thought would be useful for them in the future. She was also consid-ering moving to Cameroon. The climate is easier there and she preferred the Cam-eroonian mentality. It would teach her children proper French. In Bangui she had

---

53 Conversation with Raouda, N'Djaména, 26 February 2013.

run a strict household. The children were not allowed to *'promenade'* around the city. They would leave for school in the morning, come home, go to Qur'ān lessons in the afternoon, and come straight home again. Some children had tutors who would come to the house to provide extra lessons. Raouda herself never made it past the first few classes of secondary school, and she has worked hard to get to where she is now. Her plan is to take some kind of adult education classes which will provide her with a diploma and open new doors for her. She is a businesswoman at heart, always looking for opportunities and willing to work hard for them.

When we met again in February 2014, she was renting a concession for herself, the children, and the others in her household for whom she provides (mostly young women and children). The concession was well built, consisting of *deux salons, deux chambres*, an annex, and outhouse, with a lovely green garden and bougainvillea. It reminded me of the concession she had lived in in Bangui. She explained that she was looking to start up something in N'Djaména, something she could invest in or build up, but she was not sure what. She knew about veterinarian products, so that could be an option. She had looked into furniture, curtains, and so on, but said it was *haram* – sellers were tripling prices for customers and she did not want to be involved in that, earning *haram* money.[54] Adoum suggested she look into building a petrol station in Ati or Mongo. Mongo is practically connected by asphalt, and once it gets to Ati, well . . . it could be a wise move. Raouda asked Adoum's advice on getting into the cattle trade; but he said no, there was a lot of fraud going on and it was not a sector you could trust people in.[55]

In March 2014 Raouda showed us the plot of land she had started constructing on. It lay past Farsha in a very newly built-up area, including a freshly tarmacked road complete with electricity poles along it. The plot is actually 25 × 45 m, but she had divided it in two and had now started building on one half. Once complete, it will provide housing for her and her children. The other plot she will also construct and rent out. Her plot has a *forage* (deep well), and the water tank has already been connected to a generator. This will provide water for both plots, hers and the rental. Up until now, she has invested 30 million CFA (approx. 45,735 EUR), saying that N'Djaména was proving expensive in terms of construction. One bag of cement alone costs 12,000 CFA (approx. 18 EUR). Initially, she had planned to construct on both plots at the same time; but after having thought it over, she decided to first build a home for her and her children to live in. This way they would no longer have to pay a monthly rent and could *rester tranquilles* while she constructed the

---

54 Recorded conversation with Raouda, her mother, and Adoum, N'Djaména, 24 February 2014.
55 Chad has many businesses and sectors which are extensively monopolized by a small number of people. Cf. Debos (2016) on the monopoly of power and favouritism within the politico-military context.

second plot and two little shops along the road adjacent to the property. This should provide her with a healthy monthly income to live off, allowing her to follow a course to acquire the diploma she desired. The lack of a diploma was making it harder to find work; on paper she did not have the right qualifications for an office job. Setting up a trading business (import, export) like she had had in Bangui was almost impossible. This she had learned in the past year. She owns another plot of land on which she wants to build and had had an appointment at the bank the day before to get the money for this. She did not need a loan, as her deceased husband's money had been held frozen at the bank. She was planning to use a part of it and hold the rest for their children.[56]

Reflection

Just like those of Nour and Howwa, Raouda's story reflects various levels of disruption throughout her life. She lost her father as a child and became responsible for a sizeable business emporium when she came of age, ultimately providing her with a certain level of inclusion among Bangui's elite circles. Before and after the coup, her connections helped her get her affairs in order, securing her family's assets and businesses as best she could before violence broke out. While Raouda has the benefit of being financially well endowed, this also makes her vulnerable and cautious in terms of investments made for her future. In contrast, Howwa's lack of wealth and loose family ties give her a certain freedom – a freedom that Nour misses while being well looked after by her father's family.

Where can we then place Raouda's story, in relation to those of Howwa and Nour? She too, has been confronted with shifting circles of belonging, due to personal and external crises. Her personality includes a certain level-headedness (groundedness) while faced with such extraordinary circumstances. Over the years, she has taken an almost patriarchal role in the family, being responsible for the welfare of both assets and family members. In so doing she has become a connecting factor within her family, someone who provides a certain groundedness to her direct relations.

The place of family and belonging amidst disruption

When family members of the Walad Djifir, living as third-generation immigrants in CAR, were confronted with violence in the months following the March 2013 coup, the consequences could not yet be foreseen. In the coup's aftermath, patterns

---

56 Based on fieldnotes, N'Djaména, 22 March 2014.

emerged, shining light on the duality of family, gender, and access to wealth in daily life. Alongside the massive impact of external factors such as drought, cattle loss, and outright political violence in the specific case of what happened in CAR – the impact of a family on an individual should not be underestimated. Familial relationships form the context in which experiences are navigated and lived. In acting as a connector, these relationships simultaneously create disconnections: familial expectations, obligations, and loyalty can create conflicting feelings within an individual. Family can thus simultaneously function as safe haven and *creator* of disruption. As in all relationships, the importance of family and loyalty are paired with complicatedness and inconsistency (Bouman 2003). Through a specific focus on these familial relations, within a situation of disruption – namely the 2013 coup in CAR – we see several layers of connectivity become prominent, ultimately forming a certain groundedness for each of the women in the way they provide feelings of belonging and offer practical solutions for the future.

One would expect a level of uprootedness after the CAR coup, a feeling of being 'betwixt and between' (Haour 2013). While this was certainly the case for many of Chadian origin, the extent to which this took shape varied per individual. What elements contributed to that are what this chapter has explored. In a context where mobility is the norm, with people, goods, and political intentions moving in and between the two countries, family obligations and expectations are one of the tentacles that anchor the extraordinary into the everyday (Das 2007; Grabska 2014).

Disruption and belonging

From the stories told by Chadians born and raised in CAR, their position was not ideal, but it had become better than it was in the 1990s. Men still felt harassed by the authorities at times, even if they possessed Centrafricain nationality – people with a Muslim name were often targeted – yet some said that this was partly due to the wave of new migrants who were ruining their rapport and to the current political developments. These sentiments were further put to the test and eventually acted upon when, in the aftermath of the coup, waves of violence escalated between several different parties. The three case studies do not provide specific answers to why the Chadian population in CAR was among those targeted. The stories of those in the camp in Gawwi do show how, like so many other Chadians who fled CAR to 'return', people found themselves 'betwixt and between' – even if only for a short period. In most cases there was no real 'return', as many had never set foot in Chad to begin with. The sense of belonging they had previously felt as Chadians in CAR was uprooted. Even if only for a brief period (as in the case of Howwa), people no longer felt welcome in CAR. At the same time, through their status as 'repatriates', being physically housed in a camp away from the city centre and with very little support from the Chadian state, they also did not feel welcomed in their country of origin. So what elements contributed to the way people coped in these situations?

People rely on the networks and assets they have to help them create new futures. So too was the case with the Walad Djifir who migrated to CAR and then found themselves returning. In understanding what role these networks and assets have played and what they are made up of, Giuffrida's (2010: 30) description of mobility, stasis, and networks is helpful:

> [T]he existence of networks depends on both moving and staying in one place. Nuclei of kin residing in one locality are points, knots or nodes in the web to which movers can return if they so wish. Their presence ensures claiming rights over land and territories that represent, in the mind of those who stay and go, an imaginary homeland or territory.

For each of the three women, their feelings toward such an imaginary homeland have been tested. For Howwa, this 'homeland' seems to be in Bangui; that is where she feels most 'at home' and where she has the best chances of making a living for herself and her family – despite her 'nuclei of kin' being dispersed. For Raouda, it is unclear where her 'heart' lies. Bangui feels like the home she has left. At the same time, she is keen on finding somewhere safe and stable to raise her children. For Nour, the shift of 'belonging' to both Bangui or Sassileh and the ferīkh setting has happened more gradually. It was a process that was started through the familial visits (aunt and uncle coming to CAR) and mainly through her own longer stay in Chad after the death of her father. Her family ultimately has a connecting role, providing a focus for creating stability amidst disruption. The place of family plays out differently for each of the three women owing to the extent to which they can make individual decisions and access wealth with which to support these decisions. This brings us back to the notion of flexibility discussed in Chapter Four. Here, flexibility is informed by the differing levels of access the three women have to economic and social (familial) resources[57] – but also by being able to 'belong' to and thus access various communities: both Chadian and Centrafrican societies, as well as the communities from which their families originated, such as the Misseria Rouges. At the same time, it is precisely this belonging which defines some of the disruption in their lives. Despite having been born and raised in CAR, all three women have had

---

57 See de Bruijn (1995) on how various social categories, with different access to natural, economic, and social resources, are related to rules of behaviour, norms, and values in Fulani society. In a way, Howwa's case resonates with the intentional actions in times of uncertainty and crisis of the Cameroonian women Johnson-Hanks (2005) describes. Howwa knows how to play the rules of the game, even if the future of where this game will lead her are unknown.

to flee due to the violence and general disruption, but also due to their own Chadian backgrounds. Once in Chad, they face a different level of not quite belonging.

Family as two sides of the same coin?

'Family' as a resource seems to go hand in hand with both the restrictions and freedoms gender hierarchies and wealth can provide. For each of the three women, the diverse natures of the relations with their kin have had different implications in terms of the degree to which they are 'bounded' by family (as a source of support and constraint). When can such a connection or binding be interpreted as entailing 'constraint', or perhaps even 'duress', for those individuals taking part in it?

While I hesitate to link the concept of violence to the analysis of the place of family in moments of crisis (within the context of these case studies), ideas surrounding 'ordinary violence' as 'silent violence' do provide useful insights. Using the term violence would not do justice to the genuine feelings of concern family members have for those in trouble or disrupted by CAR's political events. Yes, their expectations can be demanding, but the intentions are not malicious. It is the emphasis on the ordinary and the silent, and perhaps even the mundane elements of everyday tensions, which I find useful. While the violence and disruption which ensued after the coup was very much a physically observable one, there were other more nuanced and less visible disruptions which require reflecting upon. In describing why and how ordinary violence is silent in the context of Africa, Bouju and de Bruijn (2014) point to a vulnerability informed by status and inequality:

> In Africa, ordinary violence is silent because it is not 'loud' (i.e. not 'public'). It is private and takes place in intimate settings between individuals in face-to-face social interactions that are often undermined by poverty, jealousy, exploitation or injustice. Vulnerable persons (such as widows, unmarried mothers, childless women, unemployed young men/husbands, dishonoured family heads) may be subordinated and even subjugated by powerful persons of authority. [. . .] Actually, vulnerability to ordinary violence would seem to depend on the unpredictable combination of a structurally weak social and economic status together with certain external circumstances. To change something in what they consider to be an alienating relationship, they try to distance themselves from the conventional values and conservative meanings of norms. But as they lack the appropriate resources to cope with their situation, they often engage in a transgression of the norms. (Bouju & de Bruijn 2014: 7)

The emphasis of studies on structural violence[58] thus often lies on individual resilience, and at times the lack thereof, within the context of ordinary violence.

---

58 See Scheper-Hughes (1993, 2008); Das (2007); Bouju & de Bruijn (2014).

Ayimpam (2014) analyses this further when examining kinship solidarity and violence within a Congolese family, in relation to economic wealth. She argues that dominating situations are reversible: 'Indeed, whatever a family member's initial status, one's dominant position will be related to one's economic situation' (p. 102). Such attention to one's economic situation is useful when analysing the place of family amidst disruption.

One may expect women like Nour, Howwa, and Raouda to be more vulnerable when faced with such uprootedness as that caused by political and communal disruption. It is true that both Nour and Howwa are somewhat dependent on their husbands for support. Even if Howwa makes her own way, it is partly out of need that she does so, due to her husband not providing as expected. At the same time, this need to be provided for, and his absence, give her a certain freedom (even if it is hard work). Nour has the familial support, while not really being in charge of her own destiny. It is unclear to what extent she and Youssouf discuss and plan their own futures. At the time they seemed caught between 'doing the right thing', vis-à-vis expectations of family in the ferīkh, and having their own vision or wishes for the future. This brings us to the notion of a 'constrained agency'. Howwa's need to provide for herself and her family constrains her choices while also giving her a certain agency (freedom). What could be dominating situations of vulnerability have, in her case, indeed become reversible, if not assets. Raouda's agency lies in her widowed status[59] and access to wealth. The latter also constrains her somewhat, as it makes her cautious and feel vulnerable.

People, then, and all that they embody, are as much connectors as they are providers of both support and constraint, whether for others or for themselves. It is perhaps a little like the idea of trust and mistrust discussed in the previous chapter – trust itself is linked to a certain dependency and the evaluation of risks (Carey 2017). So too, interactions with family can entail both dependency and possibilities, both unbridled caring and expectations which restrict. The more dependency a woman feels she has in relation to her family – whether it is she being dependent on a husband or other extended family, or whether she has family dependent on her as in the case of children or less well-off individuals – the stronger both levels of constraint and support can become.

∗∗∗

---

59 See Casciarri (1995: 111) on the relative freedom of those (pastoral Ahamda) women who were widowed, divorced, or of too poor an economic status to work 'outside' their nomadic camps and thus provide for themselves.

What role, therefore, do familial relationships play in providing (in)security and possibilities for (new) futures within a context of political and non-political disruption and mobility? This chapter has explored the relationship between three women's socio-economic environments, constituted simultaneously of vulnerability and normalcy, and those moments in life when panic, political violence, sadness, and insecurity reign. Their stories provide a nuanced insight into what life was like for those of Chadian origin after the coup in CAR in 2013. Layers of national and familial connectivity shifted, some such processes having already started before the violence broke out and providing a form of security and support. At the same time, a certain 'mundane' continuity can be discerned amidst so much potential change. This continuity is linked to the role of family in the way it can provide support, as well as a motivation for seeking economic stability and security. It is this that provides a certain groundedness to the ability of Nour, Howwa, and Raouda to cope with disruption, with their modernizing social and economic situations ultimately determining the level of independency in which decisions can be made.

Chapter 7
The everyday wilderness

The physical ferīkh is imbued with aspects of the Sahel's terrain. Tents are constructed under the most shady trees, thorny bushes are hacked away and used to create the *zerribas* which hold the smaller animals. The uneven terrain, in the tents' immediate vicinity, is swept clean of sticks, spikes, and dung. Walad Djifir make use of that which the terrain they live in offers. They adapt it as much as they can to match their needs. It is not necessarily the most ideal situation a human being can find themselves in, life is tough – especially on child-bearing women, school-going children, the sick, and the elderly. On everyone really, though in varying degrees. The point is that the terrain – whether it be the direct vicinity of the nomadic camps, a little further afield in local market towns, or even more distant in the capital city, or a different nation-state – consists of usable elements. These elements are not only physical entities like grass for the cattle, or shallow ground water. They are also all the different forms of infrastructure (transport, communication, trade, education, religious), support networks (both state and communal), and flows of information.

By approaching this nomadic group through the variety of ways in which their daily lives in the nomadic camp are linked (connected) to the world outside their camp, this ethnography departs from nomadic studies that focus on the more classical aspects of pastoral-nomadic life: livestock issues such as diseases, market dynamics, public health, ecological issues such as drought and scarcity, access to resources, sedentary–nomadic conflicts, sedentarization and displacement, and marginalization in relation to the state. Instead, it seeks to contribute to a 'nomadology' (Fischer & Kohl 2010) which looks at the interconnectedness of these aspects, including dynamics which are no longer either 'typically' sedentary or nomadic and are bound neither geographically nor economically. Walad Djifir are part of a contemporary 'wilderness', a world which sees people coming in contact with new technologies and moving in and out of the physical nomadic setting. The 'wilderness' is not a local phenomenon *pur sang*. In it we find familiar global characteristics that have been there all along, whether it be on an ecological level, infrastructural, or in terms of the movement of people, goods, and ideas. Although the Chadian 'wilderness' has experienced much positive change, contemporary (nomadic) life continues to include a lack of (access to) proper healthcare and high infant mortality rates coupled with high birth rates. Men and women alike often complain about headaches, aching limbs, and heartburn. Access to basic primary education is a work in progress yet far from being prioritized and possible for most children. Illiteracy remains high amongst both men and women. Even if benefits are slow to reveal themselves, Chad and the region in general are part of global processes of social

https://doi.org/10.1515/9783110714685-007

change. The wilderness as concept was developed as a way to understand the perceived chaos as holder and producer of both insecurity and belonging. It is this exact 'disorder' (Debos 2016) which has caused specific power relations and socio-economic hierarchies to emerge. By framing contexts of daily life as chaos, disorder, or conflict-based, we lose site of what other dynamics are at play.

García et al. (2023), for example, use the notion of the drylands (which includes such arid environments as the Sahel) as a 'frontier' to examine how 'global interests and narratives' are entangled 'with the local struggles that have always existed in the drylands' (p. 1). The frontier is introduced as both a place and a narrative (space) of opportunity or potential transformation. This opens up discussions on whom (and what) is excluded within narratives of opportunities and the so-called 'need' for development or protection: the political economy and historical roots of problems become depoliticized, and the labelling of situations as ones of religious extremism, ecological or humanitarian crisis legitimizes their subsequent interventions. For those 'frontiers' of the world often defined in terms of conflict, crisis, and chaos, social connections remain a part of people's wilderness and influence their mobility and flexibility (agency). Just as uncertainty can be productive and mistrust can be a positive social phenomenon, so too do social connections in situations of duress and chronic crisis provide (constrained) agency. Spaces, or circles, of insecurity and belonging go hand in hand, overlapping and intertwining more often than not. These visible and invisible infrastructures (or networks) can be seen as tools or spaces of insecurity and connectivity. It challenges the notion of a wilderness being defined only in line with its historical meaning of a disorderly and unwelcoming nature. Instead, the globalizing wilderness posits those situations that are often deemed chaotic and untameable as ones that are simultaneously not necessarily unstructured or unmanageable, precisely through the way they are anchored in the everyday.

The creation of the term wilderness, which I juxtapose with connectivity and belonging, is also a critique of those networks and technologies which are meant to support pastoral nomads like the Walad Djifir. Instead, these infrastructures seem to play a dual role in the way feelings of belonging are framed towards them, and in the way they simultaneously act as creators of insecurity. An analogy between the state and the wilderness, for example, touches upon the themes of marginality and insecurity. In Chad, the idea of the state calls up feelings of belonging and loyalty, while its reality catches people off-guard with its destructive, predictably unpredictable nature, resulting in fear and frustration. Its actions and non-actions create a certain agency and dependency all in one, felt by marginal communities and by those associated with those in power. Throughout the various chapters the role of the state has, at times, been noticeably absent or perhaps more correctly, something Walad Djifir seem to opt in and out of, if and when the need arises. The role of the state as protector of rights is tapped into, for example in the case of the Walad Djifir land ownership question (see Chapter Three). In other situations, opting out is not an option and the more oppressive nature of the state's actors, or those ostensibly acting in the name of the state, are revealed. The lack of state presence in a lot of the fieldwork narratives is telling in and of itself. The state is merely part and parcel of the globalizing wilderness which surrounds the ferīkh and its people, impacting upon them in both negative and positive ways. The state's presence as a source of insecurity, disruption, and marginality does not necessarily mean there is no logic to the dynamics surrounding it. As Debos (2016) and Schouten (2022) point out, the crux of the question is not whether the state is weak, or whether or not it is present. It is rather 'how power is exercised' and where people turn to for protection. The idea of the wilderness provides a way to understand that where and how, by providing a methodological and analytical space for such local dynamics of marginality and insecurity to be seen within the context of broader regional and global processes of connectivity. There are numerous formal and informal networks and connections which inform such things as social relations, hierarchical dynamics, physical movement, and the exchange of goods and ideas. Walad Djifir are not solely defined by their marginality in relation to the state, or by the level of security it provides them. As such, they are also not solely defined by their nomadic way of life, nor by the arid Sahelian environment of the Guéra, nor by the disruptive coup in CAR. Walad Djifir have been and still are part of numerous networks of connectivity.

Walad Djifir connectivity

A focus on the everyday (lives as lived) determined which networks of connectivity were currently most prevalent and on which 'connectors' they were centred. On a daily basis, conversations and actions revolved around such things as the caring for livestock (camels, cattle, sheep, and goats), the phone calls received from a brother or husband engaged in wage labour elsewhere, phone calls with these same or other family members when money was being sent, and physical meetings to discuss how to handle a land issue. These daily issues all had interlinked themes running through them which were identified as connectors – namely, Leaders, Cattle, Remittances, and Family. This book has been structured around these different connectors, as a way of understanding the daily life negotiations found within the ferīkh setting and the way they are informed by dynamics taking place 'outside' the physical nomadic camp. The ferīkh thus acted as both a concept and the physical place in which research was carried out. The unavoidable 'entering the field' moment took place within a nomadic setting characterized by small glasses of tea under shade-giving trees while waiting for the sun to move down, with the slaughter of a sheep near the camp grounds, followed by dinner in an open space surrounded by the tents of my hosts. At first the ferīkh was thus very much a physical place: the nomadic camp – a camp which moved around only a few times a year, depending on the needs of its livestock and people regarding access to pastures, water, and agricultural land. Soon, through focusing on the daily lives of those living in the ferīkh, the ways in which the camp itself was connected to goings-on outside of its physical space became apparent. These connections to the 'outside' included not only the more obvious interactions with local markets (for livestock and daily needs), but also the staying in touch with family members working in N'Djaména or even further afield, in CAR and Libya. From a 'mere' physical place, the ferīkh as research field grew to one representing an analytical space which embodies all these different networks of Walad Djifir connectivity.

Making use of the Walad Djifir's own stories to describe past and present local politics, Chapter Two details aspects of how they came to be in the Guéra and Batha regions. These past mobile itineraries have continued to a certain degree in the present day and are both the subject of the research and the tool with which it was carried out. Walad Djifir 'live their lives' in multiple locations, whether due to the needs of their livestock, to visit family members, or when carrying out wage labour. Fieldwork was therefore also carried out in various locations: different ferīkhs in the Guéra and Batha regions; in Mongo, Ati, and Koundjaar; in the capital N'Djaména; in Bangui (CAR); and in a remote village to the west of Bangui. These places were not chosen at random. Each contained either the same person I had been spending time with earlier but who had travelled; a family member (or more) related to people I had come to know during the first fieldwork sessions in 2011 and 2012; or was a site which provided context for the 'connectors' around which the chapters are written – such as a weekly market or a money transfer office. This 'following' of people and connectors allowed for an holistic understanding of Walad Djifir connectivity in relation to different places and spaces.

Chapter Three introduced the reader to Walad Djifir navigations through a sedentary-oriented political system. With 'leaders' as its connector, it looked at the decisions (actions) surrounding land ownership and familial strife by focusing on local leaders and moments of negotiation. In dealing with such issues as leadership strife, land ownership, and the forming or strengthening of allegiances, members of the ferīkh are faced with remnants of administrative changes under the French and with the more contemporary dynamics linked to Chad's system of governance. In the case of the death of Hassan's son and his own brother's unwillingness to follow custom, the family became torn and one of their groups pushed to start following a different *sheikh*. The value of sticking together as a family and group proved difficult to uphold; or, rather, each party had their own ideas on what was right. In the face of land-ownership strife between Walad Djifir and the *sheikh* of the Misseria

Rouges, the overarching group to which they belong, there was a general consensus on how to act. The consensus was to stick together as Walad Djifir and to fight to regain their ancestral wet-season grazing land, although options for the means of fighting differed – some talked of taking up arms, while others argued for the legal route. Traditional leaders' positions are coming into question (often owing to their own actions), and others have started taking their places. These others tend to be men literate in both Arabic and French and knowledgeable about urban political ways. Literacy and the sharing of information have led to the employment of specific tactics to fight for the land they believe is theirs. A certain fission and fusion can be discerned – the alternative splitting or coming together at various levels of social organization, depending on the position and need of the individual, family, and tribal unit. This is a group dynamic typical of nomadic-pastoral societies and reflects an historical continuity amidst change, a flexibility while falling back on specific 'ways of doing'. In this sense, the ferīkh functions as a point of reference (a socially constructed space) in relation to which people justify their actions, however ambiguous and inconsistent these appear to be. In dealing with historical and contemporary issues of leadership and land, the fission and fusion nature of connectivity has created a certain flexibility to either link up to bureaucratic representations of the state, or to steer clear of them.

While there is a certain ambiguity in how socio-political issues are tackled, decisions about issues surrounding another traditional 'nomadic' subject – namely, that of cattle or livestock in general – appear to be more unanimous. Chapter Four looked at what changes and continuities exist in the way Walad Djifir adhere to a 'nomadic way' of life, in light of modern economic developments, political and ecological insecurity, and regional mobility. The commodification of livestock and the search for alternative forms of income – such as labour migration to Libya, commercial endeavours in CAR, or seasonal wage labour in N'Djaména – are analysed through Walad Djifir perceptions of and attitudes to these processes. A focus on livestock as connector revealed flexibility in the logics surrounding economic activities such as cattle rearing, wage labour, and income and wealth generation. This flexibility characterizes the norms and values linked to actions and decisions made by Walad Djifir wanting to supplement their livelihood (e.g. Moustapha deciding to take up work in N'Djaména), those deciding where and how to invest their capital (e.g. Adoum and Nour's father), and those faced with a physical threat to their families and wealth (e.g. Youssouf in CAR). There is an element of individual control in this flexibility. A control guided by the will to protect and grow collective and individual wealth so as to ensure the future of any children. Together these strategies contribute to groundedness for Walad Djifir, a groundedness linked to ideas/practices about wealth (in livestock, land, social networks), mobility, and flexibility vis-à-vis economic diversification. It is a continuation of a 'nomadic way' of doing things, framed within a personal 'walk of life' amidst change. Cattle, or livestock, remain the lingua franca, even when its economic importance shifts in relation to other economic opportunities in the pastoral economy. The nomad's economy, today, includes a diaspora and relatively new technologies of communication.

Chapter Five introduces changes in the form of technologies and methods surrounding the transfer of money between Walad Djifir, both across national boundaries and within Chad. Between 2011 and 2015, most of the remittances received came from Libya. The case studies shine light on the existing ways in which money is sent through both traditional and digital means, and the reasons for choosing specific methods. New communication technologies, such as mobile phones and the services of MTOs, do not land in a blank media space. On the contrary, they are complemented by existing practices of connectivity, within contexts of insecurity and over geographical distances, such as those found between CAR, Chad and Libya. In this new mediascape, new patterns of appropriation and flexibility emerge – patterns which replicate former ways of relating and connecting built on social relations of trust and mistrust. Walad Djifir base decisions about how to send money on the potential of deception and risk – that is, on the mistrust of those outside their familial networks. It is precisely this mistrust that provides them with a tool, a groundedness, to be able to appropriate the changes in a world of fast-developing technologies. Their attitude (of mistrust) *is* their strategy (Carey 2017). The nature of a connectivity informed by 'mistrust' and coupled with practicality shows the continuing importance of familial networks when it comes to the digital transfer of money. At the same time, these new technologies of communication and sending money do also very much lead to new mobilities and new connections. However, the newness is relative as the old mobilities of the Walad Djifir are also facing social change and Walad Djifir have always combined old and new connections to face the ever-globalizing world.

In Chapter Six we see a role for the connectors previously described, coupled with the continuing role of family as creators of both support and constraint in times of disruption. The setting is that of CAR, a country hosting first-, second-, and third-generation Walad Djifir. This chapter describes the dynamics of migration out of the ferīkh and into CAR, and the processes surrounding the eruption of violence following the 2013 coup in CAR. Family and the emotion of belonging are the factors which seem to ground people within such a disruptive context – belonging to a family while also belonging to two nations at the same time (CAR and Chad). Family – not only in the form of obligations and expectations, but also in relation to the need or will to provide for them – is seen as presenting two sides of the same coin, both limiting and liberating the three women whose case studies are discussed. Despite everything, people remain the basis of all connections, allowing the ferīkh to exist as it always has: an entity flexible in its relations with and reactions to a globalizing wilderness.

Photo 7.1: Setting of a camp in Fadjé, March 2014. This is where family members were awaiting news about Youssouf's fate. The group was located a little more south along the Bambam compared to where they had been the year before, and further *en brousse*. It was not easy to reach by car but once there the trees opened up and the ferīkh was widely set up. There is a routine every time a camp is moved: the ground around the tents are swept clear of thorns and grass, shelters are built for the smaller animals, donkeys and horses, and places are found and created to hang provisions and clothes.

Photo 7.2: The inside of Khadidja's *barsh*, Al-Berekeh April 2012. This was a temporary move, driven by the needs of a herd of camels, and made possible by the flexible nature of their belongings. The structures used to transport possessions can be seen inside the tent. Khadidja and her children's health suffered while there, with access to a social support network too far away.

Photo 7.3: *Barsh* and hanging belongings, Fadjé, March 2012. The wilderness provides thorny shrubs to block unwanted visitors from entering a tent, clothes and bedding can be hung between trees. It is easy to loose your bearing amidst these close-set trees. The tents itself become camouflaged when seen from a distance.

Photo 7.4: Camels drinking, Fadjé, March 2012. The camels had just been given blocks of *natron* (salt), mixed with water. Livestock remain the main livelihood for Walad Djifir.

Photo 7.5: The remains of tea preparation, Fadjé, March 2012. The preparing and drinking of tea is a ritual in itself and such a staple part of daily life.

Groundedness amidst rupture

The nature of the connections and the behaviours attached to each layer of connectivity reveal tendencies which together 'ground' Chadian Walad Djifir within the globalizing wilderness of the twenty-first century. The visual story which runs throughout this book alternatively acts as a counterbalance to, and nuancing of, the written narrative. A first shallow encounter (a brief stay) in a nomadic camp calls up thoughts on how similar or different lives are now as compared with thirty, fifty, or one hundred years ago. In such an initial observation lies the basis for teasing out or untangling the feeling that there is a groundedness in the way Walad Djifir live their lives. Some may call it structure; but, to me, this implies something fairly static and unanimous for all. But groundedness is relative and adaptable. It varies per personality, per situation, and per connector. If it is so variable, why is it even relative or useful for us as researchers? The cases presented in this book have shown that the networks that 'work', or characterize groundedness, can and do at times add to feelings of insecurity. Yet it is an insecurity that does not mean flying off the side of the earth, floating around aimlessly in space, a feeling of being lost. Rather, in most cases – even the case of Howwa (Chapter Six) and her family in the repatriate camp in Gawwi – however desperate and traumatized they were, people had something to fall back on, to keep them going on a daily basis: the need to provide for themselves, phone calls with family and friends, a concern with what was to become of them and what they could do. Howwa took up what she knew best: her small market trade. An uncle of hers, who studied socio-linguistics at the University in Bangui, became a teacher at a refugee camp in Sido (southern Chad). These are not success stories *per se*, since life was still hard and they were poor and did not have many or varied meals. Nor did they at that time have an idea of how to get out of the situation and improve it. But one day did move into the next. It is the same with the young Farina: her days in the nomadic camp (Chapter Four) moved from one into another. The disruptions in her life were of a different order and cannot be compared to those Howwa's little boy Umar had gone through. The addition of many camels to her family's herd meant she found herself living far from the other children she would otherwise have been able to spend the evenings with. To what extent she perceived this as a disruption is difficult to tell. The point is that the walk of life throws up change, both positive and negative, both expected and unexpected. And motivations or reasons for belonging vary per person and situation.

Walad Djifir conceptualize the ferīkh through that which it stands for: family and cattle (wealth). So many of the conversations and discussions held centred or involved family in some way or another. This in no way means that there was some kind of idyllic relationship between all family members, or that they always listened to each other. Nevertheless, many decisions and happenings revolved around protecting, supporting or disagreeing with close and extended family members. The safe-keeping of wealth and the family's future are large motivators when making decisions amidst changing situations. To what extent these two values or assets will continue to be linked to the nomadic setting varies per individual. For most of the Walad Djifir whose stories run through the chapters, the means of safeguarding their wealth and family (their future) resonates with the norms and values we find in the physical pastoral-nomadic setting of the ferīkh. The shape this safeguarding takes, however, has been changing amidst modernizing economies, expanding networks, and developing technologies. The majority still carry out some form of nomadic pastoralism, complementing this with other means of making a living, such as through agriculture or wage labour. Some first-, second-, and third-generation Walad Djifir associate with their pastoral-nomadic roots but have left the nomadic camp behind and set up commercial businesses in an urban or rural town, or have taken up another form of income-generation. Experiences of living 'outside' the pastoral-nomadic setting – as in the case of Adoum, Nour's father, and Howwa – have seen people investing in land and the building of houses for their offspring, rather than in livestock alone. The importance of an education has become more prominent, although this is certainly also a dynamic we find among several Walad Djifir within the camps. The extended family still plays an important role in motivations for decisions concerning the future, yet we also observe a subtle shift taking place – a shift which sees the individual and his or her children gaining a more central role.

Nomadic connectivity

In an interconnected region pervaded by rupture and continuity, the mundane and the extraordinary go hand in hand. Despite the variety of changes, less or more severe, that Walad Djifir are facing, there is a certain 'way of doing things' in their daily lives which is linked to the ferīkh on numerous levels. It is this historical dynamic which informs and explains their groundedness and ability to persist amidst socio-political disruption (e.g. issues of land and leadership, a political coup), expected and unexpected insecurities (e.g. periods of drought, cattle disease, travelling across borders), and technological developments (e.g. in relation to communication networks and means of sending money long-distance). This persistence, in a pastoral-nomadic sense, is flexible and non-static, rooted in feelings of belonging and the practical nature of the connectivity. Reactions to extraordinary and mundane insecurity vary and are not consistent. Reactions of mistrust (Chapter Five), constrained agency (Chapter Six), flexibility (Chapter Four), and fission and fusion (Chapter Three) are temporal and dependent on historical contexts.

Despite being caught in the middle of these local, regional, and global processes, Walad Djifir have not been experiencing rupture due to their connectors and the tenacity of the networks, norms, values, and behaviours they embody. Rupture is circumvented through the connectors' consistent flexibility and adaptability to change, while not loosing their meaning and role of support (or constraint). The ferīkh as network and space (through the connectors) shares these same characteristics and has continually navigated insecurities and changes because of them. As such, 'the ferīkh' has found a way to survive and live by creating its own 'éspace' (Retaillé & Walther 2011). An *éspace* which works with the state when forming alliances with sedentary *chefs de canton* to ensure land-use rights and the building of schools, but which also stands apart from this state through their role in the cattle trade, which largely remains informal (Krätli et al. 2018). It is a space which makes use of digital means of sending money but also functions without them. Formal networks exist but Walad Djifir have the option and tendency to continue using more traditional (and less formal) means of sending money. This ability to remain mobile and flexible when it comes to governing bodies, communication technologies, conflict and changing economies is an inherent part of Walad Djifir groundedness. It directly contributes to their perseverance in avoiding large ruptures amidst the everyday wilderness. Living within a dysfunctional state, Walad Djifir have a need to fall back on their own system. A system embodied by the ferīkh.

The ferīkh *is* its connectors. It is Islam and the Arabic language. It is its people and all they contain, their wants and wishes and the places they occupy. It is a space in which the state does not necessarily have a role and the basis of nomadic life – group dynamics, mobility, and flexibility – continues to thrive. I would even argue that all that the 'tent' or ferīkh stands for is very much internalized and embodied (as an emotion of belonging) by the person him or herself, allowing the wilderness to have the possible characteristics of 'home'. It is perhaps this which informs a certain ambivalence toward the immediate environment and which will ultimately help us understand what life in a globalizing twenty-first century entails, in the context of the Chadian Walad Djifir. Walad Djifir roaming away from their camp (ferīkh) do not leave their baggage of knowledge and experience behind. In their flexible interactions with nature, with roads, markets, and other people, the ways they were taught from childhood onward will play a role. Whether he or she adheres to them or not. It is these customs – which entail norms, values, and logics of doing – which connect the individual with his or her community and which directly and indirectly provide groundedness.

Bibliography

Abakar, G.O. (2010) 'Le commerce exterieur du Tchad de 1960 de nos jours', PhD thesis, University of Strasbourg, [http://scd-theses.u-strasbg.fr/2034/01/GONI_OUSMAN_Abakar_2010.pdf], accessed 8 June 2018.

Abderamane, M.A. & D. Halley des Fontaines (2011) 'Elevage transhumant et dynamique des marchés à bétail au Tchad', in I.O. Alfaroukh, N. Avella & P. Grimaud (eds) *La politique sectorielle du pastoralisme au Tchad: Quelles orientations?*, Actes du colloque national, 1–3 March, N'Djaména, pp. 114–122.

Abu-Lughod, L. (1991) 'Writing against culture', in R. Fox (ed.) *Recapturing anthropology: Working in the present*, Santa Fe, NM: School of American Research Press, pp. 137–62.

Abu-Lughod, L. (2008) *Writing women's worlds: Bedouin stories*, Berkeley and Los Angeles, CA: University of California Press.

Africa Research Institute (17 January 2014) 'Somali money matters – an update on the remittance saga', [http://www.africaresearchinstitute.org/blog/somali-money-matters-an-update-on-the-remittances-saga-by-edward-paice/], accessed 21 November 2014.

Alfaroukh, I.O., N. Avella & P. Grimaud (eds) (2011) *La politique sectorielle du pastoralisme au Tchad: Quelles orientations?*, Actes du colloque national, 1–3 March, N'Djaména.

Alio, K. (2008) 'Conflict, mobility and language: The case of migrant Hadjaraye of Guéra to neighboring regions of Chari-Baguirmi and Salamat (Chad)', ASC working paper 82.

Amadou, A. (2012) 'Entre la "détresse" et l'inter-connectivité: Le cas des Mbororo réfugiés sur les frontières Cameroun-Centrafrique' [Between duress and interconnectivity: Mbororo refugees at the Cameroun–CAR border], PhD research, [http://www.connecting-in-times-of-duress.nl/adamou-amadou-ma-entre-detresse-et-linter-connectivite/], accessed 2 November 2018.

Amadou, A. (2015) 'CAR: Les répercussions de la crise centrafricaine au Cameroun: Des tensions déjà perceptibles', [http://www.connecting-in-times-of-duress.nl/wd-car-les-repercussions-de-la-crise-centrafricaine-au-cameroun-des-tensions-deja-perceptibles/], accessed 23 November 2018.

Amadou, A., M.E. de Bruijn, E. Lewa Doksala & B. Sangaré (2016) 'Mobile pastoralists in Central and West Africa: Between conflict, mobile telephony and (im)mobility', *Revue Scientifique et Technique (International Office of Epizootics)*, 35(2): 649–657.

Amit, V. & N. Rapport (2002) *The trouble with community: Anthropological reflections on movement, identity and collectivity*, London: Pluto Press.

Ankogui-Mpoko, G.F., K. Passingring, B. Ganota & D. Kadekoy-Tigague (2009) 'Insécurité, mobilité et migration des éleveurs dans les savanes d'Afrique central', in *Savanes africaines en développement: Innover pour durer, Garoua: Cameroun. Cirad.* [http://www.inter-reseaux.org/IMG/pdf/Savanes_africaines_en_developpement_actes_2009.pdf], accessed 10 December 2018.

Appadurai, A. (ed.) (1986) *The social life of things: Commodities in cultural perspective*, Cambridge: Cambridge University Press.

Appadurai, A. (1990) 'Disjuncture and difference in the global cultural economy', in M. Featherstone (ed.) *Global culture: Nationalism, globalization and modernity*, London: Sage, pp. 295–310.

Appadurai, A. (1996) *Modernity at large: Cultural dimensions of globalisation*, Minneapolis, MN and London: University of Minnesota Press.

Appadurai, A. (1997) 'Fieldwork in the era of globalization', *Anthropology and Humanism*, 22(1): 115–118.

https://doi.org/10.1515/9783110714685-008

Archambaud, L., I. Tidjani & B. Lallau (2020) 'Peut-on encore être éleveur en République centrafricaine? Éléments de réponse dans la région de Batangafo (Ouham)', in E. Chauvin, O. Langlois, C. Seignobos & C. Baroin (eds) *Conflits et violences dans le bassin du lac Tchad*, Marseille: IRD, pp. 197–213.

Arditi, C. (1999) 'Paysans sara et éleveurs arabes dans le sud du Tchad: Du conflit à la cohabitation', in C. Baroin & J. Boutrais (eds) *L'homme et l'animal dans le bassin du lac Tchad*, Paris: IRD, pp. 555–573.

Arditi, C. (2003) 'Les violences ordinaires ont une histoire: Le cas du Tchad', *Politique africaine*, 91: 51–67.

Argenti, N. & K. Schramm (2010) 'Introduction: Remembering violence: Anthropological perspectives on intergenerational transmission', in N. Argenti & K. Schramm (eds) *Remembering violence: Anthropological perspectives on intergenerational transmission*, New York and Oxford: Berghahn Books, pp. 1–42.

Aubague, S., D. Djialta, A.A. Fizzani & A.A. Mannany (2006) 'Du fleuve Batha au Sud Guera: Diagnostic pastoral', a report by Programme d'hydraulique pastorale au Tchad Central 'Almy Al Afia', ANTEA, IRAM & AFD, [https://docplayer.fr/39862743-Programme-d-hydraulique-pastorale-au-tchad-central-almy-al-afia.html], accessed 10 December 2018.

Ayimpam, S. (2014) 'The cyclical exchange of violence in Congolese violence relations', in J. Bouju & M.E. de Bruijn (eds) *Ordinary violence and social change in Africa*, Leiden and Boston, MA: Brill, pp. 101–116.

Azarya, V. (1996a) *Nomads and the state in Africa: The political roots of marginality*, Research Series 9, Leiden: African Studies Centre.

Azarya, V. (1996b) 'Pastoralism and the state in Africa: Marginality or incorporation?', *Nomadic Peoples*, 38: 11–36.

Azarya, V., A. Breedveld, M. de Bruijn & J.W.M. van Dijk (eds) (1999) *Pastoralists under pressure? Fulbe societies confronting change in West Africa*. Leiden, Boston, MA, and Cologne: Brill.

Azevedo, M.J. (2004) *Roots of violence: A history of war in Chad*, Abingdon: Routledge.

Azouzou, M. (1999) 'Les activités commerciales en Oubangui-Chari de 1930 à 1945', Master's thesis, Université de Bangui.

Barraud, V., O.M. Saleh & D. Mamis (2001) 'L'élevage transhumant au Tchad oriental', N'Djaména, Chad: Vétérinaires Sans Frontières/SCAC Ambassade de France.

Basso, K.H. (1996) 'Wisdom sits in places: Notes on a Western Apache landscape', in S. Feld & K. Basso (eds) *Senses of Place*, Santa Fe, NM: School of American Research, pp. 53–90.

Bauman, Z. (2007) *Liquid times: Living in an age of uncertainty*, Cambridge and Malden, MA: Polity Press.

Behrends, A. (2011) 'Fighting for oil when there is no oil yet: The Darfur-Chad border', in A. Behrends, S.P. Reyna & G. Schlee (eds) *Crude domination: An anthropology of oil*, New York and Oxford: Berghahn Books, pp. 81–106.

Behrends, A., J.P. Heiß & S.P. Reyna (eds) (2007) 'Crisis in Chad: Approaching the anthropological gap', *Sociologus*, 57(1): 1–9.

Behrends, A. & R. Hoinathy (2014) 'Does rationality travel? Translating the World Bank model for fair oil revenue distribution in Chad', in A. Behrends, S.J. Park & R. Rottenburg (eds) *Travelling models in African conflict management: Translating technologies of social ordering*, Leiden: Brill, pp. 76–91.

Ben Yahmed, D. (ed.) (2006) *Atlas du Tchad*, Atlas de l'Afrique, Paris: Les Éditions J.A.

Benda-Beckmann, F. von & K. von Benda-Beckmann (1994) 'Coping with insecurity', *Focaal*, 22/23: 7–31.

Berckmoes, L. (2014) 'Elusive tactics: Urban youth navigating the aftermath of war in Burundi', PhD dissertation, Vrije Universiteit Amsterdam.

Berg, P. (2008) 'The dynamics of conflict in the tri-border region of the Sudan, Chad and the Central African Republic', Country Conflict-Analysis Studies, Berlin: Friedrich Ebert Foundation.

Beuving, J.J (2006) 'Lebanese traders in Cotonou: A socio-cultural analysis of economic mobility and capital accumulation', *Africa*, 76: 324–351.

Binsbergen, W. van & P. Geschiere (eds) (2005) *Commodification: Things, agency, and identities (The social life of things revisited)*, Münster: LIT Verlag.

Boesen, E. (2007) 'Pastoral nomadism and urban migration: Mobility among the Fulbe Wodaabe of Central Niger', in H.P. Hahn & G. Klute (eds) *Cultures of migration: African perspectives*, Beiträge zur Afrika-Forschung, Münster: Lit Verlag, pp. 31–60.

Boesen, E. & L. Marfaing (eds) (2007) *Les nouveaux urbains dans l'espace Sahara-Sahel: Un cosmopolitisme par le bas*, Paris: Karthala.

Boesen, E., L. Marfaing & M. de Bruijn (2014) 'Nomadism and mobility in the Sahara-Sahel: Introduction', *Canadian Journal of African Studies/La Revue canadienne des études africaines*, 48(1): 1–12.

Boggero, M. (2009) 'Darfur and Chad: A fragmented ethnic mosaic', *Journal of Contemporary African Studies*, 27(1): 21–35.

Bonfiglioli, A.M. (1988) *DuDal, histoire de famille et histoire de troupeau chez un groupe de WoDaaBe du Niger*, Cambridge: Cambridge University Press.

Both, J. (2017) 'Conflict legacies: Understanding youth's post-peace agreement practices in Yumbe, north-western Uganda', PhD dissertation, University of Amsterdam.

Both, J., C.M. Mouguia, W.V. Poukoule, M.L. Tchissikombre & C. Wilson (2022) 'Staying away from arms? The non-violent trajectories of youth in times of conflict in the Central African Republic', in A. Iwilade & T.M. Ebiede (eds) *Youth and non-violence in Africa's fragile contexts*, London: Palgrave Macmillan, pp. 15–38. https://doi.org/10.1007/978-3-031-13165-3_2.

Bouju, J. & M.E. de Bruijn (eds) (2014) *Ordinary violence and social change in Africa*, Leiden and Boston, MA: Brill.

Bouman, A. (2003) 'Benefits of belonging: Dynamics of Iklan identity, Burkina Faso', PhD dissertation, Universiteit Utrecht.

Brahim, M.T. (1988) 'Etude monographique des Missiries du Batha', Memoire de fin du premier cycle, Ecole Nationale d'Administration et de Magistrature (ENAM) au N'Djamena.

Braukämper, U. (1996) 'Strategies of environmental adaptation and patterns of transhumance of the Shuwa Arabs in the Nigerian Chad Basin', *Nomadic Peoples*, 39: 53–68.

Braukämper, U. (2000) 'Management of conflicts over pastures and fields among the Baggara Arabs of the Sudan Belt', *Nomadic Peoples*, 4(1): 37–49.

Brenner, N. (1999) 'Beyond state-centrism? Space, territoriality, and geographical scale in globalization studies', *Theory and Society*, 28: 39–78.

Brenner, N. (2000) 'The urban question as a scale question: Reflections on Henri Lefebvre, urban theory and the politics of scale', *International Journal of Urban and Regional Research*, 24(2): 361–378.

Brenner, N. (2001) 'The limits to scale? Methodological reflections on scalar structuration', *Progress in Human Geography*, 25(4): 591–614.

Bruijn, M. de (1994) 'The Sahelian crisis and the poor: The role of Islam in social security among Fulbe pastoralists, central Mali', *Focaal*, 22/23: 47–65.

Bruijn, M. de (1995) 'A pastoral woman's economy in crisis: The Fulbe in central Mali', *Nomadic Peoples*, 36/37: 85–104.

Bruijn, M. de (1997) 'The Hearthhold in pastoral Fulbe society, central Mali: Social relations, milk and drought', *Africa*, 67(4): 625–651.

Bruijn, M. de (1999) 'The pastoral poor: Hazard, crisis and insecurity in Fulbe society in Central Mali', in V. Azarya, A. Breedveld, M. de Bruijn & H. van Dijk (eds) *Pastoralists under pressure? Fulbe societies confronting change in West Africa*, Leiden: Brill, pp. 285–312.

Bruijn, M. de (2004) 'From chiefs to silenced people: A family history through the period of civil war in Chad, Central Africa', Paper presented at the EASA Conference in Vienna, Leiden: African Studies Centre.

Bruijn, M. de (2013) 'Mobile telephony and socioeconomic dynamics in Africa', in G.K. Ingram & K.L. Brandt (eds) *Infrastructure and land policies*, Cambridge, MA: Lincoln Institute of Land Policy, pp. 61–83.

Bruijn, M. de (2014) 'The itinerant Koranic school: Contested practice in the history of religion and society in Central Chad', in J. Bouju & M.E. de Bruijn (eds) *Ordinary violence and social change in Africa*, Leiden and Boston, MA: Brill, pp. 63–84.

Bruijn, M. de (2015) 'New ICT and mobility in Africa', in N. Sigona, A. Gamlen, G. Liberatore & H. Neveu Kringelbach (eds) *Diasporas reimagined: Spaces, practices and belonging*, Oxford: Oxford Diasporas Programme, pp. 140–145.

Bruijn, M. de, A. Amadou, E. Lewa Doksala & B. Sangaré (2016) 'Mobile pastoralists in Central and West Africa: Between conflict, mobile telephony and (im)mobility', *Revue Scientifique et Technique (International Office of Epizootics)*, 35(2): 649–657.

Bruijn, M. de & J. Both (2018) 'Realities of duress: Understanding experiences and decisions in situations of enduring hardship in middle Africa', *Conflict and Society - Advances in Research*, 4(1): 186–198.

Bruijn, M. de & I. Brinkman (2012) 'Research practice in connections: Travels and methods', in M. de Bruijn & R. van Dijk (eds) *The social life of connectivity in Africa*, New York: Palgrave Macmillan, pp. 45–63.

Bruijn, M. de, I. Butter & A.S. Fall (2017) 'An ethnographic study on mobile money attitudes, perceptions and usages in Cameroon, Congo DRC, Senegal and Zambia', Final Report, ASC/ IFC, [http://www.ascleiden.nl/sites/default/files/final_report_ethnographic_study_on_mobile_ money_march_2017.pdf].

Bruijn, M. de & H. van Dijk (1997) *Arid ways: Cultural understandings of insecurity in Fulbe society, central Mali*, Amsterdam: Thela Publishers.

Bruijn, M. de & H. van Dijk (2007) 'The multiple experiences of civil war in the Guéra region of Chad, 1965–1990', *Sociologus*, 57(1): 61–98.

Bruijn, M. de, H. van Dijk & H.N. Djindil (2004) 'Central Chad revisited: The long-term impact of drought and war in the Guéra', Leiden: African Studies Centre, [http://www.ascleiden.nl/pdf/ seminar120204.pdf], accessed 25 April 2018.

Bruijn, M. de & J.W.M. van Dijk (2003) 'Risk positions and local politics in a Sahelian society: The Fulbe of the Hayre in Central Mali', in B. Mosely & L.B. Ikubolajeh (eds) *(Inter)National political economies and local ecologies: Rural African livelihoods in a political ecology context*, Aldershot: Ashgate, pp. 140–161.

Bruijn, M. de, J.W.M. van Dijk & R. van Dijk (2001) 'Cultures of travel: Fulbe pastoralists in central Mali and Pentecostalism in Ghana', in M. de Bruijn, D.W.J. Foeken & R.A. van Dijk (eds) *Mobile Africa: Changing patterns of movement in Africa and beyond*, Leiden: Brill, pp. 63–88.

Bruijn, M. de & R. van Dijk (2012) 'Connectivity and the postglobal moment: (Dis)connections and social change in Africa', in M. de Bruijn & R. van Dijk (eds) *The social life of connectivity in Africa*, New York: Palgrave Macmillan, pp. 1–20.

Bruijn, M. de, F.B. Nyamnjoh & T. Angwafo (2010) 'Mobile interconnections: Reinterpreting distance and relating in the Cameroonian grassfields', *Journal of African Media Studies*, 2(3): 267–285.

Bruijn, M. de, F.B. Nyamnjoh & I. Brinkman (2009) *Mobile phones: The new talking drums of everyday Africa*, Bamenda: Langaa Publishers.

Buijtenhuijs, R. (1977) 'La dialectique nord-sud dans l'histoire tchadiennes', *African Perspectives*, 2: 43–62.

Buijtenhuijs, R. (1978) *Le Frolinat et le révoltes populaires du Tchad, 1965-1976*, Den Haag, Paris and New York: Mouton.

Buijtenhuijs, R. (1987) *Le Frolinat et les guerres civiles du Tchad (1977–1984)*, Paris: Karthala.

Buijtenhuijs, R. (2001) 'The Chadian Tubu: Contemporary nomads who conquered a state', *Africa*, 71(1): 149–161.

Burnham, P. (1999) 'Pastoralism under pressure? Understanding social change in Fulbe society', in V. Azarya, A. Breedveld, M. de Bruijn & J.W.M. van Dijk (eds) *Pastoralists under pressure? Fulbe societies confronting change in West Africa*, Leiden, Boston, MA, and Cologne: Brill: pp. 270–283.

Carayannis, T. (2008) 'Elections in the DRC: The Bemba surprise', Special Report 200, Washington, DC: United States Institute of Peace.

Carayannis, T. & L. Lombard (eds) (2015) *Making sense of the Central African Republic*, London: Zed Books.

Carbou, H. (1912) *La région du Tchad et du Ouaddaï*, Paris: Leroux.

Carey, M. (2017) *Mistrust: An ethnographic theory*. Chicago, IL: HAU Books.

Carey, M. & M.A. Pedersen (2017) 'Introduction: Infrastructures of certainty and doubt', *Cambridge Journal of Anthropology*, 35(2): 18–29.

Casciarri, B. (1995) 'The role of women in the changing family and social organization of Ahamda pastoralists (Central Sudan)', *Nomadic Peoples*, 36/37: 105–118.

Castells, M. (1996) *The information age: Economy, society and culture*, vol. 1, *The rise of the network society*: Cambridge, MA and Oxford: Blackwell.

Castells, M. (1997) *The information age: Economy, society and culture*, vol. 2, *The power of identity*, Cambridge, MA and Oxford: Blackwell.

Castells, M. (1998) *The information age: Economy, society and culture*, vol. 3, *End of millennium*, Cambridge, MA and Oxford: Blackwell.

Catley, A. & Y. Aklilu (2013) 'Moving up or moving out? Commercialization, growth and destitution in pastoralist areas', in A. Catley, J. Lindy & I. Scoones (eds) *Pastoralism and development in Africa: Dynamic change at the margins*, London and New York: Routledge, pp. 85–97.

Catley, A., J. Lind & I. Scoones (eds) (2013) *Pastoralism and development in Africa: Dynamic change at the margins*, London and New York: Routledge.

Cerulo, K.A. (1997) 'Identity construction: New issues, new directions', *Annual Review of Sociology*, 23: 385–409.

Certeau, M. de (2011) *The practice of everyday life*, translated by Steven F. Rendall, 3rd ed., Berkeley, CA: University of California Press.

Chapelle, J. (1980) *Le peuple Tchadien, ses racines, sa vie quotidienne et ses combats*, Paris: Harmattan.

Chatty, D. (ed.) (2006) *Nomadic societies in the Middle East and North Africa: Entering the 21st century*. Leiden: Brill.

Chauvin, E. (2009) 'Rivalités ethniques et guerre urbaine au coeur de l'Afrique – Bangui (1996–2001)', *Enjeux*, 40: 30–38.

Chauvin, E. (2018) 'La guerre en Centrafrique à l'ombre du Tchad: Une escalade conflictuelle régionale?', AFD – Agence Française de Développement, Observatoir Pharos, [https://www.afd.fr/fr/la-guerre-en-centrafrique-lombre-du-tchad-une-escalade-conflictuelle-regionale], accessed 21 June 2018.

Chauvin, E., O. Langlois, C. Seignobos & C. Baroin (eds) (2020) *Conflits et violences dans le bassin du lac Tchad*, Marseille: IRD.

Chéneau-Loquay, A. (2012) 'La téléphonie mobile dans les villes africaines: Une adaptation réussie au contexte local', *L'Espace géographique*, 1(41): 82–93.

Ciabarri, L. (2010) 'Trade, lineages, inequalities: Twists in the northern Somali path to modernity', in M. Hoehne & V. Luling (eds) *Peace and milk, drought and war: Somali culture, society and politics*, London: Hurst, pp. 67–85.

Clifford, J. (1997) 'Travelling cultures', in J. Clifford (ed.) *Routes: Travel and translation in the late twentieth century*, Cambridge, MA: Harvard University press, pp. 17–46.

Collelo, T. (ed.) (1988/1990) *Chad: A country study*. Washington, DC: GPO for the Library of Congress.

Collins, P. (1998) 'Negotiating selves: Reflections on "unstructured" interviewing', *Sociological Research Online*, 3(3), [http://www.socresonline.org.uk/3/3/2.html], accessed 10 September 2018.

Cooper, E. & D. Pratten (2015) *Ethnographies of uncertainty in Africa*, London and New York: Palgrave Macmillan.

Cordell, D.D. (1985) 'The Awlad Sulayman of Libya and Chad: Power and adaptation in the Sahara and Sahel', *Canadian Journal of African Studies/Revue Canadienne des Études Africaines*, 19(2): 319–343.

Courtecuisse, L., J. Croquevieille, R. Gros, J. Latruffe, G. Serre & J. Vossart (1971) *Quelques populations de la république du Tchad*, Paris: Centre de Hautes Études Administratives sur l'Afrique et l'Asie Modernes (C.H.E.A.M.).

Cunnison, I. (1966) *Baggara Arabs: Power and the lineage in a Sudanese nomad tribe*, Oxford: Clarendon Press.

Cunnison, I. (1972) 'Blood money, vengeance and joint responsibility: The Baggara case', in I. Cunnison & W.R. James (eds) *Essays in Sudan ethnography*, London: Hurst, pp. 105–125.

Dalby, N. (2015) 'A multifaceted business: Diamonds in the Central African Republic', in T. Carayannis & L. Lombard (eds) *Making sense of the Central African Republic*, London: Zed Books, pp. 123–141.

Dalen, D. van (13–14 January 2018) 'Franse kapmesmoorden verdelen Tsjadische moslims', *NRC*.

Dangbet, Z. (2015a) 'Des transhumants entre alliances et conflits, les Arabes du Batha (Tchad): 1635–2012', Doctoral thesis, d'Aix-Marseille Université.

Dangbet, Z. (2015b) 'Des pasteurs transhumants entre alliances et conflits au Tchad: Les Arabes Salamat Sifera et les Arabes Djaatné au Batha', *Afrique contemporaine*, 3(255): 127–143.

Dangbet, Z. (2020) 'Les adaptations des éleveurs transhumants aux insécurités: La trajectoire des Arabes du Batha (Tchad) depuis 1966', in E. Chauvin, O. Langlois, C. Seignobos & C. Baroin (eds) *Conflits et violences dans le basin du lac Tchad*, Marseille: IRD, pp. 109–119.

Das, V. (2007) *Life and words: Violence and the descent into the ordinary*, Berkeley, CA: University of California Press.

Debos, M. (2008) 'Fluid loyalties in a regional crisis: Chadian "ex-liberators" in the Central African Republic', *African Affairs*, 107(427): 225–241.

Debos, M. (2016) *Living by the gun in Chad: Combatants, impunity and state formation*, London: Zed Books.

Decalo, S. (1980a) 'The roots of centre-periphery strife', *African Affairs*, 79(317): 490–509.

Decalo, S. (1980b) 'Political decay, and civil strife in Chad', *The Journal of Modern African Studies*, 18(1): 23–56.

Desjarlais, R. & C.J. Throop (2011) 'Phenomenological approaches in anthropology', *Annual Review of Anthropology*, 40: 87–102.

Dijck, J. van (2013) *The culture of connectivity: A critical history of social media*, Oxford: Oxford University Press.

Dijk, H. van (1995) 'Farming and herding after the drought: Fulbe agro-pastoralists in dryland central Mali', *Nomadic Peoples*, 36/37: 65–84.

Dijk, H. van (2003) 'War and land tenure in central Chad', Paper prepared for the conference, Competing Jurisdictions: Settling Land Claims in Africa, 24–26 September 2003, Free University of Amsterdam, unpublished.

Dijk, H. van (2008) 'Political instability, chronic poverty and food production systems in central Chad', in M. Rutten, A. Lelieveld & D. Foeken (eds) *Inside poverty and development in Africa: Critical reflections on pro-poor policies*. Leiden: Brill, pp. 119–143.

Dijk, H. van & M. de Bruijn (2023) 'Religious movements in the drylands: Ethnicity, jihadism and violent extremism', in A.K. García, T. Haller, H. van Dijk, C. Samimi & J. Warner (eds.) *Drylands facing change: Interventions, investments and identities*, London and New York: Routledge, pp. 155–173. https://doi.org/10.4324/9781003174486.

Dijk, J.W.M. van (1994) 'Livestock transfers and social security in Fulbe society in the Hayre', in F. von Benda-Beckmann, K. von Benda-Beckmann & H. Marks (eds) *Coping with insecurity: An 'underall' perspective on social security in the Third World*, Yogyakarta: Pustaka Pelajar and Focaal Foundation, pp. 97–112.

Dijk, J.W.M. van (1999) 'Ecological insecurity and Fulbe pastoral society in the Niger Bend', in A. Breedveld, M.E. de Bruijn, J.W.M. van Dijk & V. Azarya (eds) *Pastoralists under pressure: Fulbe societies confronting change in West Africa*, Leiden: Brill, pp. 236–265.

Djama, M. (2010) 'The political anthropology of "pastoral democracy": Scope and limitations of a political ecology', in M. Hoehne & V. Luling (eds) *Milk and peace, drought and war: Somali culture, society and politics*, London: Hurst, pp. 105–115.

Djindil, S.N. and M. de Bruijn (2009) 'The silent victims of humanitarian crises and livelihood (in) security: A case study among migrants in two Chadian towns', *JAMBA Journal of Disaster Risk Studies*, 2(3): 253–272.

Djohy, G., H. Edja & N. Schareika (2017) 'Mobile phones and socio-economic transformation among Fulani pastoralists in northern Benin', *Nomadic Peoples*, 21: 111–135.

Elliot, H. (2010) 'Somali displacements and shifting markets: Camel milk in Nairobi's Eastleigh Estate', in A. Hammer (ed.) *Displacement economies in Africa: Paradoxes of crisis and creativity*, London and New York: Zed Books, 127–144.

Evans-Pritchard, E.E. (1940) *The Nuer: A description of the modes of livelihood and political institutions of a Nilotic people*, Oxford: Oxford University Press.

Evans-Pritchard, E.E. (1949) *The Senusi of Cyrenaica*, Oxford: Clarendon Press.

'Express Union Tchad', [http://www.expressunion.net/en/ag_tchad.php], accessed 12 June 2013.

Fabian, J. (2003) 'Forgetful remembering: A colonial life in the Congo', *Journal of the International African Institute*, 73(4): 489–504.

Faier, L. & L. Rofel (2014) 'Ethnographies of encounter', *Annual Review of Anthropology*, 43: 363–377. https:doi.org/10.1146/annurev-anthro-102313-030210.

Fischer, A. & I. Kohl (eds) (2010) *Tuareg society within a globalised world: Saharan life in transition*, New York: Palgrave Macmillan.

Fuchs, P. (1996) 'Nomadic society, civil war, and the state in Chad', *Nomadic Peoples*, 38: 151–162.

Gaibazzi, P. (2015) 'Introduction', in *Bush bound: Young men and rural permanence in migrant West Africa*, New York and Oxford: Berghahn Books, pp. 1–27.

Galvin, K. (2009) 'Transitions: Pastoralists living with change', *Annual Review of Anthropology*, 38: 185–198.

García, A.K., T. Haller, H. van Dijk, C. Samimi & J. Warner (eds) (2023) *Drylands facing change: Interventions, investments and identities*, 1st ed. London and New York: Routledge. https://doi.org/10.4324/9781003174486.

Gertel, J. (2007) 'Mobility and insecurity: The significance of resources in pastoral Morocco', in J. Gertel & I. Breuer (eds) *Pastoral Morocco: Globalizing scapes of mobility and insecurity*, Wiesbaden: Dr. Ludwig Reichert Verlag, pp. 11–30.

Gertel, J. & R. Le Heron (2016a) 'Introduction: Pastoral economies between resilience and exposure', in J. Gertel & R. Le Heron (eds) *Economic spaces of pastoral production and commodity systems*, London and New York: Routledge, pp. 3–24.

Gertel, J. & R. Le Heron (eds) (2016b) *Economic spaces of pastoral production and commodity systems*, London and New York: Routledge.

Geschiere, P. (2009) *The perils of belonging: Autochthony, citizenship, and exclusion in Africa and Europe*, Chicago, IL and London: University of Chicago Press.

Giddens, A. (1991) *Modernity and self-identity*, Stanford, CA: Stanford University Press.

Gille, Z. and S. Ó Riain (2002) 'Global ethnography', *Annual Review of Sociology*, 28: 271–295.

Giuffrida, A. (2010) 'Tuareg networks: An integrated approach to mobility and stasis', in A. Fischer & I. Kohl (eds) *Tuareg society within a globalised world: Saharan life in transition*, New York: Palgrave Macmillan, pp. 23–39.

Goody, J. (2002) 'The anthropology of the senses and sensations', *La Ricerca Folklorica*, 45, *Antropologia delle sensazioni* (April): 17–28.

Grabska, K. (2014) *Gender, home and identity: Nuer repatriation to southern Sudan*, Suffolk: James Currey.

Granovetter, M. (1985) 'Economic action and social structure: The problem of embeddedness', *American Journal of Sociology*, 3: 481–510.

Graw, K. & S. Schielke (2012) 'Introduction: Reflection on migratory expectations in Africa and beyond', in K. Graw & S. Schielke (eds) *The global horizon: Expectations of migration in Africa and the Middle East*, Leuven: Leuven University Press, pp. 7–22.

Greeley, B. (23 May 2013) 'Kenyans find the unintended consequences of mobile money', *Bloomberg Businessweek*, [http://www.businessweek.com/articles/2013-05-23/kenyans-find-the-unintended-consequences-of-mobile-money], accessed 23 May 2013.

Greenough, K. (2012) 'Mobility, market exchange and livelihood transition: Fulbe flexibility in Tanout, Niger', *Nomadic Peoples*, 16(2): 26–52.

Gupta, A. & J. Ferguson (1992) 'Beyond "culture": Space, identity, and the politics of difference', *Cultural Anthropology*, 7(1): 6–23.

Gupta, A. & J. Ferguson (1997) 'Discipline and practice: The "field" as site, method and location in anthropology', in A. Gupta & J. Ferguson (eds), *Anthropological locations: Boundaries and grounds of a field science*, Berkeley, CA: University of California Press, pp. 1–46.

Hahn, H.P. & G. Klute (eds) (2007) *Cultures of migration: African perspectives*, Beiträge zur Afrika-Forschung, Münster: Lit Verlag.

Hammar, A. (ed.) (2014) *Displacement economies in Africa: Paradoxes of crisis and creativity*, London and New York: Zed Books.

Hammar, A., L. Landau & J. McGregor (eds) (2010) 'Special issue: The Zimbabwe crisis through the lens of displacement', *Journal of Southern African Studies*, 36(2): 263–510.

Hammar, A. & G. Rodgers (2008) 'Introduction: Notes on political economies of displacement in southern Africa', *Journal of Contemporary African Studies*, 26(4): 355–370.

Hampshire, K. (2002) 'Networks of nomads: Negotiating access to health resources among pastoralist women in Chad', *Social Science and Medicine*, 54: 1025–1037.

Hannerz, U, (2003) 'Being there. . .and there. . .and there!: Reflections on multi-site ethnography', *Ethnograph*, 4(2): 201–216.

Haour, A. (2013) *Outsiders and strangers: An archeology of liminality in West Africa*, Oxford: Oxford University Press.

Harvey, D. (1989) *The condition of postmodernity*, Oxford: Blackwell.

Harvey, D. (1993) 'From space to place and back again: Reflections on the condition of postmodernity', in J. Bird, B. Curtis, T. Putnam, G. Robertson & L. Tickner (eds) *Mapping the futures: Local cultures, global change*, London: Routledge, pp. 3–29.

Hashimshony-Yaffe, N., Q. Zhang & A. Alhuseen (2023) 'Making cities in drylands: Migration, livelihoods, and policy', in A.K. García, T. Haller, H. van Dijk, C. Samimi & J. Warner (eds) *Drylands facing change: Interventions, investments and identities*. London and New York: Routledge, pp. 174–192. https://doi.org/10.4324/9781003174486.

Hicks, C. (2018) *The trial of Hissène Habré: How the people of Chad brought a tyrant to justice*, London: Zed Books.

Hodgson, D.L. (1999) 'Women as children: Culture, political economy, and gender inequality among Kisongo Maasai', *Nomadic Peoples*, 3(2): 115–130.

Hoinathy, R. (2013) *Pétrole et changement social au Tchad: Rente pétrolière et monétisation des relations économiques et sociales dans la zone pétrolière de Doba*, Paris: Karthala.

Holtzman, J. (2009) *Uncertain tastes: Memory, ambivalence and the politics of eating in Samburu, northern Kenya*. Berkeley and Los Angeles, CA: University of California Press.

Holy, L. (1974) *Neighbours and kinsmen: A study of the Berti people of Darfur*, New York: St. Martin's Press.

Hugot, P. (1997) *La transhumance des arabes Missiriés et les batailles interminables d'Oumhadjer de 1947*, Paris: L'Harmattan.

IFAD (International Fund for Agricultural Development) (2007) 'Sending money home: Worldwide remittance flows to developing and transition countries', IFAD report, [https://www.ifad.org/fr/web/knowledge/publication/asset/39408693], accessed 28 October 2014.

IFAD (International Fund for Agricultural Development) (2009) 'Sending money home to Africa: Remittance markets, enabling environment and prospects', IFAD report, [http://www.ifad.org/remittances/pub/money_africa.pdf], accessed 12 June 2013.

IOM (International Organisation for Migration) (2013) 'Chadian migrants expelled from Libya a "growing concern", says IOM', [https://www.iom.int/cms/en/sites/iom/home/news-and-views/press-briefing-notes/pbn-2013/pbn-listing/chadian-migrants-expelled-from-l.html], accessed 28 October 2014.

IRIN News (27 February 2013) 'Africans pay high prices to send money home', [http://www.irinnews.org/report/97557/african-migrants-pay-high-prices-to-send-money-home], accessed 28 February 2013.

IRIN News (25 March 2013) 'CAR coup comes amid deepening humanitarian crisis', [http://www.irinnews.org/Report/97721/CAR-coup-comes-amid-deepening-humanitarian-crisis], accessed 26 April 2013.

IRIN News (18 June 2013) 'Insecurity in Bangui increases food prices, lay-offs', [http://www.irinnews.org/report/98250/insecurity-in-bangui-increases-food-prices-lay-offs], accessed 21 June 2013.

Irwin, K. (2006) 'Into the dark heart of ethnography: The lived ethics and inequality of intimate field relationships', *Qualitative Sociology*, 29(2): 155–175.

Jackson, M. (2004) *In Sierra Leone*. Durham, NC: Duke University Press.

Jackson, M. (2013) *The wherewithal of life: Ethics, migration, and the question of well-being*, Berkeley and Los Angeles, CA and London: University of California Press.

Joffe, E.G.H. (1982) 'The international consequences of the civil war in Chad', *Review of African Political Economy*, 25: 91–104.

Johnson, S. (2015) 'Informal financial practices and social networks: Transaction genealogies. Other', Nairobi and Bath: FSD Kenya and University of Bath.

Johnson-Hanks, J. (2002) 'On the limits of life stages in ethnography: Toward a theory of vital conjunctures', *American Anthropologist*, 104(3): 865–880.

Johnson-Hanks, J. (2005) 'When the future decides: Uncertainty and intentional action in contemporary Cameroon', *Current Anthropology*, 46(3): 363–385.

Julien de Pommerol, P. (1997) *L'arabe tchadien: Emergence d'une langue véhiculaire*. Paris: Karthala.

Julien de Pommerol, P. (1999) *Dictionaire arabe tchadien-français*. Paris: Karthala.

Kaag, M. (2007) 'Aid, Umma, and politics: Transnational Islamic NGOs in Chad', in B.F. Soares & R. Otayek (eds) *Islam and Muslim politics in Africa*. New York: Palgrave Macmillan, pp. 85–102.

Kaag, M. (2012) 'Connectivities compared: Transnational Islamic NGOs in Chad and Senegal', in M. de Bruijn & R. van Dijk (eds) *The social life of connectivity in Africa*. New York: Palgrave Macmillan, pp. 183–201.

Käihkö, I. & M. Utas (2014) 'The crisis in CAR: Navigating myths and interests', *Africa Spectrum*, 1: 69–77, [https://journals.sub.uni-hamburg.de/giga/afsp/article/viewArticle/715].

Kassambara, A.A. (2021) 'Vie d'errance et crise identitaire des immigrés tchadiens musulmans en Centrafrique: le cas des retournés de Gaoui, au Tchad, de 2012 à 2019', *Canadian Journal of African Studies / Revue canadienne des études africaines*, 55(3): 609–633. DOI:10.1080/00083968.2021.1928521.

Khazanov, A.M. (1994) *Nomads and the outside world*, 2nd ed. Madison, WI: University of Wisconsin Press.

Kilembe, F. (2015) 'Local dynamics in the Pk5 district of Bangui', in T. Carayannis & L. Lombard (eds) *Making sense of the Central African Republic*, London: Zed Books, pp. 76–101.

Köhler, F. (2016a) 'Transhumant pastoralists, translocal migrants: Space, place and identity in a group of Fulɓe Woɗaaɓe in Niger', Dissertation thesis, Martin-Luther-Universität Halle-Wittenberg, Faculty of Philosophy.

Köhler, F. (2016b) *The sedentarization of dwelling: Continuity and change in the habitat of Fulɓe Woɗaaɓe pastoralists and urban migrants in Niger*. Text and photo essays, Department 'Integration and Conflict' Field Notes and Research Projects, vol. 15, Halle (Saale): Max Planck Institute for Social Anthropology.

Kosnaye, M.N., G.N. Gatta, M.S. Yacoub, H. Coudray, M. Hissène & N. Yamassoum (eds) (1998) *Contentieux linguistique arabe-français*, N'Djaména: Al Mouna.

Koussou, M.O. (2013) 'Economie et fiscalité pastorale: Quels obstacles au developpement equitable de la filiere betail?', Paper presented at, La contribution de l'élevage pastoral a la securité et au developpement des espaces Saharo-Saheliens, Colloque Regional de N'Djaména, 27–29 May 2013, [https://www.pasto-secu-ndjamena.org/classified/J2-3-12-Koussou-fiscalite_et_exportation_sur_pied.pdf], accessed 8 June 2018.

Koussou, M.O. & S. Aubague (2011) 'Economie et fiscalité pastorales: Le cas du commerce d'exportation de bovins sur pied du Tchad vers le Nigeria', in I.O. Alfaroukh, N. Avella & P. Grimaud (eds) *La politique sectorielle du pastoralisme au Tchad: Quelles orientations?*, Actes du colloque national, 1–3 March, N'Djaména, pp. 107–113.

Krätli, S., P. Sougnabé, F. Staro & H. Young (2018) 'Pastoral systems in Dar Sila, Chad: A background paper for Concern Worldwide', Feinstein International Center, Tufts University, Boston, MA.

Ladiba, G. (2011) *L'émergence des organisations Islamiques au Tchad: Enjeux, acteurs et territoires*, Paris: L'Harmattan.

Latruffe, J. (1949) 'Un problème politique au Tchad: Les Arabes myssyrié', *Mémoires du CHEAM* 1388.

Lecocq, B. (2010) 'Tuareg city blues: Cultural capital in a global cosmopole', in A. Fischer & I. Kohl (eds) *Tuareg society within a globalised world: Saharan life in transition*, New York: Palgrave Macmillan, pp. 41–58.

Lemarchand, R. (1980) 'The politics of Sara Ethnicity: A note on the origins of the civil war in Chad', *Cahiers d'Etudes Africaines*, 20(4): 449–471.

Lemarchand, R. (1981) 'Chad: The roots of Chaos', *Current History*, 80(470): 414–438.

Lemarchand, R. (1985) 'The crisis in Chad', in G. Bender, J.S. Coleman & R. Sklar (eds) *African crisis areas and the US foreign policy*, Berkeley and Los Angeles, CA: University of California Press, pp. 239–256.

Lemarchand, R. (1986) 'The misadventures of the North–South dialectic', *African Studies Review*, 29(3): 27–41.

Le Rouvreur, A. (1989) *Sahariens et Sahéliens du Tchad*, Paris: L'Harmattan.

Levy, S. (2006) 'Public investment to reverse Dutch disease: The case of Chad', Development Strategy and Governance Division (DSGD) Discussion paper 35. Washington, DC: International Food Policy Research Institute (IFPRI).

Lindley, A. (2010) *The early morning phone call: Somali refugees' remittances*, New York and Oxford: Berghahn Books.

Little P.D., H. Mahmoud & D.L. Coppock (2001) 'When deserts flood: Risk management and climatic processes among East African pastoralists', *Climate Research*, 19: 149–159.

Lombard, L. (2011) 'Rébellion et limites de la consolidation de la paix en République centrafricaine', *Politique Africaine*, 125: 189–208.

Lombard, L. (2014) 'A brief political history of the Central African Republic', Hot Spots, *Cultural Anthropology Online*, 11 June, [https://culanth.org/fieldsights/539-a-brief-political-history-of-the-central-african-republic].

Lombard, L. (2016) *State of rebellion: Violence and intervention in the Central African Republic*, London: Zed Books.

Lucas, C. & S. Manfredi (eds) (2020) *Arabic and contact-induced change*, Contact and Multilingualism 1, Berlin: Language Science Press. DOI:10.5281/zenodo.3744565.

Lydon, G. (2009) *On trans-Saharan trails: Islamic law, trade networks, and cross-cultural exchange in nineteenth-century Western Africa*, Cambridge: Cambridge University Press.

Mahmoud, H.A. (2013) 'Pastoralists' innovative responses to new camel export market opportunities on the Kenya/Ethiopia borderlands', in A. Catley, J. Lindy and I. Scoones (eds) *Pastoralism and Development in Africa: Dynamic change at the margins*, London and New York: Routledge, pp. 98–107.

Malkki, L.H. (1992) 'National geographic: The rooting of peoples and the territorialization of national identity among scholars and refugees', *Cultural Anthropology*, 7(1): 24–44.

Manfredi, S. & C. Roset (2021) 'Towards a dialect history of the Baggara Belt', *Languages*, 6(146). DOI:10.3390/languages6030146.

Manoli, C., V. Ancey, C. Corniaux, A. Ickowicz, B. Dedieu & C.H. Moulin (2014) 'How do pastoral families combine livestock herds with other livelihood security means to survive? The case of the Ferlo area in Senegal', *Pastoralism: Research, Policy and Practice*, 4: article 3.

Marchal, R. (2006) 'Chad/Darfur: How to merge two crises', *Review of African Political Economy*, 33(106): 467–482.

Marchal, R. (2008) 'The roots of the Darfur conflict and the Chadian civil war', *Public Culture*, 20(3): 429–436.

Marchal, R. (2015) 'CAR and the regional (dis)order', in T. Carayannis & L. Lombard (eds) *Making sense of the Central African Republic*, London: Zed Books, pp. 166–193.

Marcus, G.E. (1995) 'Ethnography in/of the world system: The emergence of multi-sited ethnography', *Annual Review of Anthropology*, 24(1): 95–117.

Marfaing, L. (2014) 'Quelles mobilités pour quelles ressources?', *Canadian Journal of African Studies/La Revue canadienne des études africaines*, 48(1): 41–57.

Markakis, J. (ed.) (1993) *Conflict and the decline of pastoralism in the Horn of Africa*, London: Sage.

Marston, S. (2000) 'The social construction of scale', *Progress in Human Geography*, 24(2): 219–242.

Marty, A., A. Eberschweiler & Z. Dangbet (2009) *Au coeur de la transhumance: Un campement chamelier au Tchad central. Septembre 2006–avril 2007*, Paris: Karthala.

Maru, N. (2020) 'A relational view of pastoral (im)mobilities', *Nomadic Peoples*, 24: 209–227. DOI:10.3197/np.2020.240203.

Massey, D. (1994) 'Double articulation: A place in the world', in A. Bammer (ed.) *Displacements: Cultural identities in question*, Bloomington and Indianapolis, IN: Indiana University Press, pp. 110–121.

Matsutake Worlds Research Group (2009) 'A new form of collaboration in cultural anthropology: Matsutake worlds', *American Ethnologist*, 36(2): 380–403.

Mayneri, A.C. (2014) 'La Centrafrique, de la rébellion Séléka aux groupes anti-balaka (2012–2014): Usages de la violence, schème persécutif et traitement médiatique du conflit', *Politique africaine*, 134 (June): 179–193. [http://www.cairn.info/resume.php?ID_ARTICLE=POLAF_134_0179].

Mbembe, A. & J. Roitman (1995) 'Figures of the subject in times of crisis', *Public Culture*, 7(2): 323–352.

Meagher, K. (2014) 'Smuggling ideologies: From criminalization to hybrid governance in African clandestine economies', *African Affairs*, 113(453): 497–517. https://doi.org/10.1093/afraf/adu057.

Mintz, S.W. (1989) 'The sensation of moving while standing still', *American Ethnologist*, 16(4): 786–796.

'Mobile money: East African governments are targeting telecoms firms' (22 June 2013) *The Economist*.

Mobile Payments Today website (18 June 2012) 'Airtel launches mobile money in Chad', [http://www.mobilepaymentstoday.com/article/196055/Airtel-launches-mobile-money-in-Chad], accessed 12 June 2013.

'MoneyGram store locator in Chad', [http://moneygrampoint.in/locations/chad], accessed 12 June 2013.

Monod, T. (1975) *Pastoralism in Tropical Africa*, London: Oxford University Press.

Morley, D. (2001) 'Belongings: Place, space and identity in a mediated world', *European Journal of Cultural Studies*, 4(4): 425–448.

Mravili, A., E. Abdelfettah & H. Abdourahamane (2013) 'Étude sur les abatoirs d'animaux de boucherie en afrique centrale: Cameroun, Congo, Gabon, Tchad', *Serie État des Lieux*, FAO, [http://www.fao.org/3/i3317f/i3317f.pdf], accessed 17 July 2019.

Nader, L. (2011) 'Ethnography as theory', *HAU Journal of Ethnographic Theory*, 1(1): 211–219.

Næss, M.W. (2013) 'Climate change, risk management and the end of Nomadic pastoralism', *International Journal of Sustainable Development & World Ecology*, 20(2): 123–133, DOI:10.1080/1350 4509.2013.779615.

Nolutshungu, S.C. (1996) *Limits of Anarchy: Intervention and state formation in Chad*, Charlottesville, VA: University Press of Virginia.

Nyamnjoh, H.M. (2014) *Bridging mobilities: ICTs appropriation by Cameroonians in South Africa and the Netherlands*, Leiden: African Studies Centre and Langaa RPCIG.

Olwig, K.F. & K. Hastrup (1997) *Siting culture: The shifting anthropological object*, London and New York: Routledge.

Onyx, J. & J. Small (2001) 'Memory-work: The method', *Qualitative Inquiry*, 7(6): 773–786.

Orabank website [http://www.orabank.net/en/], accessed 19 July 2013.

Pantuliano, S. (2010) 'Oil, land and conflict: The decline of Misseriyya pastoralism in Sudan', *Review of African Political Economy*, 37(123): 7–23.

Peters, E. (1960) 'The proliferation of segments in the lineage of the Bedouin of Cyrenaica', *The Journal of the Royal Anthropological Institute of Great Britain and Ireland*, 90(1): 29–53.

Peters, E. (1967) 'Some structural aspects of the feud among the camel-herding Bedouin of Cyrenaica', *Africa*, 37(3): 261–282.

Petitdemange, C. (2021) 'Bricoler au rythme du politique: L'ambivalence des islams au Tchad', Doctoral dissertation, l'Université de Genève & l'École des Hautes Études en Sciences sociales.

Pink, S. (2009) *Doing sensory ethnography*. London: Sage.

Pink, S. (2012a) *Advances in visual methodology*. London: Sage.

Pink, S. (2012b) 'The visual in ethnography: Photography, video, cultures and individuals', in S. Pink, *Doing visual ethnography*, London: Sage, pp. 16–29.

Prussin, L. (1995) *African nomadic architecture: Space, place and gender*, Washington, DC and London: Smithsonian Institute Press and The National Museum of African Art.

Rense, M. (2006) 'Des contrées ainsi deshéritées: Het Franse koloniale beleid in de Guéra in Tsjaad 1900–1945', Master's thesis, Vrije Universiteit Amsterdam.

République du Tchad (2009) Deuxième Recensement Général de la Population et de l'Habitat (RGPH2 2009): Résultats Globaux. Njamena: Ministère de l'Economie et du Plan.

Retaillé, D. (2014) 'De l'espace nomade à l'espace mobile en passant par l'espace du contrat: Une expérience théorique', *Canadian Journal of African Studies/La Revue canadienne des études africaines*, 48(1): 13–28.

Retaillé, D. & O. Walther (2011) 'Spaces of uncertainty: A model of mobile space in the Sahel', *Singapore Journal of Tropical Geography*, 32: 85–101.

Reyna, S.P. (2011) 'Constituting domination/constructing monsters: Imperialism, cultural desire, and anti-Beowulfs in the Chadian petro-state', in A. Behrends, S.P. Reyna & G. Schlee (eds) *Crude domination: An anthropology of oil*, New York: Berghahn Books, pp. 132–162.

Reynolds Whyte, S. (2008) 'Discrimination: Afterthoughts on crisis and chronicity', *Ethnos*, 73(1): 97–100.

RFI English (2 March 2013) 'Deby confirms AQIM's Abou Zeid dead: France stays mum', [http://www.english.rfi.fr/africa/20130302-deby-confirms-aqims-abou-zeid-dead-france-stays-mum], accessed 26 April 2013.

RFI English (3 March 2013) 'Chad claims to have killed AQIM's Mokhtar Belmokhtar', [http://www.english.rfi.fr/africa/20130303-chad-claims-have-killed-aqims-mokhtar-belmokhtar], accessed 26 April 2013.

Richards, P. (ed.) (2005) *No peace no war: An anthropology of contemporary armed conflicts*, Oxford: James Currey.

Rivoal, I. & N.B. Salazar (2013) 'Contemporary ethnographic practice and the value of serendipity', *Social Anthropology*, 21(2): 178–185. https://doi.org/10.1111/1469-8676.12026.

Robertson, R. (1995) 'Glocalization: Time-space and homogeneity-heterogeneity', in M. Featherstone, S. Lash & R. Robertson (eds) *Global Modernities*, London: Sage, pp. 25–44.

Roitman, J. (1998) 'The garrison-entrepôt', *Cahiers d'Études Africaines*, 38(150/152): 297–329.

Roitman, J. (2001) 'New sovereigns? Regulatory authority in the Chad Basin', in T.M. Callaghy, R. Kassimir & R. Latham (eds) *Intervention and transnationalism in Africa: Global-local networks of power*, Cambridge: Cambridge University Press, pp. 240–263.

Roitman, J. (2005) *Fiscal disobedience: An anthropology of economic regulation in Central Africa*, Princeton, NJ: Princeton University Press.

Roitman, J. (2013) *Anti-crisis*, Durham, NC: Duke University Press.

Rosen, S.A. (2017) *Revolutions in the desert: The rise of mobile pastoralism in the southern Levant*, Routledge: New York.

Salazar, N.B. (2010) 'Towards an anthropology of cultural mobilities', *Crossings: Journal of Migration and Culture*, 1(1): 53–68.

Salzman, P.C. (1995) 'Studying nomads: An autobiographical reflection', *Nomadic Peoples*, 36/37: 157–166.

Schapendonk, J. (2011) 'Turbulent trajectories: Sub-Saharan African migrants heading north', [http://repository.ubn.ru.nl/handle/2066/91326].

Schelling, E., S. Daoud, D.M. Daugla, P. Diallo, M. Tanner & J. Zinsstag (2005) 'Morbidity and nutrition patterns of three nomadic pastoralist communities of Chad', *Acta Tropica*, 95: 16–25.

Scheper-Hughes, N. (1993) *Death without weeping: The violence of everyday life in Brazil*. Berkeley, CA: University of California Press.

Scheper-Hughes, N. (2008) 'A talent for life: Reflections on human vulnerability and resilience', *Ethnos*, 73(1): 25–56.

Scheper-Hughes, N. & P. Bourgois (eds) (2004) *Violence in war and peace: An anthology*, Malden, MA: Blackwell.

Schouten, P. (2022) *Roadblock politics: The Origins of Violence in Central Africa*, Cambridge: Cambridge University Press.

Seli, D. (2012) *(De)connexions identitaires hadjeray: Les enjeux des technologies de la communication au Tchad*, Bamenda and Leiden: Langaa and African Studies Centre.

Shehu, D.J. & W.A. Hassan (1995) 'Women in dairying in the African savanna: Their contribution to agro-pastoral household income in the dry southwest of Nigeria', *Nomadic Peoples*, 36/37: 53–64.

Sheller, M. & J. Urry (2006) 'The new mobilities paradigm', *Environment and Planning A*, 38(2): 207–226.

Sheperd, B. & P. Melly (2016) 'Stability and vulnerability in the Sahel: The regional roles and internal dynamics of Chad and Niger', NOREF Report, April 2016.

Siele, D., J. Swift & S. Krätli (2013) 'Reaching pastoralists with formal education: A distance learning strategy for Kenya', in A. Catley, J. Lind & I. Scones (eds) *Pastoralism and development in Africa: Dynamic changes at the margins*, London and New York: Routledge, pp. 206–214.

Sigona, N.A., A. Gameln, G. Liberatore & H. Neveu Kringelbach (2015) 'Introduction', in N.A. Sigona, A. Gameln, G. Liberatore & H. Neveu Kringelbach (eds) *Diasporas reimagined: Spaces, practices and belonging*, Oxford: Oxford Diasporas Programme, pp. xvii–xxiii.

Smith, M.P. (2001) *Transnational urbanism: Locating globalization*, Oxford: Blackwell.

Smith, N. (1996) 'Spaces of vulnerability: The space of flows and the politics of scale', *Critique of Anthropology*, 16: 63–77.

Smith, S.W. (2015) 'CAR's history: The past of a tense present', in T. Carayannis & L. Lombard (eds) *Making sense of the Central African Republic*, London: Zed Books, pp. 17–52.

Souleymane, A.A. (2017) 'Communication et violences au Tchad: Le cas du Moyen-Chari et du Guera (1900–2010)', Doctoral dissertation, Leiden University.

Stasik, M. (2010) 'DISCOnnections: Popular music audiences in Freetown, Sierra Leone', Research Master's thesis: African Studies Centre, Leiden University.

Stoller, P. (2011) 'Introduction: A return to the senses', in *The taste of ethnographic things: The senses in anthropology*. Philadelphia, PA: University of Pennsylvania Press, pp. 3–13.

Strathern, M. (1991) *Partial connections*, Savage, MD: Rowman & Littlefield.

Strathern, M. (1996) 'Cutting the network', *The Journal of the Royal Anthropological Institute*, 2(3): 517–535.

Swift, J. (2011) 'L'éducation des éleveurs nomades', in I.O. Alfaroukh, N. Avella & P. Grimaud (eds) *La politique sectorielle du pastoralisme au Tchad: Quelles orientations?*, Actes du colloque national, 1–3 March, N'Djaména, pp. 123–128.

Szabó, T.P. & R.A. Troyer (2017) 'Inclusive ethnographies: Beyond the binaries of observer and observed in linguistic landscape studies', *Linguistic Landscape: An International Journal*, 3(3): 306–326. https://doi.org/10.1075/ll.17008.sza.

Telegeography website (14 January 2013) 'Tigo launches mobile money in Chad', [http://www.telegeography.com/products/commsupdate/articles/2013/01/14/tigo-launches-mobile-money-in-chad/], accessed 12 June 2013.

'Tentative de déstabilisation au Tchad: de nouvelles arrestations, le cerveau présumé identifié' (3 May 2013), Radio France International, [http://www.rfi.fr/afrique/20130503-tentative-destabilisation-tchad-nouvelles-arrestations-cerveau-presume-identifie], accessed 3 May 2013.

Thébaud, B. (1990) 'Politique d'hydraulique pastorale et gestion de l'espace au Sahel', *Cahiers des Sciences Humaines*, 26(1–2): 13–31.

Thomas, F.C. (1959) 'The Juhaina Arabs of Chad', *Middle East Journal*, 13(2): 141–155.

Tsing, A. (2000) 'The global situation', *Cultural Anthropology*, 15(3): 327–360.

Tubiana, J. (2011) 'Renouncing the rebels: Local and regional dimensions of Chad-Sudan Rapprochement, *Small Arms Survery*, [http://www.smallarmssurveysudan.org/fileadmin/docs/working-papers/HSBA-WP-25-Local-and-Regional-Dimensions-Chad-Sudan-Rapprochement.pdf], accessed 14 November 2018.

Tubiana, J. & M. Debos (2017) 'Déby's Chad, political manipulation at home, military intervention abroad, challenging times ahead', Peace Institute, 12 December, [https://www.usip.org/publications/2017/12/debys-chad].

Tumblety, J. (2013) *Memory and history: Understanding memory as source and subject*, Abingdon: Routledge.

Turner, M.D. (1999) 'The role of social networks, indefinite boundaries and political bargaining in maintaining the ecological and economic resilience of the transhumance systems of Sudan-Sahelian West Africa', in M. Niamir-Fuller (ed.) *Managing mobility in African rangelands*, London: Food and Agriculture Organization of the United Nations and Beijer Institute of Ecological Economic, pp. 97–123.

Unusa, H. (2012) 'The new pastoralism: Absentee owners, new technologies, economic change and natural resource management in the Sahelian region of far north Cameroon', PhD thesis, University of Leiden.

Urry, J. (2000) *Sociology beyond societies: Mobilities for the twenty-first century*, London: Routledge.

Urry, J. (2004) 'Connections', *Environment and Planning D: Society and Space*, 22(1): 27–37.

Urry, J. (2007) *Mobilities*, Cambridge: Polity Press.

Urry, J. (2010) 'Mobile sociology', *The British Journal of Sociology*, 61(1): 347–366.

Vansina, J. (1980) 'Memory and oral tradition', in J.C. Miller (ed.) *The African past speaks: Essays on oral tradition and history*, Folkestone: Dawson, pp. 262–279.

Vigh, H. (2006) 'Social death and violent life chances', in C. Christiansen, M. Utas & H. Vigh (eds) *Navigating youth, generating adulthood: Social being in an African context*, Uppsala: Nordiska Afrikainstitutet, pp. 31–60.

Vigh, H. (2008) 'Crisis and chronicity: Anthropological perspectives on continuous conflict and decline', *Ethnos*, 73(1): 5–24.

Vigh, H. (2009) 'Motion squared: A second look at the concept of social navigation', *Anthropological Theory*, 9(4): 419–438.

Vries, L. de (2018) 'Navigating violence and exclusion: The Mbororo's claim to the Central African Republic's margins', *Geoforum*. https://doi.org/10.1016/j.geoforum.2016.03.014.

Vries, L. de & T. Glawion (2015) 'Speculating on crisis: The progressive disintegration of the Central African Republic's political economy', CRU Report, Netherlands Institute of International Relations 'Clingendael', [http://www.clingendael.nl/pub/2015/speculating_on_crisis/].

Wehr, H. (1994) *A dictionary of modern written Arabic*, ed. J. Milton Cowan, 4th ed., Wiesbaden: Harrasowitz.

Weyns, Y., L. Hoex, F. Hilgert & S. Spittaels (2014) 'Mapping conflict motives: Central African Republic', Mapping Conflict Motives, IPIS, [http://reliefweb.int/sites/reliefweb.int/files/resources/20141124_CAR.pdf].

Wiese, M. (2004) *Health-vulnerability in a complex crisis situation: Implications for providing health care to nomadic people in Chad*, Studies in Development Geography 26, Saarbrücken: Verlag für Entwicklungspolitik.

Wiese, M. (2011) 'Livestock production and pastoral livelihood security in Western Chad', in J. Gertel & R. Le Heron (eds) *Economic spaces of pastoral production and commodity systems: Markets and livelihoods*, Abingdon: Routledge, pp. 55–78.

Wilson Janssens, M.C. (2018) 'Spatial mobility and social becoming: The journeys of four Central African Students in Congo-Kinshasa', *Geoforum*. https://doi.org/10.1016/j.geoforum.2018.05.018.

Wilson Janssens, M.C. (2019) 'Conflict (im)mobiles: Biographies of mobility along the Ubangi River in Central Africa', Doctoral dissertation, Leiden University.

Wilson, M.C. (forthcoming) *Conflict (im)mobiles: Biographies of mobility along the Ubangi River in Central Africa* (working title), Berlin and Boston, MA: de Gruyter Oldenbourg.

Yorbana, S. (2017) 'Representations of oil in Chad: A blessing or a curse?', *Africa Spectrum*, 52(1): 65–83.

Youssouf, I.A, A.D. Grimshaw & C.S. Bird (1976) 'Greetings in the desert', *American Ethnologist*, 3(4): 797–824.

Yuval-Davis, N. (2006) 'Belonging and the politics of belonging', *Patterns of Prejudice*, 40(3): 197–214. DOI:10.1080/00313220600769331.

Zeltner, J.C. (1979) *Les Arabes dans la region du Lac Tchad: Problemes d'origine et de chronologie*, Sarh: Centre d'Etudes Linguistique.

Zeltner, J.C. & H. Tourneux (1986) *L'Arabe dans le bassin du Tchad: Le parler des Ulâd Eli*, Paris: Karthala.

Glossary of Chadian Arabic and French terms

Abāla Those that rear camels.

Ahaliéh Alliances between communities.

Ammar al-bir / Kabīr al-bir The one that manages the pastoral well.

Baha'īm The herd (of cattle).

Baqqara Cattle herders; lit. cattle.

Barāda A metal tea pot which is used to brew the tea as well as serve it. When I learned the word for tea kettle (barada), it made me laugh. In Arabic, sokhun means that something is warm, while baarid means something is cold. The sokhaan, however, holds cool water, while the barada is used to heat water.

Barsh A nomadic tent. The roof used to be made of woven mats but has now often been replaced by a heavy tarp. The roof is supported by wooden sticks, carved into v-shapes at the top so as to hold another stick across them.

Bidon Jerry-can.

Bir A well.

Boule Cooked like porridge and then rolled into a ball, this staple food can be accompanied by different sauces. In Chad *boule* is often made from sorghum, maize, millet, rice, cassava, or peanuts, depending on which crop is in season locally.

Collecteur In CAR, used to refer to those that go from mine to mine collecting diamonds to then sell them on to larger companies.

Dabanga A granary.

Da'inéh A grouping of several ferīkhs for displacement during the transhumance, mainly for security reasons.

Damréh A more or less permanent nomadic camp, or a village of pastoralists.

Darat Typically between October and November, the time after the rainy season during which food crops mature and are harvested.

Delou A tool used to extract water from a well, made of leather and able to hold 8, 20, or 30 litres, depending on the animal or person pulling it up. The ones the Walad Djifir typically use by hand hold approximately 20/30 litres, as it usually only takes two 'pulls' to fill one jerry tank (40 litres).

Djallabeya A long, loose-fitting piece of clothing.

Doungous Used to refer to the territory of a *kashim beyt* (lineage and sub-lineage). In general use, it refers to old ancestral villages.

'Eidd An area or zone with many ground-water wells (a zone where ground water is easily reached).

Fakīr An Arabic word for a Sufi Muslim who has devoted himself to poverty and worship.

Ferīkh (pl. furkhān) Nomadic camp.

Gaiysh Pasture (herbaceous vegetation).

https://doi.org/10.1515/9783110714685-009

Goz A fairly sandy terrain on which the penicillary millet (*doukhoun*) is cultivated.

Habīl Rope.

Kabīr hana ferīkh Head of the nomadic camp (*kabīr 'an al-ferīkh*).

Khalīfa The administrative representative of a sultan, a chief of a canton, or of a nomadic group's chief in a specific locality. Typically in charge of collecting and paying taxes in the name of the group.

Kharīf Rainy season, between July and September.

Khashim beyt (pl. khashim buyūt) A subdivision of a lineage within a group. A distinction can be made between the *khashim beyt kabir* (larger lineage) and the *khashim beyt saghir* (smaller sub-lineage).

Kouzi A round hut made of stone bricks and a straw roof, most often used by sedentary populations – and thus it is interesting to see the nomadic Walad Djifir building such homes of their own in their permanent villages. These villages are characterized by both *kouzis* and traditional nomadic tents (*barsh*).

Makharaf (pl. makhārif) Place where pastoralists, sedentary and transhumant, stay during the rainy season.

Māl The animals or herd.

Marabout An Arabic word for a teacher of Islam and at times a religious leader as well. One who has studied the Qur'ān.

Murhal (pl. marāhil) Transhumance corridor.

Naga Typically, clayey and flat bare ground which is floodable. Once the rainy season starts, camps will be moved away from such terrain.

Qabīla Group or larger familial lineage.

al-Rūha Pastoralism; lit. the travel.

Rushāsh The start of the rainy season, around the month of June.

Seyf The dry season.

Shittéh The cold season, between December and February.

Sokhān (sokhaan in text) The *sokhaan* can be found in every Chadian household. They are usually made of plastic and look like a kettle, having a handle and spout. They come in various colours, sizes, and qualities. The *sokhaan* is filled with water and used to wash one's hands before a meal, for Muslims to carry out their ablutions, and also to take with you to the 'bathroom'.

Wādi dry river bed.

Zerrība Animal enclosure – in the case of the Walad Djifir, mostly for smaller animals such as sheep, goats, and young calves – keeping them safe from predators at night. The *zerrība* is often found in the middle of a group of tents (a camp), with the tent openings facing outwards.

Index

https://doi.org/10.1515/9783110714685-010